20 Strategies for STEM Instruction

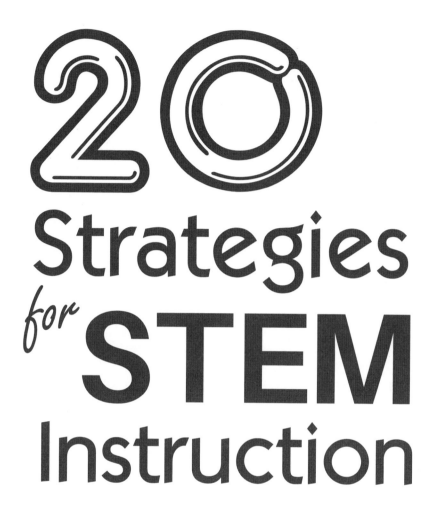

20
Strategies
for STEM
Instruction

William N. Bender

LearningSciencesInternational

LEARNING AND PERFORMANCE MANAGEMENT

1400 Centrepark Blvd, Suite 1000
West Palm Beach, FL 33401
717-845-6300

email: pub@learningsciences.com
learningsciences.com

Printed in the United States of America

21 20 19 18   2 3 4 5 6

Library of Congress Control Number: 2016945698

Publisher's Cataloging-in-Publication Data
provided by Five Rainbows Cataloging Services

Names: Bender, William N.

Title: 20 Strategies for STEM Instruction / William N. Bender.

Description: West Palm Beach, FL : Learning Sciences, 2016. | Includes bibliographical references and index.

Identifiers: ISBN 978-1-941112-78-6 (pbk.) | ISBN 978-1-941112-88-5 (ebook)

Subjects: LCSH: Science--Study and teaching. | Technology--Study and teaching. | Engineering--Study and teaching. | Mathematics--Study and teaching. | Teacher effectiveness. | Education--Study and teaching. | BISAC: EDUCATION / Teaching Methods & Materials / Science & Technology. | EDUCATION / Teaching Methods & Materials / Mathematics.

Classification: LCC Q181 .B51 2016 (print) | LCC Q181 (ebook) | DDC 507--dc23.

TABLE OF CONTENTS

SECTION I
Project- and Inquiry-Based Learning | 17

SECTION II
Technology in STEM Classes | 83

SECTION III

Collaborative and Cooperative Learning in STEM | 151

CHAPTER 12: Social Learning Networks for STEM Instruction 163

CHAPTER 13: Wikis for STEM Instructional Units 171

CHAPTER 14: Mindfulness in STEM Classes. 181

CHAPTER 15: Classwide Peer Tutoring 187

CHAPTER 16: Reciprocal Teaching. 193

SECTION IV
Differentiated STEM Instruction | 199

INTRODUCTION

STEM, an acronym for science, technology, engineering, and mathematics, represents one of the most impactful instructional perspectives in schools today (Myers & Berkowicz, 2015; Slavin, 2014). Over the last decade, STEM instruction has been sweeping schools throughout the United States, Great Britain, Canada, Australia, and most of the rest of the world, as educators increasingly choose to emphasize more rigorous instruction in these "hard science" subjects (Jolly, 2014; Markham, 2011; Myers & Berkowicz, 2015; National Science Board, 2012). The primary rationale for increasing the rigor of instruction in these topics in particular has been based on research showing that the United States and other Western nations are falling behind certain other countries in the areas of science and mathematics (Jolly, 2014; National Science Board, 2012; U.S. Department of Education, 2011; Venkataraman, Riordan, & Olson, 2010).

While that rationale is both comprehensive and compelling, it is not the focus of this book. Here we will not spend a great deal of time on comparing U.S. school performance to that of other nations or describing how other nations instruct students. Rather, this book is intended for educators seeking practical instructional strategies that help foster STEM instruction in the classroom, and I intend to present the latest STEM instructional trends and specific teaching techniques.

Parameters of STEM

As with most innovative instructional perspectives, proponents do not always agree on the definition or parameters of STEM (Myers & Berkowicz, 2015; Zubrzycki, 2015). For some educators, STEM represents merely a restructuring of instruction in the four subject areas of science, technology, engineering, and mathematics, while stressing 21st century technology tools for teaching and student learning. Other educators suggest that all school subjects become STEM focused, while still others argue that STEM represents nothing less than a fundamental restructuring of the instructional process in all subjects. The latter group proposes to focus on constructing understandings by cooperatively solving real-world problems while exposing students to content as needed within that solution process. Myers and Berkowicz (2015) summarize this comprehensive view of STEM as follows:

> The STEM shift encourages reimagining schools from kindergarten through the 12th grade, including the way curriculum is designed, organized, and delivered. (p. 8)

As shown by this quote, some STEM proponents see STEM as a profound reorganization of schools, a complete restructuring, which they believe is required by the demands of the global marketplace. In fact, there is a rationale for this view of STEM. As most educators realize, our current school curriculum has not been fundamentally restructured since the work of John Dewey in the early 1900s (see https://en.wikipedia.org/wiki/John_Dewey for a discussion of Dewey's work).

Dewey advocated for what he referred to as a vocational curriculum focused on math, science, history, and English, rather than the classics-based curriculum of the day—a historical curriculum utilized in the colonial period, which emphasized the great works of history and philosophy, as well as Greek and/or Latin studies. Dewey's version of the vocational curriculum has been the main thrust of how schooling has been conducted since the 1920s or so, and we've structured our current school courses around those practical application topics emphasized by Dewey, including math, science, history, and language as our core studies. While a technology course, a course in home economics, or a course or two specializing in automotive or other vocational skills (*vocational* as used herein reflects the current meaning of that term) may have been added, we are, in general terms, still teaching using Dewey's course structure.

In contrast to these subject-defined curricula, some of the more extreme proponents of STEM education advocate something quite different—a complete restructuring of schools to emphasize the STEM process in all areas (Bender, 2012; Myers & Berkowicz, 2015). In this view, STEM involves student-driven, scientifically grounded instruction based on real-world problems to be solved by students working in teams and using the scientific method. Such a reorganization may do away with daily lesson plans, units of instruction, or even our current course structures (Myers & Berkowicz, 2015).

> STEM involves student-driven, scientifically grounded instruction based on real-world problems to be solved by students working in teams and using the scientific method.

Here is an example. The Minnesota New Country High School has been restructured based on student-initiated research projects that are not tied to specific courses. Students are provided with the required educational standards, and they must negotiate with the faculty to complete a series of STEM projects to address all of the standards. Students may work individually or in groups and are required to regularly present their various projects to a faculty committee, describing how their work should earn them the required credits (ten credits per year are required). In this successful school, students are studying content within their own interest areas but must show how they are meeting the required curricular standards while completing the ten credits. This usually translates to between eight and twelve projects each year. To better understand this STEM example, I'd encourage all educators to view the following video: www.bing.com/videos /search?q=project+based+learning+mummified+chicken&FORM=VIRE1#view=detail &mid=34E95753BCE0516773C434E95753BCE0516773C4.

While this is one of the most extreme examples of school restructuring based on project-based instruction in STEM, it is quite impressive to consider that in the Minnesota New Country School, students rather than teachers are responsible for documenting their mastery of the content. Further, documentary evidence presented in the video shows that students are doing well on state and national assessments.

In terms of legislation, the definition of STEM is a bit more restricted but was expanded in October of 2015. Federal legislation on STEM funding includes computer science, in addition to the four original areas of science, technology, engineering, and mathematics (Zubrzycki, 2015).

As one might expect, these widely divergent visions of STEM represent part of the difficulty in discussing STEM. Definitions of STEM range from those that are overly focused on a few courses to those that are expansively broad, such as the example above, which exemplifies fundamental restructuring of both the curriculum and the school organization.

At this point, let me reassure you that the expansive definition of STEM does not represent the vast majority of STEM instruction. While that example can provide for a challenging reflection for educators, the strategies provided within this book will not require such a major rebuilding of school structures. For our purposes, we'll focus on strategies that can be applied by a single teacher working alone in his or her science, mathematics, technology, or engineering classroom. We'll use a definition of STEM that is somewhat toward the center of these extreme examples. STEM can best be understood as a concerted, systematic effort to increase the instructional rigor in science, technology, engineering, mathematics, and other classes, utilizing the scientific method to solve real-world problems as the basis for instruction in order to position U.S. students to better compete with other students in a world economy (National Science Board, 2012; U.S. Department of Education, 2011). As this definition suggests, STEM is broader than merely a new way to teach mathematics or science, and STEM should certainly impact all courses in the school. Throughout this book, I will discuss strategies for the hard sciences of STEM classes, as well as STEM approaches to instruction in other subject areas, in an effort to provide a vision of what a STEM-based school might look like.

> STEM is a concerted, systematic effort to increase the instructional rigor in science, technology, engineering, mathematics, and other classes, utilizing the scientific method to solve real-world problems as the basis for instruction in order to position U.S. students to better compete with other students in a world economy.

However, educators moving into STEM instruction should not plan on rebuilding schools from the ground up; rather, they should move more tentatively and explore the strategies presented herein that seem to best fit within their current teaching assignments. As those are shown to be successful in the classroom, teachers may choose to explore more innovative approaches and/or school restructuring options for STEM instruction.

With this definition of STEM in mind, I should again point out that broad discussions of the implementation of STEM at the school level or of research supporting the STEM movement are not the primary emphasis of this book. Rather, this book is intended to provide specific instructional practices for teachers in science, mathematics, technology, engineering, and other classes across the grade levels. Further, in addition to providing detail on the best practices for STEM classes, this book will give teachers specific instruction on how to effectively implement these strategies in a manner consistent with the expectations of STEM instruction.

Efficacy of STEM

While an expansive exploration of the research basis for STEM is beyond the scope of this book, some general discussion of the STEM literature and research is warranted, since this will prepare teachers to explore STEM instruction. While many research studies, as well as a variety of books, have focused on STEM across the grade levels, most of these have emphasized either the need for more robust instruction in these topics (Berkowicz & Myers, 2015) or methods for school administrators to effect the movement toward STEM (Myers & Berkowicz, 2015; Slavin, 2014). Only a few books have looked specifically at STEM strategies for teachers in the classroom, and those tend to be somewhat lacking in specificity.

Research studies have focused on the efficacy of STEM instruction, and while not all results are positive (Goodwin & Hein, 2014), the research generally documents increased school achievement in science and mathematics as a result of STEM instruction (Grier, Blumenfeld, Marx, Krajcik, Fishman, Soloway, et al., 2008; Hansen, 2014; Hattie, 2012; Judson, 2014; Vega, 2012). The research documents that STEM instruction does engage students at a higher level in the subjects of science, engineering, and mathematics, and that students exposed to STEM do perform better academically (Hansen, 2014; Judson, 2014; Subotnik, Tai, & Almarode, 2011; Venkataraman, Riordan, & Olson, 2010, September; Wiswall, Stiefel, Schwartz, & Boccardo, 2014, June; Young, House, Wang, Singleton, & Klopfenstein, 2011). STEM students are also more likely to specialize in these subjects in higher education. Additional research results are presented for each of the specific strategies presented.

Teaching Ideas in STEM Classes

Many educators have provided general suggestions for teaching in the STEM classroom (Gorman, 2015; Jolly, 2014; Markham, 2011; Slavin, 2014; Vega, 2012), and while these are not specific instructional strategies for STEM, these suggestions do encompass many useful ideas on how a teacher should conduct STEM instruction. A brief introductory discussion of these ideas should help readers better understand the broader instructional approaches embedded within the STEM instructional process.

Instructional Emphases for STEM Classes

- Focus on real-world problem.
- Frame learning using engineering design principles.
- Emphasize open-ended, hands-on inquiry.
- Make teamwork/collaboration the primary instructional approach.
- Emphasize rigorous math and science content.
- Allow for multiple right answers, and encourage students to learn from failure.

First, STEM lessons should focus on the application of the scientific method to real-world issues and problems (Gorman, 2015; Jolly, 2014; Vega, 2012). This often involves a project that might benefit the school or community (for example, turning a grassy area into a landscaped green space or development of a vegetable garden for the school). The focus in STEM is to find a challenging student-selected problem that will help someone in the students' environment and engage students in the academic tasks. The real-world problem should likewise focus students on the specific content to be mastered as they develop a product to solve the problem and/or answer the question (Barell, 2007; Myers & Berkowicz, 2015).

Next, many proponents of STEM suggest that lessons be guided by the engineering design process (Jolly, 2014). Specifically, students should build something in the process of their learning, using the engineering principles and process steps that work in industry (Breeden, 2015; Markham, 2011). These might include developing multiple approaches to solving a problem or using parallel student groups to develop various problem-solution options. In STEM discussions today, innovations such as 3-D printing, augmented reality, and robotics are central to the discussion and are emphasized to stress the need to engineer solutions to real-world problems using the most modern scientific and technological tools available (De Gree, 2015; Myers & Berkowicz, 2015; Smith, 2015).

Third, STEM lessons thrust students into open-ended explorations and hands-on inquiry (Jolly, 2014). Markham (2011) suggests that all STEM lessons should begin with a question that students discuss while they brainstorm possible solutions. Once those possible solutions to the presenting problem are generated, they become the basis for hypothesis testing. Student reflection is emphasized, as students note which hypotheses were proven and which must be modified or discarded.

Fourth, almost all proponents of STEM suggest that the STEM process should be based on effective student collaboration and communication (Jolly, 2014; Markham, 2011; Myers & Berkowicz, 2015). Students should engage in productive teamwork to attack the presenting problem, using the same scientific language, procedures, and modern communication tools. Teamwork and cooperative endeavors are stressed throughout the STEM process, and in that sense, STEM instruction is more closely aligned with the modern work environment than more traditional, teacher-led instruction (Jolly, 2014; Vega, 2012).

Fifth, STEM lessons must emphasize rigorous math and science content (Jolly, 2014; Vega, 2012). Teachers should purposely connect and integrate content from math, science, and technology. Teachers in STEM classes often collaborate with other math and/or science teachers to gain insight into how course objectives can be interwoven in a given STEM lesson. Many STEM lessons are interdisciplinary because students should understand that science and math are not isolated subjects and that they can work together to solve real-world problems in history or science. That is why STEM is frequently undertaken within an interdisciplinary or cross-disciplinary framework. Many STEM projects couple history with science and mathematics to help students develop projects and ideas. This interdisciplinary focus, coupled with an emphasis on rigorous content, adds relevance to the content, as students apply mathematics, science, and engineering to various problems and course projects. This will also increase students' engagement with the Common Core standards overall.

Finally, STEM lessons frequently allow for multiple right answers, as student teams find different ways to approach problems. Further, STEM allows students to learn from mistakes, from failure, and from hypotheses that don't work out (Jolly, 2014). Students should learn that multiple approaches to problems are often productive and that even when an idea fails, it may be the basis for the development of more effective strategies in the future. Over time, this type of instruction should foster student creativity, as students feel empowered to explore options that may not prove effective. Students are expected to take risks, to learn from what goes wrong, and try again. Reflective thinking is a hallmark of STEM instruction, and in the STEM classroom, failure is considered a positive step on the way to discovering and designing solutions.

Foundational Instructional Approaches in STEM

While a large variety of instructional strategies have been used in STEM classes, most STEM theorists discuss several broad foundational approaches that form the basis for most STEM instruction (Judson, 2014; Subotnik, Tai, & Almarode, 2011; Vega,

2012; Venkataraman, Riordan, & Olson, 2010; Young, House, Wang, Singleton, & Klopfenstein, 2011). These broad instructional approaches will provide the structure for this book. They include: inquiry/project-based instruction, technology-rich instruction, cooperative/collaborative instruction, and differentiated instruction.

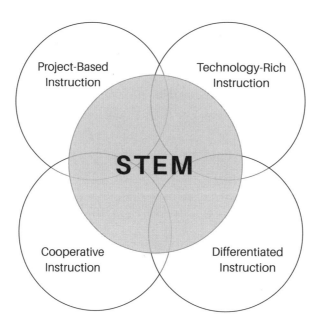

Figure I.1: Foundational approaches for STEM.

As presented in figure I.1, STEM instruction overlaps with the instructional practices mentioned and employs many strategies within each of these four areas. Of course, the figure is not intended to show the various areas of overlap among these four instructional approaches themselves but rather to represent the fact that STEM instruction is central to many of the strands of research within these four areas. Each of these broad instructional approaches is discussed below, in the context of the STEM classroom.

Inquiry/Project-Based Instruction

Because of the emphasis on solving real-world problems in the STEM movement, problem-based learning, inquiry-based instruction, and project-based learning have received increasing emphasis in STEM classrooms and represent perhaps the most important instructional approach for STEM (Bender, 2012; Berkowicz & Myers, 2015; Gorman, 2015; Markham, 2011; Myers & Berkowicz, 2015; Vega, 2012). While various proponents might differentiate between inquiry-based, problem-based, and project-based learning, for purposes of this book these terms will be considered roughly synonymous. This is based on the fact that each of these approaches focuses on student-driven inquiry as the basis for content instruction and requires the students to produce an idea, product, or project that addresses the question they select. Further, each of these approaches leads to increased student engagement with the content and increased student achievement (Barell, 2007; Bender, 2012; Hattie, 2012).

For example, the meta-analysis of John Hattie showed that problem-based instruction was among the top twenty-five instructional strategies that positively influenced academic achievement. Specifically, students receiving this type of instruction improved by over half a standard deviation on academic skills, with an effect size of 0.61. (Effect sizes higher than 0.50 are interpreted to mean that the instructional approach is highly effective. For more information on interpreting effect sizes, see appendix A in this book, Hattie [2012], or Marzano, Pickering, & Pollock [2001].)

Within this broad inquiry/project-based learning framework, this book presents five specific strategies, Strategies 1 through 5: project-based learning; building/engineering something; summarizing, prediction, and hypothesis testing; rubric-based feedback; and the flipped classroom.

Technology-Rich Instruction

A second major instructional emphasis in the STEM discussions is an emphasis on technology-rich instruction (National Science Board, 2012; U.S. Department of Education, 2011; Vega, 2012). While instructional technology has long been used in a variety of instructional areas, developments in science are providing a much richer array of technology options that will assist students in learning and, more specifically, in engineering solutions to problems in their science or mathematics classes. Specifically, innovations such as 3-D printing and robotics are becoming routine in math and science classes, as students create solutions for student-selected problems (Davis, 2015; Breeden, 2015). These cutting-edge innovations are bringing new emphasis to the "engineering" options in various classes, as well as to the momentum for moving to STEM instruction (Berkowicz & Myers, 2015; Davis, 2015; De Gree, 2015; Politis, 2015; Slavin, 2014; Smith, 2015).

Within this broad arena of technology applications for instruction, five strategies will be presented in the second section of the book, Strategies 6 through 10: technology-rich teaching, coding and robotics, animation, gaming and simulations, and augmented reality.

Cooperative Instruction

Another consistently recommended instructional approach in the STEM literature is the application of collaborative instructional approaches such as cooperative learning instructional practices (Berkowicz & Myers, 2015; Jolly, 2014). Cooperative instruction is an effective instructional strategy and does increase academic achievement over time

(Hattie, 2012; Markham, 2011; Marzano, 2007, 2009a; Myers & Berkowicz, 2015; Thurston, 2014). In fact, Hattie demonstrated that cooperative instruction was among the top thirty-five instructional strategies that positively influenced achievement and that students receiving this type of instruction improved by over half a standard deviation on academic skills (effect size of 0.54). Marzano's work (2009; Marzano et al., 2001) documents that cooperative instruction, when implemented well, increases academic achievement by 23 percent.

However, the aim of cooperative instruction has been raised somewhat by STEM teachers. First, the new instructional emphasis on cooperative instruction is focused on building teamwork, while using social media in the learning process. Clearly social media have dramatically increased the options for cooperation in learning endeavors, and several social media instructional procedures are presented herein.

Further, while it has long been realized that schools needed to implement more cooperative instruction generally within the STEM literature, these cooperative instructional practices are focused on moving beyond mere group cooperation, toward a true collaboration—a teamwork focus for most classroom activities. This cooperative approach should go far beyond the jigsaw type of cooperative strategies that have been practiced for the last several decades. Rather, modern cooperative instruction must closely approximate the collaborative practices found in most work environments. In particular, Markham (2011) cautions educators developing STEM lessons to not become locked into older approaches to cooperative instructional procedures. Rather, educators should use cooperative learning processes to move toward students' development of true collaborative, team-based problem-solving skills.

Strategies 11 through 16 provide teachers with several options for increasing collaborative instruction in the STEM classroom. These specific strategies include cooperative learning, social learning networks, teaching with wikis, mindfulness, classwide peer tutoring, and reciprocal teaching.

Differentiated Instruction

Differentiated instruction has been recommended as a STEM instructional approach on a more limited basis than the other approaches discussed above (Haldane & Smith, 2014; Slavin, 2014). However, when one considers the instructional strategies consistently discussed in the STEM literature, one thing becomes obvious: many of these strategies represent the best ideas from the differentiated instructional literature (Bender, 2013a; 2013b; Bender & Waller, 2011; Haldane & Smith, 2014). Haldane and Smith (2014) did recommend that teachers use differentiated instructional strategies for STEM instruction, and for that reason, several strategies for differentiating instruction, Strategies 17 through 20, are presented. These differentiated instructional strategies are particularly germane to STEM instruction and include differentiating instruction, metacognitive instruction, peer evaluation and feedback, and goal-setting/self-evaluation.

STEM or STEAM?

For several decades, there has been a running battle between the hard sciences on the one hand and humanities and the arts on the other. That conflict is often brought to the fore-front in tough budgetary times when cuts in certain course offerings are required. Simply put, art, music, and other such creative subjects are often on the budgetary chopping block first, as opposed to the hard sciences, such as biology, chemistry, and mathematics.

Perhaps for this reason, teachers in the arts have sought to demonstrate that the arts are in fact critical within STEM, because visual arts and/or digital visual arts often help represent concepts in the hard sciences. Further, the creativity that is stressed within the arts and humanities is certainly essential in developing new ideas within the hard sciences. Thus, for many educators, the arts must be a major emphasis in STEM instruction. Many educators advocate the acronym STEAM, with the *A* representing the arts as they might be embedded within STEM instruction (Myers & Berkowicz, 2015; Slavin, 2014). Markham (2011) points out that STEM instruction becomes STEAM with the addition of the emphasis on art, presentation efficacy using modern communication technologies and design principles.

Other proponents of STEM have suggested the use of the acronym STREAM, with the addition of an *R* to represent the concept of ongoing research within the learning process (Myers & Berkowicz, 2015).

While I do concur that both research and the arts are critical in 21st century STEM instruction, I've chosen to use the more traditional acronym, STEM, for several reasons. First, most STEM proponents are not shifting their terminology to these newer terms as yet, though most do agree with the need to include both a research emphasis and the arts (Jolly, 2014; Vega, 2012). Second, I do not intend to spend a great deal of time in this book on these theoretical discussions about STEM. The discussion of twenty best practices for STEM classrooms is quite enough for this book. With that noted, I concur with the emphasis placed on artistic creativity in STEM, as shown in the discussion of various strategies included. I also concur with the emphasis on research, as represented by the scientific process of exploration, prediction, hypothesis testing, reflection, and revision in the modern STEM classroom.

In fact, I would suggest that STEM teachers in particular hold a special responsibility to not only teach about research procedures but also to *actually practice action research in the classroom*. Imagine how engaged students in STEM classes might become if they realize that teachers are using them in action research to test the efficacy of one instructional procedure or another. For this reason, I have provided a number of separate case studies to demonstrate the type of action research that teachers should undertake in STEM classes. Such action research will demonstrate both the efficacy of a particular teaching strategy and how research on a real-world question might be conducted. Each of these case studies includes a data chart of some type to illustrate how action research should lead to data, which in turn leads to increased efficacy of instruction. In short, in STEM classes, we should teach about scientific research by doing research and sharing that with the students.

Recurring Concerns in Transitioning to STEM

Because many teachers have already begun the transition to STEM instruction, educators have been able to identify several consistent concerns teachers face as they consider how to implement STEM (Bender, 2012; Markham, 2011; Myers & Berkowicz, 2015; Slavin, 2014). These concerns seem to be constant, and they present some tentative conflict in virtually every instance, so an awareness of these issues will help teachers better prepare for their own transition to STEM instruction. These issues include the linear nature of traditional educational standards, including the Common Core standards and the teacher's control of the classroom.

Rigid, Linear Curricular Standards

One issue teachers have to confront when they move toward STEM instruction is the rather rigid, linear nature of the Common Core State Standards or, in some states (e.g., Texas and Alaska), the state list of curricular standards. In short, most lists of educational standards are linear and fairly rigid in nature, with one topic logically following the previous topic in an understandable, orderly fashion. Traditional instruction has likewise followed this linear, rigid nature of the standards, introducing topics in a set, predictable order.

However, teachers involved in the STEM process soon understand that STEM instruction may be much less linear in nature than the curricular standards would suggest. In fact, when engaged in a STEM project, and in particular in an interdisciplinary project, students will probably be exposed to content (and thus to content standards) in any order but that prescribed by the curriculum. A project in a grade 5 science class might require students to learn some content that is normally covered in grade 6 mathematics, as one example. Further, while doing a project in grade 5, students may develop a method to do the project that does not require them to master all of the standards required for the fifth grade.

For many teachers, this nonlinear approach to learning can be somewhat disquieting, since in traditional instruction the teacher alone controlled when students were exposed to and were required to master specific standards. Teachers were free to follow the prescribed order. Thus, the transition to STEM instruction makes some teachers feel uncomfortable, with a less organized approach to learning the content in a systematic fashion.

However, even in STEM instruction, there are things teachers can do to exert some control over when students are exposed to content. This can be done by delineating specific rubrics during the ongoing STEM process, rubrics that require students to cover content standards that are required during a given year and are related to the student-selected STEM projects. Even while students exercise choice on what projects they undertake, teachers can and should recommend the addition of certain tasks and provide rubrics for them that will require students to cover some content that they may not have considered. Thus, the use of specific rubrics can allow students to focus on the specific task at hand and can also help the teacher exert some control over when students are taught specific content.

Still, teachers moving into STEM teaching for the first time should realize that, because of the emphasis on student voice and student choice in most STEM instruction, students will not be mastering content standards in as orderly a fashion as in the traditional classroom. Rather, students will seek out knowledge as project development makes that knowledge relevant to their ongoing learning process.

I should point out that this "less-ordered" curriculum is one strength of STEM instruction. Because students seek out the knowledge (i.e., course content standards) they need when they need it, they are much more likely to be meaningfully engaged in mastering those content standards that are essential for their STEM project. Students are learning on a need-to-know basis in STEM classes, and this results in higher student engagement (Bender, 2012; Vega, 2012). This will result in increased academic achievement overall. Further, getting students to pay attention in a STEM class is not nearly as time consuming for the teacher as in traditional instruction, and that is one big advantage in a less rigid curriculum.

Teacher Control of the Classroom

The issue of dealing with curricular standards in a less linear fashion is, in reality, one exemplar of a larger issue teachers face when moving toward STEM instruction—the issue of teacher control of the class (Bender, 2012). When students exercise choice over what they study, teachers will have less control in the classroom, and again, this places many teachers outside of their comfort zone. As a teacher myself, I can assure the reader, I would not have been comfortable moving away from the tight discipline and curricular control I maintained in my classroom; yet had I attempted the move toward STEM instruction, I would have had to relinquish some of that control.

However, over time, teachers exploring STEM instruction will realize that STEM instruction and student choice do not mean classroom chaos. Rather than a lack of control, the shift to STEM instruction really involves the teacher sharing some control of the ongoing classroom operations with students who, over time, will grow to take those responsibilities seriously.

To help teachers in this transition, I advocate several strategies. First, most teachers will be more comfortable if they move into STEM instruction slowly and somewhat tentatively. In the discussions of specific strategies, I will suggest ways for teachers to move into STEM in a manner that allows them to engage in smaller steps outside of their comfort zone, while still transitioning in a meaningful way to STEM instruction.

Here is another tactic I recommend to all teachers making that transition to STEM: *Do it together!* In your first STEM teaching, you should work with another teacher for a two- or three-week interdisciplinary STEM project. In that fashion, teachers can effectively resource each other, collectively deciding what works and what doesn't. This collaborative teaching idea, more so than any other idea I'm aware of, will allow teachers to experience the types of learning activities that characterize the STEM classroom with some degree of comfort, and yet will also help teachers, over the long term, embrace the shared control over their classroom that is characteristic of STEM classes. In such a shared-control environment, the vast majority of students can and do rise to the occasion and become successful at maintaining class decorum while moving increasingly into STEM.

Using This Book

This book is intended for teachers across the grade levels who are moving into STEM instruction. In various strategy sections, I have included both classroom examples and case studies that include examples in various subjects across the grade levels. In order to ensure practicality of this work, I have also invited several teachers to make brief contributions on how they use specific strategies in their classes. Each of these text features is clearly identified in the various strategies.

Of course, teachers are always looking for efficient time-saving ideas, and this book is structured to facilitate efficiency of study. First, while research evidence is cited throughout, the primary purpose here is to provide teachers with practical, effective, and time-efficient instructional strategies that are proven in the classroom. Teachers should feel free to select individual strategies that they wish to consider for their own classroom and read those sections of the book first and consult the research cited as they wish. Also, teachers are invited to skip around in the book as they like. However, given the general importance of project-based learning in STEM instruction generally, I would encourage teachers to read through that first strategy initially, and then select the strategies and topics that interest them, based on their particular teaching situations.

In various sections, I've included some specific related information in boxed form, and that should generally be considered as sidebar information. I've also included several figures and data charts throughout the text to assist in your understanding of the case studies.

This book also provides many sets of specific instructional guidelines, or step-by-step instructions for various strategies. Please understand that for most of these strategies, there are a variety of ways they may be implemented and that such instructions or guidelines as may be presented here are exactly that—guidelines. While almost all teachers realize that these are guidelines, I do want to state up front that the readers of this book (i.e., you!) are very likely to be highly effective teachers already. You are most certainly a group of highly trained teachers, and as such, you should take these strategies and make them your own. Feel free to adapt these ideas, to merge these strategies, or to modify them in any reasonable and ethical manner that works in your classroom.

With that noted, I would also make one request: drop me a line or two via email (williamnbender@gmail.com) and let me know how any of these strategies worked for you. Let me know of your modifications and adaptations of these ideas and how and why they worked, if they did, in your classroom. Please understand that this is more than merely a polite invitation. I truly enjoy interacting via email with teachers who have used my work to further their own, and I seriously invite you to contact me about the topics included herein. I sincerely hope that this work is useful in your move toward STEM instruction, and as a classroom teacher myself, I understand your time constraints, as well as the job you are doing. Further, I recognize the importance of that job.

With that awareness in mind, let me join the many parents and students who, I'm sure, have told you in the past: *Thanks for what you do! You are making a difference!*

Section I

Project- and Inquiry-Based Learning

No instructional strategy is as closely identified with STEM instruction as project-based learning (Myers & Berkowicz, 2015). Perhaps for this reason, project-based learning (PBL), which is sometimes referred to as inquiry learning or problem-based learning, is the basis for many of the examples of STEM instruction one finds in the literature (Vega, 2012). Also, project-based learning and STEM share many of the same instructional emphases, including the stress placed on student collaboration, the emphasis on solving real-world problems, student choice, and actual construction of a project based on the learning content (Myers & Berkowicz, 2015).

For this reason, I've chosen to discuss PBL as the initial strategy in this book, and while many of the subsequent strategies will stand on their own in either PBL or more traditional classrooms, teachers are well advised to explore the exciting options presented by PBL. This represents the best instruction for the next century.

In addition, PBL instruction incorporates several additional instructional strategies that are particularly germane for STEM instruction. These include: building something/engineering, summarization and hypothesis testing/prediction, rubric-based instruction, and the flipped classroom. Each of these will be described in this section as strategies supportive of PBL in the STEM classroom.

STRATEGY 1

Project-Based Learning

Project-based learning (PBL) in the 21st century involves much more than merely planning a project within a given unit of instruction. Most proponents of PBL argue that true project-based learning involves basing all or most of the instruction on student-selected projects, such that the projects rather than lesson plans or lesson units drive the curriculum (Bender, 2012; Boss & Krauss, 2007; Larmer, Ross, & Mergendoller, 2009). Stressing this focus, PBL may be defined as using authentic, real-world projects as the basis for all or most instruction, with such instruction founded on student-selected, highly motivating, and engaging questions, tasks, or problems, and resulting in a product or project that addresses the driving question (Bender, 2012, 2013a).

> PBL may be defined as using authentic, real-world projects as the basis for all or most instruction, with such instruction founded on student-selected, highly motivating, and engaging questions, tasks, or problems, and resulting in a product or project that addresses the driving question (Bender, 2012, 2013a).

Within a PBL framework, each project is likely to take considerable time—often a number of weeks—and should be developed jointly by the teacher and students in order to teach academic standards within the context of students working cooperatively to solve a real-world problem and complete a real-world project (Barell, 2007). Individual projects may, on occasion, be found in PBL classes, but most projects are undertaken by teams of students. Also, student choice and student inquiry in a team decision-making process must be heavily integrated into project-based learning. Because students have choices in selecting the methods they use to develop their projects, they tend to be much more engaged and more highly motivated to work diligently toward a solution (Boss & Krauss, 2007; Larmer, Ross, & Mergendoller, 2009; Mergendoller, Maxwell, & Bellisimo, 2007; Vega, 2012). This increased engagement typically results in higher levels of academic achievement than more traditional instruction (Barell, 2007; Hattie, 2012; Larmer & Mergendoller, 2010; Mergendoller et al., 2007). A number of brief introductory videos on PBL are available at the website Edutopia.org/project-based-learning, and these are strongly recommended as a quick introduction for PBL.

Real-World Projects and Project Scope

In the majority of cases, PBL is implemented by individual teachers. However, some projects are interdisciplinary and involve two teachers and their classes, while other projects are much larger in scope and may involve whole-school efforts. As one example of a PBL implementation with a larger scope, the following YouTube video shows teachers discussing a schoolwide PBL implementation for Sammamish High School: https://www.youtube.com/watch?v=nMCCLB9gOag.

Of course, not every project can involve the whole school or community. However, sometimes projects grow in scope during implementation. For example, Boss (2011) provides an excellent example of a single class project that became a project for the whole school. When studying deforestation resulting from erosion, one upper-elementary science teacher in Indiana made an extra effort and introduced his students to a professional colleague who was headmaster of a school in Haiti. In that locale, tree cutting had led to flooding problems. The Indiana students explored how deforestation had led to flooding just prior to the several hurricanes that hit Haiti in 2011. After one hurricane struck Haiti, the Indiana students heard stories of school students who could not get clean drinking water for days. The class was determined to help their friends in Haiti obtain clean drinking water, and that became a focus for a PBL study in science. Students focused on the question, "How can we get our friends in Haiti some clean drinking water?"

Students then began to study water purification, factors that made water unsafe, and so forth. Several teams of students were formed to research those questions (Boss, 2011). Another group of students focused on the actual construction of simple water purification devices (Boss, 2011). That group consulted a retired local engineer and obtained a patented water purification device, which they immediately dismantled for study. They investigated its operation, testing the electrolysis device with various salts and different voltages (Boss, 2011). The team then sought ways to both simplify the device and improve it.

Another team began a campaign to invest their community in the project. They chose to refer to this as "investing" rather than fund-raising, because they wanted their community to care about, and become involved in, the cause of water purification for Haiti. All of these student teams presented their work each Friday to every other group, and after yet another massive earthquake struck Haiti, the whole school became involved in this exciting PBL project. Ultimately eight students, selected competitively, and eight teachers used community-generated funds to travel to Haiti along with a number of simple water purification devices, which were then given to their new friends in Haiti.

Again, few PBL projects hold this scope or involve this much time and community commitment; indeed, most projects are much more modest in scale and do not involve fund-raising or international travel at all. Many PBL examples are presented on the web, and the following site presents a compendium of forty-six websites with specific PBL examples: www.learningreviews.com/Project-Based-Learning-Lesson-Plans.html.

The following box presents several brief descriptions of PBL projects of smaller scope, as well as several additional websites that feature projects from across the grade levels. Teachers are encouraged to review several of these projects and websites and specifically compare the lesson plan examples for PBL projects.

Examples of PBL Projects/Websites

- One teacher in grade 5 utilized a grassy area behind the school and developed a vegetable garden as part of science and math studies. The students studied what vegetables would grow locally and then planted them. They watered and tended them, and harvested them the following fall.

- The Fly Me to the Moon Travel Agency is a project for kindergarten students. They study the moon environment and what they need to travel to the moon. The project culminates when they book a trip to the moon. This project is available for teachers to evaluate online: http://wveis.k12.wv.us/teach21 /public/project/Guide.cfm?upid=3266&tsele1=3 &tsele2=100.

continued →

- Two teachers in grades 5 and 6 collaborated on a project designed to prepare a school display on Native Americans in the Upstate New York area. The project covered both English language arts and social studies standards and resulted in a series of display posters, written reports, and short videos depicting various aspects of Native American PBL culture.

- Drug Movie is a project for tenth graders from High Tech High School: www.hightechhigh.org/pbl/drug-movie/sitemap.html. In this project, students investigate over-the-counter and illegal drugs, and how they impact the body. The culminating project involves the creation of a short movie on drug use and supporting materials for that video. The website presents an overview of this project and project timeline/objectives.

- BIE.org stands for the BUCK Institute for Education, a helpful website devoted to PBL. Many of the projects found there include both math and science.

- WV_Tree (http://wvde.state.wv.us/teach21/ Teach_21) is the current designation for a site developed by the West Virginia Department of Education. Select a grade level and subject area, and you will find examples of PBL projects in all STEM areas.

- Real World Math PBL (www.realworldmath.org /project-based-learning.html) provides a selection of mathematics projects.

Structure and Components of PBL Instruction

The following box presents a lesson format for a multiweek PBL project that includes most of the common components of PBL instruction. As shown here, PBL instruction often begins with the formulation of a project narrative or problem statement. This is sometimes referred to as a project anchor, since it is intended to motivate students and anchor their topic. This is typically followed by a driving question that can become the basis of a PBL project (Bender, 2012).

Project anchor—a brief paragraph narrative that excites students about a real-world problem and/or describes a real-world project to be developed.

Driving question—one or two brief questions that help set parameters for a PBL project.

Generally, teachers experienced with PBL develop the anchor and driving question and then begin the PBL process with only those components in hand. In such cases, student teams would develop the other aspects of the PBL project description that are shown here.

A Sample PBL Project

The Project Anchor

The City of Rochester has created a walking trail along an old canal within the city boundaries and has invited community organizations to contribute signage to help make this walking trail an educational experience. The nature trail features many places for animals and insects to live, and one of the topics they are interested in involves butterflies that are local to the area. The city has invited the community to construct signage about various aspects of nature that can be found along the trail.

Driving Questions

What butterflies live here along this trail?

When can these butterflies be seen here?

continued →

Necessary Resources

To understand when butterflies are here, we need to understand their life. Thus, we need information on the four cycles in the life of a butterfly.

Information on when different butterflies may be seen locally.

Contributed treated wood, plastic, and time for construction of the actual signage.

Several websites on life cycle of butterflies. Begin with this one: http://www3.canisius.edu/~grandem/butterfly lifecycle/The_Lifecycle_of_a_Butterfly_print.html

Map of the trail with locations of the signs marked.

Artifacts

Four life cycle posters: One poster about each of the four life cycles with drawings and/or pictures for each stage.

Written information on each life cycle, and/or each drawing or picture.

One poster focused on the most common butterflies seen in our area, and when.

A five-minute PowerPoint presentation of these artifacts to a committee of the city parks and recreation department.

Culminating Project/Artifact

Five finished signs, using treated wood, posters developed by the class, and plastic to cover and protect the artwork. One teacher's husband can help purchase appropriate wood and plastic and construct the actual signs. The class will do a field trip to install the signage along the trail in the spring of the academic year.

One version of this sample PBL project was developed in a workshop I conducted, by two third-grade teachers in the Rochester, New York, area. Those teachers chose to work together to help their students understand the life cycles of butterflies and the ecology that supports them, as well as to help label a greenway walk along a local canal. This sample PBL project shows the general framework for a PBL project, including a number of components: project anchor, driving question, list of necessary resources, anticipated artifacts (or specific products) and rubrics for production of these artifacts, and finally, the culminating project.

While many projects are initiated with only a project anchor and driving question in hand, others are more developed by the teacher before being shared with students. With students and teachers who are not veterans of PBL instruction, teachers tend to develop more of the components of the project description. In fact, the first time a teacher undertakes a PBL project, he or she should probably develop more of the components shown in the previous box. This "pre-development" of the basic components of the PBL project will lend more structure to the initial effort, yet still leave some choices for students to make. This process will make both teachers and students more comfortable during their first project. Later, as both students and teachers become more experienced in PBL, student collaborative teams should hold team meetings and take responsibility for developing these specific components of subsequent PBL projects. Ideally, a veteran group of students would exercise student choice and student decision making in a collaborative framework.

As shown in this example, PBL does involve some use of specific terminology. In PBL, the term *artifact* is used to mean a product developed by the students. This term is used rather than *report*, or *presentation*, or *paper*, since projects typically involve development of a large variety of products, rather than merely a written report. Artifacts may include: written work, art work, spreadsheets, video products, websites, podcasts, webquests, PowerPoint presentations, wikis, computer games and simulations, or any other product students may develop. In most PBL projects, a variety of preliminary artifacts are developed prior to the culminating artifact or project, and teachers can exercise some control over which educational standards are covered within a PBL project by stipulating specific artifacts that must be developed.

> Artifact—any product developed within a PBL project. These may include written reports, PowerPoint presentations, spreadsheets, videos, art projects, songs, poems, or any other creative product.

The culminating project may be considered as the final and most important artifact of the PBL project, and it must involve some type of publication or public display beyond the classroom. Note that in this example, student work will be presented to an outside group, and then displayed along a city walking trail for several years to come. Publication of student work is the "payoff" for PBL projects, and because students realize that many people will be reviewing their work, they are typically more invested in that work. Of course, not every project results in public signage. Rather, the culminating project may be a presentation published on a class or school website, a presentation to a school or community committee, a YouTube video posted online, or any other publication option that places student work before an outside group.

> Culminating project—the final and most important artifact of the PBL project, which will be published in some form beyond the classroom.

Most PBL projects are heavily tied to 21st century communications technologies. In this example, both PowerPoint presentations and Internet searches were included during the PBL experience. These modern teaching tools help every student access the curricular content, much more so than merely delivering this content via a textbook and lecture presentation. Rigorous use of these tools also helps prepare students for the working world of the 21st century.

Step-by-Step PBL Instruction

The following box presents a rough guide to the steps in the PBL instructional process, including specific indicators of the types of instruction that will be necessary as students and teachers move toward increased PBL instruction (Bender, 2012). While these can provide an indication of what PBL instruction involves, these steps must be considered quite fluid, and these processes often overlap during a PBL project, as both teachers and students respond to the real-time requirements of PBL.

> ### Steps in the PBL Instructional Process
>
> **Introduction of PBL Project Anchor**
>
> - Brainstorming possible problem solutions
> - Identification of specific areas of inquiry
> - Development of artifact list
> - Dividing up research responsibilities
> - Developing timeline for initial research

Initial Research Phase

- Searching for information

- Evaluation of web-based sources

- Minilessons (short whole-group lessons led by the teacher) on specific topics

Creation/Development of Initial Artifacts

- Synthesizing information

- Rubrics to evaluate initial work

- Collaborative decision making

- Begin development of culminating artifact

- Identification of additional information needed

Second Research Phase

- Additional information sought

- Modification of responsibilities and timeline

- Development of additional artifacts as needed

Development/Evaluation of Culminating Artifact Phase

- Development of culminating artifact

- Class evaluation of all artifacts including culminating artifact

Presentation/Publication of PBL Project

Introductory Planning Phase

As indicated previously, in classes where both teachers and students are experienced with PBL, the teacher may begin the PBL instructional process with only the project anchor and perhaps a driving question in hand. In those circumstances, PBL teams (usually ranging in size from four to ten students) will meet and brainstorm the anchor, creating ways to attack the problem. As they brainstorm, they will identify specific pieces of information they need, and these initial research areas will eventually become initial artifacts to be developed during the project.

One aspect of PBL that many proponents applaud is the fact that emotional intelligence, the various "people skills" that help students succeed in life, are specifically taught in most PBL classes. For example, during this first phase, teachers often spend some time teaching the brainstorming process (i.e., accept all possible ideas without criticism during initial brainstorming; compare/critique them later), as well as teamwork skills (using "I" messages and not "you" messages when criticizing, and practice active listening). These skills have collectively been referred to as "emotional intelligence," and as Myers and Berkowicz (2015) point out, emotional intelligence should be stressed in every PBL and STEM classroom because these skills dramatically impact a student's overall success in life. These skills will greatly facilitate the types of collaborative work required within the PBL experience.

We should also note that emotional intelligence skills are often overlooked in classrooms. While content standards are certainly stressed, the ability to understand and get along with other people is not often a structured part of the school curriculum, even though these skills go a long way in determining who is most successful in the workplace of the 21st century (Myers & Berkowicz, 2015). In that sense, PBL and STEM instruction offer a richer learning environment than traditional instruction, and this initial phase in a PBL project is a wonderful time to teach these essential skills.

> Emotional intelligence—a set of people skills including ability to respectfully brainstorm without criticism, and later, to criticize without rancor, using "I" messages and not "you" messages. Active listening is also included.

This introductory phase will usually take place over two or three class periods, and most of those initial days will be spent in PBL team meetings. These meetings should last between fifteen and twenty minutes, and be highly focused on developing the remaining components of the PBL project. Each team meeting should generate a set of team meeting notes that delineate specific artifacts to develop, role responsibilities for each team member, a to-do list for all students, and any decisions reached by the team. Clearly this planning of the PBL project components will take some time. Also, when students are first exposed to PBL instruction the teacher will spend more time on the emotional intelligence skills discussed above, so this phase will take more time than in later PBL experiences.

This phase ends when the team has fleshed out each of the components presented in the box earlier in this chapter. Of course, during those first days, when students are not in team meetings, research should be undertaken for the remainder of the period. Finally,

I recommend that teachers require a written summary from each team at the end of this phase that identifies each artifact needed and the responsibility of each team member, as well as a timeline for artifact and project completion. Teachers may wish to develop forms to document individual students' responsibilities as this phase is completed. Later in the PBL process, these documents will help the teacher understand the work that has been accomplished and will also keep the team focused during their subsequent work.

Initial Research Phase

Next, teams will move into the initial research phase, and as noted above, this will overlap with the introductory planning phase. During the initial research, teams will gather information on their proposed artifacts. This second phase will take multiple days, and perhaps several weeks, depending on the nature and scope of the project, since much of the work in PBL is accomplished in this phase.

During this phase, teachers often note that students from different teams seem to be having the same problem with certain concepts. Therefore, if teachers see a need, they may offer minilessons of ten to fifteen minutes on particularly difficult concepts to help team members move forward (Bender, 2012). This would resemble traditional, whole-class instruction on that particular concept, and should end with some demonstration from every student that they have mastered that content.

> Minilesson—teacher-directed group instruction, usually lasting only ten to fifteen minutes, focused on a specific topic or concept.

When determining which students may need a minilesson, teachers can use a tool like the LSI Tracker: http://www.learningsciences.com/?s=LSI+Tracker. The LSI Tracker is a mobile-enabled application, developed by Learning Sciences International, that works with any mobile device. It will help teachers to track individual student progress during the less structured instructional activities that characterize the initial instruction phase of PBL. With the LSI Tracker, teachers can input specific goals, and subordinate indicators for each goal, to document mastery of that content. Then, during the PBL lesson, or during the minilesson, the teacher can quickly check off specific indicators for individual students as they demonstrate mastery.

Here's an example. If a teacher notes that some students are having difficulty with the brainstorming skills discussed previously, that teacher might create the following goal and behavioral indicators, and input these into the LSI Tracker.

Goal: Demonstrate ability to brainstorm successfully during PBL.

Subordinate Indicators: Contribute ideas to the discussion without self-censoring.
Help to generate additional ideas through encouragement.
Respond to ideas of others with a compliment.
Do not criticize any idea during the initial brainstorming.

Using the LSI Tracker, the teacher could check off, for each individual student in the class, when that brainstorming indicator is observed. Most students will understand these behaviors of brainstorming merely by having the brainstorming process described to them, so the teacher would check off those indicators for most students during the first brainstorming session. However, other students may not follow those brainstorming guidelines and may need a minilesson on brainstorming processes.

Again, during the initial research phase, various minilessons can be provided on any content that students need help with. Strategic use of minilessons for selected groups of students helps ensure that all students reach mastery of the content, even during the less structured instruction that characterizes the PBL classroom (Bender, 2012). Note that most minilessons are typically offered when most students are engaged in research procedures. Thus, the students who are not participating in the minilesson continue their individual research.

As an additional suggestion, Bender (2012) recommends that teachers instruct students in evaluation of web-based sources during this phase of the PBL process. This may be either in a minilesson or instruction offered for the entire class. It is clear that much research will be undertaken in the future based on Internet searches, and students should understand how to evaluate the quality of information available. For example, information from governmental sources and websites is, in most cases, more reliable than information from Wikipedia, and information from both of those types of sites are more likely to be accurate than the website of an advocacy organization. Also, evaluation of the intentions behind the authors of various sources is critical, and PBL projects provide ample opportunity to teach students critical thinking and evaluation of information quality during this initial research phase. Again a tool like the LSI Tracker could be useful here. Teachers can input the indicators of information evaluation and check off when students demonstrate those behavioral indicators.

Creation of Initial Artifacts

The next phase in the process involves the actual development of initial artifacts. As students complete their initial research, they will share their information, and synthesize that information, as they begin to develop the specific artifacts required. Again, these initial artifacts may include almost anything such as artwork, graphics, spreadsheets of data, wikis, video presentations, or PowerPoint presentations. This phase will, of necessity, overlap with the previous research phase, since students typically begin artifact development while they are still doing research, and then realize they need more information. Thus, this phase is somewhat ill-defined, and students may spend considerable time here.

Rubrics can be very helpful here. (Rubrics are discussed as a separate strategy below.) Because teachers can typically tell which artifacts will be necessary (and in many cases, even before students realize it), they can develop rubrics for various artifacts even before the project begins. These can then be shared with students as they work on the initial artifacts. Thus, students will be instantly receiving feedback on their work throughout this step in the process.

Through the development of the initial artifacts, students begin the process of developing their final product. This is one reason that PBL fits so completely with STEM instruction; engineering an object that solves a real-world problem is the major goal for a PBL project, and this process emphasizes the engineering component of STEM much more forcefully than traditional instruction.

Second Research Phase

The second research phase is a catch-up phase in which students collect additional information and perhaps design and develop additional artifacts that were not previously identified. This phase will be much shorter in general than the previous phases, but it is necessary to emphasize that during the project completion process, sometimes it is necessary to return to the research material for additional information. Also, teachers typically stress reflection and self-evaluation during this phase, in order to strengthen each learner's self-reflection skills. Further, reflective thinking is a skill that will be necessary throughout life.

Development/Evaluation of Culminating Artifact

At some point, usually during the second phase, students begin the development of their artifacts. Because some or most of those artifacts will appear or be represented in some form in the culminating artifact, this development of the culminating artifact cuts across several phases of this process. The culminating artifact is often some type of combined presentation that utilizes various components from the previous artifacts and synthesizes them into a meaningful whole. Again, engineering is stressed in this process in ways that traditional instruction simply cannot match.

In addition to development of the culminating artifact, students must evaluate that artifact in the context of a "pre-publication" formative evaluation. As indicated previously, rubrics are frequently used for development of initial artifacts, and can likewise be used in this evaluation of the culminating artifact. Further, this final formative evaluation offers the opportunity for a team-based peer evaluation. Thus, this phase provides students with many opportunities to practice these skills—skills that are in demand in the 21st century workplace (Bender, 2012).

Based on this final, formative evaluation, and prior to publication, some additional work may be necessary on the culminating artifact. In some cases, one or more extra days may be required if a team identifies specific weaknesses that can be addressed with just a bit more research and project refinement.

Publication Phase

The PBL project is published in the final phase. This may be a presentation of some type to an outside body or uploading the culminating project to YouTube, a school website, or to the World Wide Web. At this point, parents should be informed of the availability of the project, and students should be encouraged to talk with their parents about their role in the PBL process. This publication to the larger world is in many ways the most powerful student motivator for PBL learning. Knowing that many persons will see the project in some form often spurs students to work harder to get the culminating artifact as strong as possible.

These phases will vary considerably from one project to another and across the grade levels. The size of the project teams will also impact this time frame, since larger PBL teams will typically require more meeting time to complete these project phases. However, most PBL projects are week-long, or multiweek projects, since that much time is required to cover these phases and develop a valuable and valid culminating artifact.

Research on PBL Instruction

Again, the primary focus of this book is not presentation of extensive research evidence on various strategies. However, some research evidence will be shared that is supportive of the strategies discussed. In this instance, research on PBL has shown it to be a very effective instructional approach (Bender, 2012; Boss & Krauss, 2007; Hattie, 2012; Larmer, Ross, & Mergendoller, 2009; Myers & Berkowicz, 2015; Vega, 2012). Hattie (2012) demonstrated that this type of instruction was among the twenty-five most effective types of instruction to positively impact student achievement. PBL has been applied in virtually every subject area and grade level, in both science and mathematics, as well as most other subject areas, and students do seem to learn more using this approach than traditional instruction (Boss & Krauss, 2007; Larmer, Ross, & Mergendoller, 2009). Because PBL increases student engagement, motivation to learn, and collaborative skills, it is recommended across the board as a 21st century teaching approach (Bender, 2012; Larmer, Ross, & Mergendoller, 2010).

Summary

PBL is presented first in this book for a reason: PBL instruction is one of the most effective instructional procedures developed over recent decades, and for some educators, PBL is virtually synonymous with STEM (Vega, 2012). Further, PBL is receiving increased emphasis in STEM classes from educators around the world, simply because it works so well. Because PBL incorporates real-world problems, and uses team decision making from the modern workplace, this instructional procedure prepares students better for the world of work in the 21st century. Further, PBL instruction involves specific instruction in skills that are not typically included in today's classes (e.g., brainstorming, teamwork), even though these are recognized as essential skills in the workplace (Bender, 2012).

As stated previously, much of the discussion of STEM instruction takes place in the context of PBL instructional practices, and one is hard-pressed to find many examples of STEM teaching that are not based on PBL. Thus, for teachers who are moving into more of a STEM instructional orientation, PBL is one instructional strategy that must be explored.

STRATEGY 2

Build Something: Engineering and Makerspace in STEM Classes

Engineers build things. They operate things such as complex pressurized systems or large engines. They build, make changes, and operate things in the man-made world. In that sense, one fundamental in both STEM and PBL involves the expectation that students will target a problem and, using principles of engineering, create a solution for that problem. In short, like most engineers, students in STEM are expected to build (Anderson, 2014; Bender, 2012; De Gree, 2015; Markam, 2011; Myers & Berkowicz, 2015; Smith, 2015; Vega, 2012). In fact, project construction, game development, model development, and refinement/improvement for specific products become the primary focal point of learning in STEM education, and students in STEM classes are routinely expected to build a solution to the selected problem or project.

In public schools, this "build something" mandate has taken on the mantel of the "makerspace" movement. Makerspace is a growing trend in business that is based on providing "space" in the community or school for employees or students to gather, invent, tinker, explore, and create things using a variety of tools and resources.

The "20% time" is a similar idea, and both concepts are receiving the attention of educators (Anderson, 2014; Yokana, 2015). Here is a brief definition of each idea:

continued →

Makerspaces—places in the classroom where students can create, explore, and make stuff. Tools, time, resources, and space to build are provided to give students freedom to creatively explore making stuff (Anderson, 2014). Teachers should explore the website MakerFaire.org for resources and ideas for makerspaces in the classroom.

20% Time—a return of 20% of the instructional time to the students for exploration of topics they select, or for designing and creating things, given resources to work with. This idea was first implemented by Google (Anderson, 2014), a company that gives its employees 20% of their time to work on something not related to their assigned area. Gmail was one of many innovations to result from that time.

As these ideas suggest, both industry leaders and educators are seeking ways to simply give students the time to create. In short, one might anticipate that within only a few years, most STEM classes will incorporate some structured time for students, either working alone or in groups to simply build something (Anderson, 2014).

However, with this broader engineering goal of "build something" in mind, educators should realize that traditional ideas for building are about to change rather drastically (Anderson, 2014; De Gree, 2015; Epps & Osborn, 2015; Smith, 2015). While most of us on the planet do not yet realize it, we are in the midst of a revolution in engineering and manufacturing, a revolution that may surpass the industrial revolution or the information age, in terms of changing the daily lives of millions of people (Smith, 2015). This creative revolution stems from one of the most innovative developments in history since the wheel: 3-D printing (De Gree, 2015; Smith, 2015).

3-D printing is, of course, an innovation that is very recent and is exactly what it sounds like—using the equivalent of digital printing technology and a wired manufacturing "printer" to work with fluid plastics or metals to actually create three-dimensional objects that can then be applied to a limitless number of problems. This is discussed in more detail later, but for now we must note that all of our older conceptualizations of what students can build, what they can do in the classroom, are likely to change because of this revolutionary technology. But this is only one of the changes in education coming from the STEM movement.

3-D printing is the use of digital printing technology and a manufacturing "printer" to work with fluid plastics or metals to actually create three-dimensional objects that can then be applied to a limitless number of problems. This development alone is revolutionizing the manufacturing process.

Teachers have long realized that technology can greatly enhance instruction in a variety of ways. While video development, storyboarding software, and presentation software options have been utilized in education increasingly in recent decades (Bender & Waller, 2013), newer technologies such as 3-D printing, augmented reality, and robotics are making newer construction options available to students in the learner-centered classroom. Construction of projects has taken on new forms that could not have been conceived of even ten or fifteen years ago (De Gree, 2015; Myers & Berkowicz, 2015; Smith, 2015), and use of these innovative technologies has, increasingly, become the hallmark of the STEM classroom.

The Engineering Design Process

In addition to the makerspace movement, another difference between STEM instruction and more traditional instruction in the physical sciences involves the emphasis on engineering and design (Jolly, 2014). The principles of engineering are very similar to the overall scientific method, thus making the creative engineering process an excellent opportunity for teaching the scientific process overall. The following box presents Jolly's synthesis of the steps in the engineering process.

The Engineering Design Process

Define the problem—A group discussion focused on reaching consensus on what the problem is and what the general construction project should do (Jolly, 2014).

Brainstorm to develop multiple ideas for solutions—Brainstorming is a critical skill in the modern, collaborative workplace and should be one of the first steps when attacking a problem in a collaborative fashion.

continued →

Conduct background research and summarize—Either a team or an individual process intended as the first step toward identification of an actual construction project/product. If undertaken as a team activity, the results of the initial instructional phase should be summarized for all team members.

State hypotheses—Scientists explore ideas from their brainstorming sessions by stating hypotheses concerning how the ideas might work. These hypotheses may then be proven or disproven with subsequent work.

Create prototypes—Engineers solve problems by creating prototypes to test their hypotheses. The development (i.e., building) process is not only foundational, it is critical to the learning process in STEM.

Evaluate the prototypes—As prototypes are developed, students begin the evaluation phase. Does the prototype work? Does it do effectively what it is supposed to do? When this evaluation shows mistakes in the design, students determine collectively how to move forward. Also, they then begin to understand that a mistake is a learning opportunity.

Redesign the prototype for the final product—The process of design, evaluation, and redesign is more convoluted than this simple list of steps suggests, and students will quickly learn that these three steps are often repeated a number of times before a project is completed—exactly as it is in the real life of an engineering project (Jolly, 2014).

In reviewing the engineering design steps above, teachers will also note the similarity to the ongoing steps previously described as the PBL process. First, delineation of the problem/product and brainstorming, next research, next product construction, and so forth. It is no accident that both engineering and project-based learning in the STEM class incorporate basically the same steps; this is the definitive example of problem solving in the modern world, and students simply must master this process in order to compete globally in the decades to come (National Research Council, 2011; National Science Board, 2012).

Building Curriculum Options for STEM

There is an array of creative makerspace curricular options available. Several are presented here and others are discussed later in this book. Below, I have discussed general resources for your STEM makerspace, as well as several of the more recent and exciting engineering/construction options: LEGOs construction, Project STEM, AutoCAD, and 3-D printing.

Stocking Your STEM Makerspace

As stated above, the intention of the makerspace is to provide space, time, and resources to encourage students to make things. Teachers in primary and elementary grades, as well as middle and high school teachers in science, engineering, and technology have to provide a "space" in their room, and place various resources for students to create things. Of course, those makerspace materials and resources will vary across the grade levels. In a primary class, teachers might place constructor sets, LEGOs, cardboard, tape, crayons, cardstock paper, clothespins, paste, and similar materials to encourage students to create stuff. I like to see small sections of ½ inch PVC plumbing pipe (a white, lightweight pipe), maybe in sections that are six inches, one foot, and two feet long, along with elbow and T connectors that can be reused.

For middle and secondary classes, the makerspace materials will be much more sophisticated. They include some of the materials above, but might also include small electric motors, wire, connections, batteries, and perhaps small robotic arms. While few teachers will have large budgets for their makerspace, teachers can accumulate these materials over time and encourage students to plan for reuse of them. A 3-D printer might be found in sophisticated makerspaces in middle and high schools, for supervised student use.

Teachers setting up a makerspace should not overlook the virtual world options. As one example, Contraption Maker is a new computer app that allows students to "make" virtual Rube Goldberg–type machines (TeachThought Staff, 2015). This app is free for schools and includes a teacher dashboard allowing teachers to track an individual student's progress. Curriculum ideas are also included. Using hamster motors, pulleys, balls, conveyor belts, and various tools presented onscreen, students will either repair machines or make new ones and test them operationally. Students can then save and share them. This app is intended for students from grade 3 up through high school and makes a great addition to any teacher's makerspace in the STEM classroom.

LEGOs: Not Just a Childhood Toy Anymore!

Most adults are quite familiar with LEGOs. (LEGO is a registered trademark of the LEGO Corporation. See http://education.lego.com/en-us.) These lock-together plastic bricks are frequently used as a play toy by our children or even by ourselves. Those same lock-together toys have been supplemented with various sensors, electric motors, and computer-based instructions to provide makerspace construction opportunities for students from kindergarten through grade 8 (Hicks, 2015). Teachers might want to review the LEGO Education podcast http://www.teachercast.net/lego-education-iste-2015/.

Of course, any parent who ever shared a set of LEGO blocks with their children has seen youngsters play with the blocks, sometimes to the near exclusion of the world around them. Certainly most students consider such LEGO play anything but school-work! However, by coupling these simple construction bricks with software and several motors and sensors, LEGO Education has provided a number of tools for teachers that will make the use of LEGO virtually a required feature in any STEM classroom at the primary and elementary level.

For example, the LEGO Machines and Mechanisms curricular program introduces students to simple machines, including gears, levers, pulleys, wheels, and axles, and they construct various projects to demonstrate concepts such as energy, force, and motion. At this level, the LEGO program parallels much of the early science content in the elementary grades. A range of additional products allows this to be extended past fifth grade and well into middle school. Using interdisciplinary, theme-based activities, students begin to develop engineering skills, as well as communication skills as they work together.

Hicks (2015) provides a list of ways to use LEGOs in the classroom, ranging from their use as counters to represent mathematics facts in the operations to the LEGO More to Math program to help students visualize the mathematics problem. Hicks (2015) also noted that simple coding (programming the computer) can be taught using LEGOs—bricks of a different size, shape, or color representing different symbols in a "code" that can then be used to control "robots"—which are in this case other students in the class. The following box presents several other instructional ideas for various subjects.

STEM Instructional Ideas Using LEGOs

Use LEGOs to teach math visually, including counting, comparing, and measuring.

LEGOs can help students visualize arithmetic problems (e.g., a square piece with four studs helps students see what 2×2 looks like. If you connect that piece to a rectangular one with eight studs, students can count out what 4+8 is. By setting different pieces side by side, you can show how fractions work: this one is ½ the size of that one, which is ¼ of the size of this other one [Hicks, 2015]). See http://www.scholastic.com/teachers/top-teaching/2013/12/using-lego-build-math-concepts.

LEGOs can show patterns and symmetry. Varied colors and shapes encourage creativity and can demonstrate symmetry.

LEGOs can illustrate a story. History lessons involve imagining historical settings, such as the attack on Bastogne in World War II or the burning of the White House in the War of 1812.

LEGOs can help teach students about classification systems. Classification can be based on color, size, shape, or combinations of these (Hicks, 2015).

As this list shows, the options provided by these LEGOs curricular materials are nearly inexhaustible (Hicks, 2015). Thus, if a primary, elementary, or middle school teacher is just beginning with STEM, a first stop should be the LEGOs website, for exploration of the many creative construction options provided by LEGOs.

Project STEM

Of course, many curricula are becoming available for STEM instruction other than the LEGOs materials presented, and an Internet search will show many scores of curricular materials for STEM. As one example, Pearson Education created Project STEM: http://www.pearsonschool.com/index.cfm?locator=PS14Kt. Project STEM is a curriculum for grades K through 8, and includes instructional guidelines to help teachers integrate the eighteen lessons into existing curricula in science and math classes. Each module follows the same traditional instructional format: introduce, teach, and evaluate. Topics in Project STEM cover life science, earth science, and physical science, while stressing curricular connections and using hands-on labs, projects, and supporting instructional materials. Specifically, programs include Designing Trails and Roads (K–2), Designing a Super Sneaker (3–5), and Designing Roller Coasters (6–8). As is obvious from these titles, the engineering design process is featured heavily in this curriculum, and the topics should help engage the students across the grade levels.

CAD for Public Education

CAD is an acronym for computer assisted design. (Sometimes the term *CADD* is used, standing for computer assisted design and drafting.) A variety of computer programs are available that help engineers plan and design all types of items, and one of the most popular is AutoCAD from Autodesk Inc. (http://www.autodesk.com/products/autocad/overview). There are also different levels of this program (e.g., AutoCAD for Beginners), and this makes CAD instruction an option for makerspaces in public schools.

AutoCAD and similar programs allow someone to draft/draw virtually anything in either 2-D or 3-D, on a single computerized drawing board. These programs are used by engineers for building anything from toys to houses, bridges to oil or gas pipelines. As the availability of engineering courses in high schools increases, these and similar programs are likely to be found in STEM high schools in the near future, if they are not already taught. Specifically, virtually all higher education engineering schools, and many two-year colleges, offer courses or certificate programs using these CAD programs to teach the skill of technical drawing and drafting. While only a few public schools are teaching with these computer design programs, some are, and, as noted above, the use of these programs is likely to increase during the high school years, with the increased emphasis in STEM overall.

Building Across the Grade Levels

As these varied makerspace options and curricula demonstrate, STEM has become a realistic instructional expectation across the grade levels. While early discussions of STEM focused on science and math classes in middle and high schools, this is no longer the case. STEM should no longer be considered merely an innovation for middle and high school science and mathematics classes. Rather, STEM as a comprehensive instructional approach must begin in kindergarten and continue throughout the school years (Hicks, 2015; Myers & Berkowicz, 2015; Slavin, 2014).

3-D Printing: Construction for the Next Century

As mentioned previously, the 3-D printing process is creating shockwaves in manufacturing plants around the world and promises to fundamentally transform our world, not to mention our educational practices (Davis, 2015; De Gree, 2015; Epps & Osborn, 2015; Smith, 2015). Printing with fluid plastic (or with fluid metals in industrial settings) rather than simply ink, a 3-D printer can create virtually any object that can be imagined and digitally described, and this technology is finding its way into public school classrooms. For example, Breeden (2015) described his use of a 3-D printer in the science classroom, noting that simple objects were created in fairly short order but that more detailed objects took time. A simple button or badge took Breeden's students about fifteen minutes to create, whereas a scale model of the U.S. Capitol building was built in slightly over twelve hours.

Of course, the implications of 3-D printing can hardly be imagined. The following box presents some real-world examples of the types of creativity and innovation resulting from this 3-D printing technology. Teachers should note that, as indicated in these examples, important engineering work using 3-D printing can be and is being done by nonengineers as well as, in some cases, elementary school students!

Examples of the 3-D Printing Revolution

An Indonesian man, Arie Kurniawan, participated in an open innovation design challenge to redesign a bracket that attaches a jet engine to an airplane wing (Smith, 2015). Mr. Kurniawan was not an engineer and had no experience in manufacturing. However, he used a 3-D printer to make his bracket. His design beat out over one thousand other submissions, and it worked perfectly, passing every single industrial test for durability, stress, and reliability. Further, it weighed 83 percent less than the part it replaced, and saving weight is a big deal in airplane construction! Soon, his bracket will be flying all over the world on the most modern jets in the sky, and you will be riding on one!

A fifth-grade student used 3-D printing and created a prosthetic hand for a needy student (this example was described by Myers & Berkowicz [2015]). Sierra Petrocelli was a fifth grader in Monkton, Virginia, and was developing a project for her school science fair. Her teacher challenged her to create something to change someone's life, and Sierra decided to "print" an affordable 3-D prosthetic hand. She contacted a company that does that type of work, and the company sent her a tutorial. She then printed a prosthetic hand that cost only $50 for a young girl in California: http://kdvr.com/2014/07/15/11-year-old-girl-uses-science-project-to-create-prosthetic-hands-for-children/.

continued →

Sixth-grade math students in North Carolina have used 3-D printing to model their mathematics work. "The Interactive Project-Based Learning Using 3-D" grant results (Epps & Osborn, 2015) present academic achievement results from a STEM project in Richmond County Schools (https://www.youtube.com/watch?v=bfT1AqO1qi8). Forty-four sixth-grade students participated in using 3-D printing in the mathematics classes in several middle schools. These students used computer programs featuring engineering design principles and a 3-D printer to engage them in their lessons by having them "build" their models. Using math modeling and a 3-D printer together seemed to engage and motivate these lower achieving students at the beginning of middle school. The students' achievement increased by 44 percent using these innovation teaching practices.

A team at General Electric used 3-D printing to create a new fuel injection system for jet engines. The previous system included twenty-one separate parts, any one of which might fail, and all of which had to be produced and shipped to the engine manufacturing factory. The new 3-D printed system had only one part and that part was many times stronger than the original. The new part increased fuel efficiency by 15 percent, thus saving over one million dollars in fuel costs per year, per jet! Additional savings are soon to be realized from saving shipping costs. Rather than have the older parts shipped in, the 3-D print process allows the company to build that new part on site (Smith, 2015).

One can only speculate what this revolution in manufacturing might mean to the world at large, or for that matter, to teachers in our mathematics and science classrooms. Some ideas have been floated about what this revolution might look like (De Gree, 2015; Smith, 2015).

- Imagine a large manufacturing base within the United States with no supply chain reaching back into Brazil or China (Smith, 2015). What does that mean for international trade? Now that is a great project-based learning idea for math and social studies, if I've ever seen one!

- Imagine beginning the manufacturing process with only raw materials fed into a 3-D printing machine in a local factory. What happens if every manufacturer worldwide simply makes parts as they are needed?

- Imagine students doing mathematical modeling, and then using this technology to print up the actual model they created mathematically.

- Imagine what happens to the distinction between manufacturer and retailer. If a local Walmart needs a lamp for a customer to purchase, why not just print one up in the back of the store?

- If 3-D printing enabled individual parts to be redesigned with massive improvements in efficiency, what other increases in efficiency might be possible in cars, stereos, boat engines, fishing rods, or … (you name the product)?

- If students can create useful, durable products while they learn, should they profit from their creative endeavors while they are in school?

- If people with no training can out-design a part in a company stocked with top engineers, what are the implications for the current global workforce (Smith, 2015)?

- If 3-D printing can reduce twenty-one parts to one, what does that mean for parts manufacturing worldwide (Smith, 2015)?

- In the world of 3-D printing, if you can think of it, you can build it. What new products might we see?

These speculations could go on, quite literally, forever, and that might be an interesting discussion, but that is not our focus here. Rather, these questions should be enough to help us all, as educators, understand the wave of change in manufacturing, as well as science and mathematics instruction, that is about to overtake us. Smith (2015) in an article for business leaders summarized it best:

> Industrial 3-D printing, also referred to as additive manufacturing, is poised to significantly and permanently disrupt global production. No longer just a tool for rapid prototyping, 3-D printing is being used for end-use part production, and adoption is growing exponentially.

For our purposes as educators, the implications of 3-D printing technology on the world at large should motivate us all to consider the world for which we are preparing our students (Davis, 2015). Will students in our math and sciences classes today be able to effectively compete in the post–3-D printing world? Are we preparing our students to build effectively, given the tools that are available? Are our students learning to use the technologies in our classes that other students worldwide are already using in theirs? One may rest assured that students in India, China, Singapore, and Europe are learning them.

As Epps and Osborn (2015) demonstrated, sixth-grade students can benefit greatly from innovative instruction in mathematics that requires them to build something using 3-D printing. These realities should motivate us all to move into STEM construction using the new 3-D printing technology.

3-D Printing in STEM Classes

Simply having a 3-D printer and learning to use it in the classroom effectively are not synonymous. Teachers must, as always, attend to a number of considerations when planning for the effective use of a 3-D printer in their class makerspace (Breeden, 2015; Davis, 2015). Still, one can only imagine the learning that might take place if students were afforded the opportunity to create actual objects, perhaps a pirate ship, as they study that period of history. How much ballast is necessary to make the ship float well, and perform well in battle? What is the weight of a ship built with wood, rather than plastic, and how does that impact calculations of the ballast? How high must the sides be for the ship to be defensible? In such a project, history, science, and mathematics merge as students hypothesize on how their ship might perform, and then test those hypotheses on objects they actually created.

As that one example indicates, the impact of building, of creation, and the educational value thereof are limited only by the minds in the classroom—both teachers and students. Still, learning how to use this technology for teaching will require long-term reflective thought on the part of the teacher. Fortunately, a number of teachers have provided guidance for using 3-D printers in the classroom (Breeden, 2015; Davis, 2015; see also the web page of Kathy Schrock: http://www.schrockguide.net/3d-printing.html). Davis (2015) presented her reflections in that regard, and some of those are presented in the following box.

Teaching Tips for Using a 3-D Printer

- Find a video about loading the filament properly, using the printer, and planning initial print jobs.

- Review all the material that comes with the printer, and then call the printer manufacturer when you need help (don't wait).

- Printers use heat that will burn fingers, so keep fingers (and students) away from the printer during the print process. Also, let items cool off once they are finished, since they will remain hot for some time.

- Play with the resolution, density, and thickness, since you can control these. Resolution involves how thick the layers are, and smaller layers make for smoother printed objects. Fill density involves how full of filament the inside of a 3-D object is—hollow objects sometimes collapse, so the inside of most 3-D jobs look like the inside of a honeycomb. Thickness involves the thickness of the outside wall of the printed object (Davis, 2015).

- Be nearby the printer during all print jobs, which means you will probably do the larger print jobs during the school day.

- Combine the smaller parts of a print job. Install print software on every computer students use, which will allow you to print smaller jobs into one print job.

- Organize your printing, deciding in advance how students submit work for printing, how you will approve that work or give feedback before printing, how students might revise work, and how you can organize print jobs efficiently.

- Let students work in teams of three or four. They will then serve as "self-correcting" partners prior to the print job, and fewer resources will be wasted.

- Start with premade items. A variety of sources (e.g., Thingiverse.com) offer downloadable instructions for premade items for students to print. Starting with those items gives students the necessary practice.

- Let students use 3-D print software that's comfortable for them. You should use the software that came with the printer, but explore other programs as well, including Google Sketchup, that might be easier. Let students test and compare the 3-D print programs (Davis, 2015).

continued →

- Plan longer-term projects by giving student teams one day with the printer. It is unlikely that students will be able to finish a print job in one class period, so planning is critical.

- Learn with your students! 3-D printers are still quite new, so teachers and students can explore applications together.

Makerbot: A 3-D Printer for the Classroom

Makerbot is a 3-D printer robot intended for STEM classroom makerspaces, as well as other educational applications (Breeden, 2015; Davis, 2015). Makerbot is available at a fairly low cost, given relative costs for such technology and the overall quality of the machine (Breeden, 2015). For example, Breeden (2015) noted that there were two heads feeding plastic into your creation in Makerbot, rather than one, as in some other 3-D printers. This allows the students to create with multiple colors rather than merely one. Makerbot comes with Tinkercard, a software program to facilitate creativity in 3-D printing. This program uses a simple drag-and-drop interface, and students will pick up that mostly intuitive program quickly. They can then create projects in fairly short order.

This product also includes a variety of makerspace activities. For example, the *scoPe* project on geography and climates allows students to take on the role of new world explorer while they print up their own new world. This involves the creation of new biome geographic areas (or "tiles") for various geographical features, including tiles for water, forest, mountains, and other landscape features. As teams of students build their worlds, they explore their new biomes and learn about the various ecosystems, resources, and the dangers in each locale. They can even learn to trade with other students who have constructed separate worlds. This PBL project allows for wide flexibility and can easily be scaled with increasing complexity and difficulty for higher grade levels. This represents only one application of Makerbot in the classroom.

Finally, Makerbot has created several sites to assist teachers in using 3-D printing in their makerspaces. First, Thingiverse is an online repository of 3-D printing designs teachers can assess. Also, Jumpstart (http://www.thingiverse.com/jumpstart) is a site devoted to helping newcomers into the world of 3-D printing in the classroom and includes various resources to get STEM teachers started. JumpStart was created specifically with early learners in mind, so primary and elementary teachers should explore these resources, as they create or continue to enrich their makerspace.

Engineering, Makerspace, and Creativity

As an author, I debated with myself about the inclusion of this "build something/makerspace" strategy. Of course, in preparing any book many choices are made regarding what instructional practices and strategies should be presented, and it could easily be argued that makerspace is not an instructional strategy in and of itself. However, I chose to present this strategy for a variety of reasons. First, both STEM and PBL stress building as an important motivator for students, specifically with the emphasis on student choices (Bender, 2012; Vega, 2012). The creativity embodied within the necessity of building something must be emphasized in 21st century classrooms, and in that sense, the research supportive of PBL is likewise supportive of this "build something" strategy (Bender, 2012). Students simply learn more when they are creating things.

Second, the amazing functionality of the technology tools we have for building things in the classroom seemed to make inclusion of this strategy necessary. Whether a teacher uses LEGOs, Project STEM, Makerbot, or other similar curricula or tools for makerspaces in the classroom, having students create—having students build—is an important engineering component and represents the skills to be stressed in science and math classrooms. These are the exact skills needed in the 21st century workplace.

Third, the level of student engagement that is facilitated by the mandate to build something is critical to the overall efficacy of both PBL and STEM (Vega, 2012). The impressive—some would say compelling—body of research demonstrating the efficacy of PBL is likewise supportive of having students create something.

However, while those reasons are important, I wanted to present this strategy of building something because of the demonstrative importance of building real-world projects in STEM instruction (Jolly, 2014; Markham, 2011; Myers & Berkowicz, 2015). STEM instruction is not STEM unless students are creating something, so the absolute mandate to build something can and should stand on its own, as one of the preeminent STEM strategies. As we collectively envision education for the next decades, building must be close to the top of our priority list. Students should no longer be passive recipients of learning in American classrooms. Rather, they must become active creators of knowledge and builders of real-world solutions, if they are to compete in a global economy. In short, students must learn to build.

Summary

One thing is certain, changes in our methods of teaching science and mathematics are about to overtake us all, as the influence of the makerspace/build something movement grows. Teachers are increasingly embracing these concepts because we all realize that we are preparing our students for a new and different world. As usual, teachers will have to move quickly to stay ahead of that curve, and effective teachers have always embraced such a challenge. Of course, the best step-by-step instruction for teaching with makerspaces is the engineering and design process itself, and since that process was discussed previously, there is no need to readdress that here. Using that design process as a background, teachers will find that students can and will embrace the necessity to create projects using these new tools that address specific real-world needs. Perhaps your students will find a way to impact the world as did the fifth grader, Sierra Petrocelli. Her construction changed the life of a girl in California; what could be a better learning experience than that?

STRATEGY 3

Summarizing and Prediction/ Hypothesis Testing

The teaching strategies of summarizing and prediction/hypothesis testing have long been recognized as effective instructional procedures (Hattie, 2012; Lewis & Thompson, 2010; Marzano, 2007, 2003; Marzano, Pickering, & Pollock, 2001; Tileston, 2004). Specifically, these strategies have been shown to be quite effective in increasing school achievement (Marzano, 2009a, 2007; Marzano, Pickering, & Pollock, 2001). For example, Marzano's work has indicated that having students summarize content is likely to increase achievement by 34 percent, and hypothesis testing will probably result in an achievement increase of 23 percent (Marzano, 2009a, 2007, 2003; Marzano, Pickering, & Pollock, 2001). For this reason, teachers have been emphasizing these skills in various STEM and other courses.

With that noted, educators most often implement these strategies independently (Marzano, 2009a) because summarization is not directly dependent on hypothesis testing or prediction. However, in STEM instruction, summarization and prediction/hypothesis are related steps within the broader scientific method, which is the very basis of STEM instruction. Therefore, in STEM instruction, both summarization and prediction take on additional meaning, and teaching these processes in a manner that emphasizes the interdependent nature of these instructional strategies makes the most sense. Below, the scientific method is briefly described, and then the specific instructional strategies of summarization and prediction are discussed.

The Scientific Method

The scientific method is fundamental in STEM instruction and serves as the basis for many lessons in the STEM class. Some science texts describe development of the scientific method within the context of the Age of Reason in Europe. However, as early as the development of rudimentary medical practices in the ancient Egyptian culture, a version of the scientific method, including observation, prediction, treatment or testing, and summary observation, was in evidence. Further, different versions of the scientific method are presented in different science textbooks, with some emphasizing the various steps or processes in different order. Of course, teachers should use the explanation of this concept that is presented in their curriculum. For our purposes, we will discuss the scientific process in terms of the steps shown in the following box, though these steps and/or the order in which they are performed certainly vary. For additional examples of the scientific method at various grade levels, teachers may wish to review several of the YouTube videos from this search: https://search.yahoo.com/search?fr=mcafee&type=C211US662D20141212&p=Scientific+Method+Videos

The Processes in the Scientific Method

1. Observe and summarize.
2. Ask a question (or questions).
3. Make a hypothesis/prediction.
4. Experiment/research to test the hypothesis.
5. Observe results.
6. Draw conclusions and summarize.

As noted previously, STEM is an instructional process based on the scientific method, and it should be used in many courses other than science, technology, engineering, and mathematics. In fact, STEM should become the basis for teaching in almost all core instructional subjects (exceptions might be the performing arts, and perhaps subjects such as creative writing). Thus, two case studies are presented below, one in science and one in social studies.

A Classroom Example: Scientific Method in Science

In a primary science class, students may be studying different states of matter (e.g., solid, liquid, gas). In particular, the process by which water becomes ice can provide a nice example for primary students of the scientific method in science class. Each step is explained below.

Observe and summarize. In the scientific method, students must be taught to use the power of observation to propose a question about the topic under discussion. Of course, this observation and question will typically be based on prior knowledge, and the student's ability to summarize both prior knowledge and new observed results is critical. Students might know that their parents make ice by freezing water but might not realize that ice and water are the same substance in different states.

Ask a question. Next students are taught to ask a question. Specifically, students must be taught to ask a question that is based on their previous summary and specifies exactly what they want to know. How do we make ice from water?

Make a hypothesis/prediction. The scientific method is founded on the statement of a hypothesis. A provable/disprovable hypothesis is critical, and students have to be taught the difference between provable and nonprovable propositions. In short, a provable hypothesis is a hypothesis that can serve as the basis for experimental exploration, the results of which must be observable and repeatable. The proposition "Storing drinking water at 31 degrees for twenty-four hours makes the water turn to ice" is a provable proposition. It is suggestive of an experimental action (actually store some water in a 31-degree environment for twenty-four hours), as well as an observable result (water either turns to ice or it doesn't).

Experiment/research to test the hypothesis. The experiment is the "testing" of the hypothesis. In the water-to-ice example, the students would store drinking water in an ice tray at 31 degrees (or colder) for twenty-four hours, and store other water in a similar container in an environment at 40 degrees for twenty-four hours. The students then would observe the results. Depending on the grade level of the class, the concept of independent variables and dependent variables might be introduced at this point. The independent variable is the variable that is intentionally manipulated to produce a specific effect (i.e., temperature of the storage bin or room), while other variables that might impact the outcome are held constant (i.e., the type of container and the length of time in this example). The dependent variable is the observed effect (ice or no ice after twenty-four hours).

Observe results. After the experiment is completed, the results are observed. In this example, ice would probably have formed in the 31-degree environment but not in the 40-degree environment. Again, the teacher would stress that these are observable effects on which all observers are likely to agree.

Draw conclusions and summarize. The drawing conclusions process in the scientific method involves basically three options: accept, reject, or modify the hypothesis. If observed results are as expected, students may accept the hypothesis as true. If not, then the hypothesis is rejected. The third option involves rejecting the hypothesis as originally stated but modifying it in a manner suggested by the observed results. This involves a change of, or a different manipulation of, the independent variable. Thus, the summary in this context is more than merely stating the important facts. It also involves suggesting possible future actions and possibly a modified hypothesis.

A Classroom Example: Scientific Method in Social Studies

The science class application of the scientific method, as described above, is fairly straightforward, but the scientific method in STEM schools should also be employed in a wide variety of non-STEM subject areas. For example, in a social studies class studying the American Revolution, the same scientific method process might apply. Here is an example.

Observe and summarize. After some study of the history of the American Revolution, the students might conclude that revolutions are more likely when a population is taxed without representation. This "cause/effect" is often stressed in most United States history courses.

Ask a question. Next students would ask a question: How many examples can we find in history where heavy taxation led to a revolution?

Make a hypothesis/prediction. In this case, the hypothesis might be, "Populations that are taxed without being represented in government are likely to revolt against that government."

Experiment/research to test the hypothesis. Whereas the sciences allow for direct experimentation and manipulation of variables, studies in the humanities do not. However, research can still be done by looking for multiple examples and nonexamples in which one variable seems to impact others. In this history example, to test the hypothesis, students would turn to other revolutions.

The teacher may, again depending on grade level, discuss the issue of independent and dependent variables in the social studies context. Of course, no variable can be intentionally manipulated in studies of history, but one can find examples in which the variables were either similar or different. For example, in this question on taxation causing revolutions, the independent variable is taxation, and the dependent variable is a subsequent revolution. Teachers might suggest that other cultural factors (other possible causal variables) be held constant as much as possible. Thus, students would seek examples of revolutions in cultures that were similar to the American colonies in 1775. In this case, students might research revolutions in Western Europe, since much of the populations of the American colonies in 1775 came from Western Europe. Thus, the French Revolution, the English Revolution, and the later Russian Revolution would be considered more appropriate comparisons than revolutions in Africa or ancient China.

Observe results. The observed results from such a comparative analysis would show several interesting things. First, in none of these other revolutions did high taxes play a significant causal role. However, there are similarities that would show up in the analysis of causes of the other revolutions. In every case above, the revolutionaries voiced what they perceived to be oppression of some type as valid reasons to reject the authority of a king, dictatorial ruler, or government.

Draw conclusions and summarize. In social sciences, like science, there are three possible conclusions related to the original hypothesis: accept the hypothesis, reject it, or reject and modify it. In this example, taxation was not a culprit in revolutions other than the American colonies, but the similarities do suggest that when populations begin to believe they are oppressed in some fashion, they become dissatisfied with a king, dictator, or other ruling elite. Thus, a variety of oppressive conditions (no food for the population, a war that the population doesn't care about but is forced to fight) may precipitate a revolution. In short, oppression of many types causes revolutions.

Summarizing in STEM Classes

In the context of the case studies of the scientific method presented above, the task of summarizing represents a significant step in learning in virtually all core subjects, and as shown above, summarization takes place at several different times during the scientific process. Further, high-ability learners realize this in the early grades and thus continually grow in the habit of summarizing their content all through the learning process, regardless of the subject under study. Summarizing is something that effective learners do without really thinking about it.

For example, when a high-achieving student reads content from a text, or a website such as Wikipedia, that student, as early as grade 2 or 3, will immediately consider any prior knowledge he or she has on that subject, and refine his or her understanding by taking the new knowledge into account. This represents the summarization process, and effective learners form that summarization habit early. They have learned over time that such integration of old information and new information helps them understand the content faster, and they summarize without really thinking about it.

For average-achieving students and students with learning challenges in the STEM class, however, these summarization procedures have not yet been mastered, and teachers will have to provide specific instructional guidance to help students master them. Students should be taught various procedures for summarizing content. Further, in the context of collaborative research that characterizes STEM classes, the ability to summarize content for one's teammates on a STEM project is even more critical.

Teaching Summarizing Skills

Summarization skills are often taught by providing an organizer strategy for summarizing. The following box provides a list and description of several strategies for summarizing main points, compiled from several sources (Lewis & Thompson, 2010; Tileston, 2004). However, this list provides only a few examples, and the reader may wish to check the various summarization strategy lists online for additional ideas (Lewis & Thompson, 2010; Teachervision, 2015). Again, research has documented that using summarization and prediction will improve comprehension (Marzano, 2009a), so all students will eventually need to master these skills.

A List of Summarization Strategies

- **3-2-1 List:** At the end of a class period, have students list three main points (or three "somethings"), two controversial ideas (or two things they disagree with), and one question related to their work that day. This works even in "research days" during the STEM process, even though students will list different things when they are researching different topics (Lewis & Thompson, 2010).

- **Ticket Out the Door/Exit Ticket:** Have students verbally answer one question on the lesson before they leave class. This can be the answer to any question about the day's work (Tileston, 2004).

- **The Important Thing:** Ask students to write several lines about the "three important ideas/things from the lesson today" and then identify the most important one (Lewis & Thompson, 2010).

- **Questions to the Teacher List:** Have students list one or two questions for the teacher to cover the next day (e.g., things the student might want clarified or discussed again [Lewis & Thompson, 2010]).

- **Headline Summaries:** Have students write a newspaper headline that gives the main points of the lesson (Lewis & Thompson, 2010).

- **Summary Journals:** Have students keep a journal of important concepts, in which they summarize their learning daily. Some teachers use prompting questions, such as the "Important Thing" idea above (Lewis & Thompson, 2010; Tileston, 2004).

- **PMI Chart:** Have students complete a PMI, in three columns with the following headings. *P* indicates three "positive" things you learned today. *M* means "minus"—or several things you didn't like or didn't quite understand, and *I* means "interesting," or things you have some information to share on (Tileston, 2004).

- **Text Scratch-Out:** When summarizing from written material, cover the page with plastic, and have students summarize by scratching out nonessential information. That usually leaves a topic sentence and a couple of main ideas (Teachervision, 2015).

- **Word Splash:** Students are given a "splash," including several key words from the lesson. They then write a summary of the lesson using these words (Lewis & Thompson, 2010).

- **Changing Points of View:** Ask students to do a quick-write about the lesson from another perspective (e.g., when discussing speeding up of plant life cycles using genetics, teachers might ask, "What would the Sierra Club say about that?"). The questions should force a student to take a different point of view (Lewis & Thompson, 2010).

- **What? So What? Now What?:** At various points in the lesson, have students answer the questions, What did we just learn? So what does that mean? And what should I expect now? As this last question indicates, summarization often leads directly to the next prediction in STEM classes (Tileston, 2004).

As indicated above, STEM is intended as an instructional approach for all subject areas, including areas other than hard sciences. With that in mind, several summarization techniques, described by Lewis and Thompson (2010), that are particularly applicable in nonscience subjects such as English, literature, and social studies are presented in the following box.

Summarization Strategies for Non-STEM Subjects

- **Carousel Brainstorming:** Using charts posted around the room, ask small groups of three or four students to respond to the question on the chart. Then, after three minutes, have the groups move on to another chart, read what has been written, and add a response to it. These charts can be used as a lesson activator or review the next day. This is a technique useful in any subject.

- **RAFT:** This is a writing summarization technique, in which students choose the Role or point of view, Audience (the specific readers to whom their summary is being written), Form (e.g., a letter, memo, list, email, etc.), and Topic (specific subject of the writing). Because of the emphasis on role and point of view, this can be particularly effective as a summarization technique in literature or English classes.

- **Dear Student Letter:** As a summary exercise, have students write a letter to an absent student telling him or her the main points of the lesson along with important details. The emphasis on writing makes this appropriate for social science classes as well as English classes.

- **What Would X Do?:** This is a great summary exercise in social studies classes, since it emphasizes perspectives and different motivations of various historical or fictional characters. Give students a situation related to the topic of or learning from the lesson. Then ask them to respond to the question, using a specific person (e.g., government official, historical figure, or scientist). This is similar to "Changing Points of View" above.

- **Cause-Effect Timeline:** Students use a timeline to summarize main events in a history or social science class. They must note for each indicator in the timeline what happened, why, and its possible effects.

- **Snowballs:** Put a problem on the SMART Board that has not been covered in class up to that point. Then each student is asked to guess the answer to the question on a small piece of paper, without signing the paper. They then wad up the paper and toss the "snowball" into a box. Next, each student in the class gets one of the tossed snowballs, and the teacher answers the question. Then each student looks at their snowball to see how many guessed the right answer in advance. The students can then work in pairs and edit the answers, making each snowball "correct." This stresses collaborative teamwork in the editing phase.

Learning Maps

In addition to point-by-point summaries and written summaries such as those above, some summarization strategies emphasize the presentation of more complex concepts—the big ideas of the unit—and these might be summarized together in pictorial form. For example, one new take on teaching summarization involves the creation of a learning map (Knight, 2013; O'Connell & Vandas, 2015). The learning map is one recent variation of the concept map, an idea that has been shown to be very effective in helping students understand difficult concepts. Hattie (2012), for example, showed that the concept map generated an effect size of .60, demonstrating that this technique was highly effective in facilitating higher achievement.

To form a learning map, one identifies a foundational concept or construct as the basis for the map. This is placed in the center, with several big ideas located around it.

The example in figure 3.1 (page 60) presents a learning map showing the concepts in an elementary earth science unit on the planet Earth. To begin a unit on the Earth, the teacher might present this learning map with only the main items (i.e., the items in bold print) on the map. Students would then be required to add the critical pieces of information under those critical concepts.

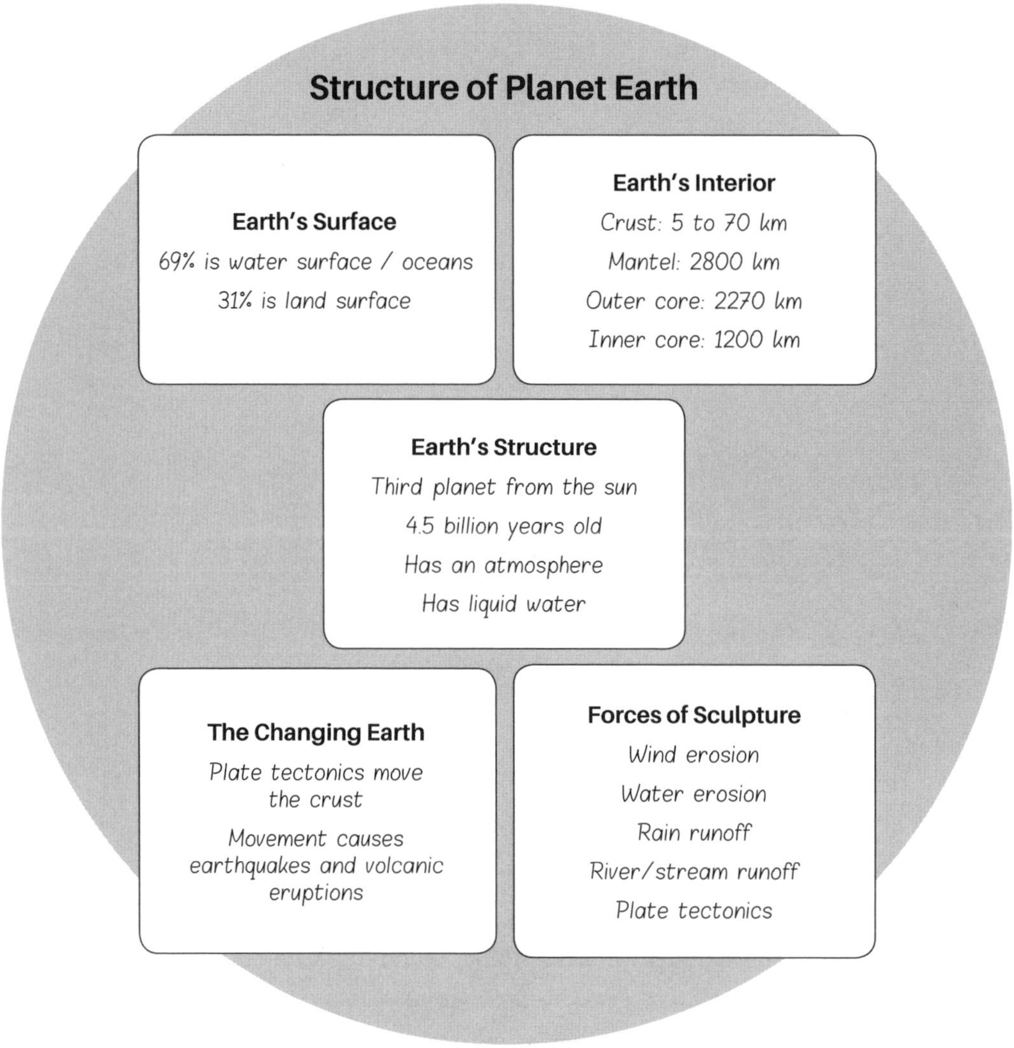

Structure of Planet Earth

Earth's Surface

69% is water surface / oceans

31% is land surface

Earth's Interior

Crust: 5 to 70 km

Mantel: 2800 km

Outer core: 2270 km

Inner core: 1200 km

Earth's Structure

Third planet from the sun

4.5 billion years old

Has an atmosphere

Has liquid water

The Changing Earth

Plate tectonics move
the crust

Movement causes
earthquakes and volcanic
eruptions

Forces of Sculpture

Wind erosion

Water erosion

Rain runoff

River/stream runoff

Plate tectonics

Figure 3.1: Planet Earth learning map.

Differentiating the instruction for students with learning challenges is relatively easy with simple adjustments to the learning map. For example, some students might begin with a learning map that included blank lines under each big idea to indicate how much information is expected.

Prediction and Hypothesis Testing

Like summarization, prediction and/or hypothesis testing is a critical skill in STEM instruction, and as indicated, summarization and prediction are often taught independently. However, pairing them makes more sense, in the context of the scientific method. For example, note that the last two summarization strategies ("Changing Points of View" and "What? So What? Now What?") each include not only a summary element but also a prediction element within the strategy itself. As this illustrates, summarization and prediction/hypothesis testing can easily be taught together.

Forming Scientific Hypotheses

In terms of the scientific method, predictions must be formulated with several factors in mind. First, as noted above, hypotheses must be provable or disprovable. Next, results of the experiment designed to test the hypothesis must be observable and repeatable. Depending on the grade level, teachers may wish to introduce the concepts of independent and dependent variables. Finally, hypotheses must include one or more indicators stating how students might measure the changes in dependent variables.

However, instruction on how to make predictions can involve more than these foundational concepts. For example, Tileston (2004) described a "prediction tree" (others have used the phrase "prediction chain") in which students make a series of predictions while noting the evidence on which that prediction was based and the proof for the accuracy of each hypothesis. In this manner, the art of hypothesis formation and testing can also include the element of chained, or sequenced, hypotheses to describe more complex phenomena. Figure 3.2 presents a prediction tree form, and the case study below provides an example from an elementary health class on sequenced predictions.

	Reason	Proof
Prediction 1		
Prediction 2		
Prediction 3		
Prediction 4		

Figure 3.2: Prediction tree form.

A Classroom Example: Using a Prediction Tree

When a student reads a lesson, or listens to and participates in a discussion in class, the student might use the prediction tree to both summarize and predict what comes next. For example, in a unit on the circulatory system, students in the class might work in pairs, and at first, they would listen as one student describes each of the four chambers of the heart and its purpose. Beginning with the right atrium, the student leading the lesson might state that this chamber of the heart receives blood from the body that has little oxygen in it, and that blood then proceeds to the right ventricle. At that point, the teacher might ask students to make their first prediction by asking: Where does the blood go from that point to get more oxygen?

That leading question can help many pairs of students make a prediction in the prediction tree: Blood flows from the left ventricle to the lungs to get more blood. They would then write that in the prediction tree, and list the reason for that prediction as: Blood needs to pick up oxygen, and it can only do that in the lungs.

Thus, the paired students in the class have made a prediction and cited their reason for it—deoxygenated blood. Next, the student leading the lesson might state that blood does then flow into the lungs to pick up oxygen and drop off carbon dioxide. At that point, the pairs of students would write that as proof of the first prediction, but they would then be asked to make a second prediction: Where does the blood go next?

If the students have paid attention, they might have picked up on the fact that the right atrium collected the blood from the body, and some might surmise that the left atrium is likewise a collection chamber within the heart. Thus, some would make the next prediction: Oxygen-rich blood from the lungs is collected by the left atrium, and then flows into the left ventricle. The lesson could continue along these lines, as students list a "tree" of sequenced predictions that describe how blood flows through the heart and lungs, and into the body.

Summary

The scientific method provides a strong basis and rationale for emphasizing the skills of summarization and prediction/hypothesis testing in STEM classes. Of course, there is certainly nothing wrong with teaching these skills independently as has been done most frequently in the past. However, the twin strategies of summarization and prediction/hypothesis testing provide a powerful combination of teaching strategies, and this partnering of strategies should be the goal for all STEM-oriented classrooms. As discussed above, these strategies are proven instructional tactics and will increase student achievement (Hattie, 2012; Lewis & Thompson, 2010; Marzano, 2007; Marzano, Pickering, & Pollock, 2001). Moreover, these skills provide tools for lifelong learning that are immediately transferable to the modern workplace, where problem solving is critical. Thus, regardless of the subject area or format of instruction (i.e., project-based learning, traditional unit-based instruction), these strategies should certainly be emphasized in virtually every STEM unit, and our students' achievement will reflect that emphasis.

STRATEGY 4

Rubrics and Feedback in STEM Classes

Providing frequent, specific feedback to learners involved in STEM projects is critical for learning (Andrade, 2000; Hattie, 2012; Marzano, 2009a, 2007; Marzano, Pickering, & Pollock, 2001; Yokana, 2015). Moreover, rubrics represent one of the most effective ways to provide effective feedback for students in PBL projects within STEM classes. In broad terms, a rubric is a set of grading or evaluation indicators that are typically made available to the students prior to beginning a project. They can be used for providing structure for STEM assignments and can also be used to evaluate virtually all STEM work (Yokana, 2015). Rubrics even provide a self-evaluation option for students to use during a STEM project. For these reasons, rubrics are one of the most recommended feedback and evaluation tools in education (Andrade, 2000; Barell, 2007; Boss & Krauss, 2007).

Rubric—a scoring guide that lists specific criteria for student performance.

Using Rubrics for Feedback

While rubrics can be quite broad, the more detailed rubrics are, the more useful they can be as both a self-evaluation tool and a feedback tool. Therefore, many proponents of project-based learning recommend sharing very specific rubrics for various artifacts in STEM projects in order to facilitate both teacher feedback and self-evaluation (Bender, 2012; Boss & Krauss, 2007; Yokana, 2015).

As an example, imagine a fifth-grade class that is about to embark on a STEM project focused on dinosaurs in their respective environments. In that project, one artifact might be an animated video in which dinosaurs describe their own environment or perhaps differences in the environments from that period. (In this example, students should have already mastered animation and video development skills, as discussed in Strategy 8.) In that situation, both the quality of the animated video and the quality and quantity of the information provided in the video can provide specific indicators for the rubric. Figure 4.1 presents an example of a rubric for such an artifact.

	Expected	Good	Excellent
Quality of Animation (30%)	three-minute video with one animated character	three-minute video with two animated characters; voice/action is synced; is engaged in dialogue	five-minute video using two or more characters; voice/action well synced with extensive dialogue and scenery
Critical Facts (20%)	eight facts from chapter presented	ten facts from chapter presented in summary form / table	twelve facts from chapter presented in logical order and in summary form and in context of scenic background
Conclusions (20%)	Three conclusions presented	All main conclusions presented	Conclusions are interwoven with factual material
Engaging (20%)	Most students engaged	All students engaged	All students engaged and enjoying / laughing or smiling
References (10%)	three references presented	five references presented	five or more references presented, including two video sources or spreadsheets

Figure 4.1: Rubric for animated dinosaur video.

The level of detail in this rubric shows that students can easily use this rubric for planning the development of their animated video. This rubric gives guidance on what the assignment requires (in the "expected" column), as well as the type of extra additions to the video that will make it a higher quality product. Of course, any of these indicators could easily be broken down into numerous, highly specific indicators that provide detail on virtually every aspect of the work, and as noted previously, more detail usually results in higher quality work. However, it is relatively easy for teachers to "detail" themselves to death when developing rubrics, and in most cases, particularly when students are working in pairs or small groups, providing highly extensive guidance will not be necessary.

Indeed, students tend to critique and to motivate themselves when working in groups, so the rubrics should give specific guidance, but not so much as to prevent creativity.

In this example, as students complete this STEM assignment, they will be referring to the rubric to ensure that they have met the expectations of the teacher on the assignment. For feedback purposes, teachers should sit individually with each student, or each pair of students, after an assignment is completed, and review the assignment, using the rubric as the basis for the discussion. This practice will emphasize the critical importance of the rubric to the students, and over time, they will make more of an effort to comply with indicators in the rubric, because they will realize that rubrics help improve their work.

Some holistic rubrics provide only general guidance for the assigned work, whereas more detailed rubrics, sometimes referred to as analytic rubrics, provide highly detailed guidance. That distinction makes analytic rubrics preferable in STEM classes. A well-designed analytic rubric provides multiple indicators that enable analysis of various specific parts of the STEM assignment, and for each indicator, a graded set of evaluation indicators is presented. More specifically, analytic rubrics are often presented as some type of grid that cross-references various aspects of the task with different levels of performance (Barell, 2007; Larmer et al., 2009).

Figure 4.1, as one example, presented a five-by-three grid with five different assignment aspects listed on the left side, and three different levels of performance listed across the top for each indicator. While the number of assignments and levels of performance might vary from one analytic rubric to another, the vast majority of rubrics include four or more task components on the left and three or four different levels of performance delineated on top of the grid.

> Analytic rubrics—analytic rubrics are often presented as some type of grid, which cross-references various aspects of the task with different levels of performance.

Creating Rubrics

When a STEM teacher has an idea for a specific artifact or assignment, he or she may begin creating the rubric by asking, "What do I expect students to know at the end of production of this artifact?" Larmer et al. (2009) describe this type of reverse planning as planning "with the end in mind." Thus, teachers would typically begin planning an artifact with a set of specific expectations about what students must do to complete the artifact. In the example of figure 4.1, the teacher clearly intended to evaluate both the quality of the cartoon, as well as the type and depth of the information provided. Those questions provided the teacher with the indicators for the left side of the grid.

Next, the teacher needed to consider what would represent acceptable work, good work, and outstanding work for each of the main indicators. In the boxes within the grid, he or she then delineated the requirements for each of the content indicators. In this case, the teacher clearly expected a high-quality animated cartoon with at least one cartoon dinosaur describing the environment in which it lived. However, the addition of more dinosaur characters, and appropriate dialogue between them, represented a higher quality cartooning effort.

Teachers can find a great deal of assistance in creating and using rubrics for STEM classes. First, most STEM curricula, including many textbooks, delineate rubrics for specific lessons, and teachers should utilize those resources first, since they directly apply to the curriculum under study. Next, many rubrics are available for teachers online, and I encourage all teachers to become familiar with these resources, particularly within STEM classes. In many cases, teachers may find a rubric that is designed for use with the type of project artifact they have planned or perhaps a rubric that can be easily modified for their use. The following box presents a number of websites that will help in designing rubrics for your STEM classes.

Websites to Assist in Designing Rubrics

- **www.csufresno.edu/irap/assessment/rubric. shtml.** This is the website from the California State University at Fresno. A variety of sample rubrics are included for a variety of subjects including science and mathematics.

- **www.jason.org.** This is a nonprofit organization that connects students to real scientific organizations and real scientists to inspire and motivate them in STEM classes. This group uses live webcasts from science labs and provides accompanying curricula including inquiry-based labs, videos, and online games, along with assessment rubrics.

- **Rubric Maker K-12.** Rubric Maker is a service of the Teachers First website, in which teachers can indicate their grade level and the topic of interest. This generates several rubrics and allows teachers to revise those or make their own. See http://www .teachersfirst.com/search_action.cfm?grade_low=4 &grade_high=5&searchtext=Planets&searchtype=all.

- **www.educationworld.com/a_curr/curr248. shtmo.** This site presents information on rubrics across the school age span, ranging from definition of a rubric to many sample rubrics. Also, the authors of this site recommend specific additional sites that will assist teachers in building rubrics.

- **http://stemincubator.org/en/resources/ becoming-stem-certified/stem-program-critera- and-rubrics/.** This site provides links to a wide variety of STEM resources, including resources for assessment using rubrics. A list of digital instructional STEM tools is also provided.

- **www.introductiontorubrics.com/samples.html.** This website is associated with a book on rubrics and presents several sample rubrics as well as rubric templates for three, four, and five performance levels. Several different types of rubrics are presented, which will help teachers understand the assessment options that rubrics provide.

- **http://rubistar.4teachers.org.** This website allows teachers to create a free rubric specifically for STEM projects. It was developed by the University of Kansas and will assist teachers in a variety of subject areas and topics including math, reading, science, writing, and oral projects. Also, this site includes an option for making your rubrics interactive, allowing the teacher to create detailed feedback for the students, and the interactive feature ties in with other class management tools such as AimsWeb and Moodle.

- **www.rubrics4teachers.com.** This website is associated with the Western Governors University site, Teacher Planet, and is intended to assist teachers with design and multimedia instruction, including rubric development. Many sample rubrics can be downloaded free and adapted for your particular use. Rubrics are provided in virtually all subject areas (Bender, 2012).

Advantages in Using Rubrics for Feedback

As shown above, there are a number of advantages to using rubrics to provide feedback to students. High-quality rubrics provide sufficient detail for individuals to self-evaluate their work during the development or work completion process, and this self-evaluation will increase the students' sense of ownership of their own work (Andrade, 2000; Barell, 2007). Next, rubrics can assist peers in evaluation of the work of others who might be working on a different aspect of the same STEM project (Boss & Krauss, 2007). Because STEM instruction stresses motivation and self-direction more so than traditional instruction, rubrics fit nicely within most STEM projects (Barell, 2007; Bender, 2012; Boss & Krauss, 2007; Larmer et al., 2009). Further, in addition to using rubrics for evaluation of individual artifacts, rubrics may also be used as a mechanism for overall evaluation of the entire STEM instructional unit.

Research on the Efficacy of Rubrics for Feedback

Research over the decades has repeatedly shown that rubrics are an effective way to provide feedback to students across the curriculum (Andrade, 2000; Hattie, 2012; Marzano, 2009a, 2007; Marzano, Pickering, & Pollock, 2001; Yokana, 2015). Hattie's 2012 research, for example, indicates that providing effective, detailed teacher feedback can enhance learning by as much as three-fourths of a standard deviation (effect size = .75). This research indicates that providing effective feedback was one of the top ten instructional strategies for increasing student achievement.

Similarly, Marzano and his colleagues (Marzano & Haystead, 2009; Marzano, Pickering, & Pollock, 2001) have recommended feedback provided through rubrics. Their research has consistently shown that providing feedback yields a 23 percent gain in achievement. In short, rubrics work as a feedback mechanism, and I typically recommend that teachers develop an analytic rubric for every anticipated artifact. For artifacts that students choose to devise on their own in a PBL project, teachers might first have students develop a rubric for that proposed artifact. That process will help them determine exactly what their goal is for the proposed artifact.

Case Study: Rubrics for Feedback

Teachers in many STEM subjects require some type of product from students with each instructional unit. Having students produce a product often provides a more accurate estimate of their knowledge than daily quizzes or unit tests. One strategy teachers might consider is pairing an analytic rubric with each required product across the instructional units.

In this action research example, an eighth-grade science teacher, Ms. Snyder, decided to investigate how rubrics impacted the quality of student work. Ms. Snyder routinely required at least two student products in each instructional unit. These were not full-blown "science fair" projects, but rather short papers on various scientists, presentations on scientific principles under study, or completions of lab assignments. Thus, Ms. Snyder had grades from several assignments in each unit of study for each student.

Like many effective teachers, Ms. Snyder often read teacher magazines and consulted with her colleagues about new strategies for the classroom. She'd read an article about using rubrics for feedback and decided to set up a data collection experiment to see if rubrics would assist students in her class. In particular, she was interested in seeing data on the efficacy of rubrics for high-achieving students, average students, and lower-achieving students.

In order to tease out these data, Ms. Snyder used the science grades for each student from the most recent report card, and divided the class into three groups: high-achieving students with grades of 90 and above, average students with grades from 75 to 90, and lower-achieving students with grades of 74 and below. In order to get some comparison data, she gathered project grades from the last two units of instruction for all the students in each group and averaged them for each unit. Thus, she had four data points (i.e., the average product assignment grades from two assignments for two units of study) for each of three groups in her class; high-achieving, average, and low-achieving students. Those data were used as the comparison data in figure 4.2 (page 70).

After creating that chart, Ms. Snyder began to produce an analytic rubric for each product assignment she made to the class. She emphasized the importance of these rubrics by holding a class meeting to review each product assignment after it was graded and returned to the students. Also, for students who did not do as well on the assignment as she would have liked, she held a private meeting to review the work and the correct use of the rubric indicators. She implemented this instructional strategy during the next four instructional units, yielding eight data points in the experimental phase of the action research. Once again, she averaged the product grades for each of the groups above. Those are presented as the experimental data in figure 4.2.

As these data show, Ms. Snyder's use of rubrics did positively impact the achievement for students in the class. The data showed that rubrics seemed to have the most impact on students who were average or low achievers. From a strictly scientific perspective, the experiment was not "fair" in the sense that lower-achieving students received a different and more intensive intervention than others in the class, since they received not only the rubric and the whole-class discussion of feedback based on the rubric, but also a private feedback session with the teacher. Still, Ms. Snyder didn't see that as a serious drawback, since she had already realized that using the rubrics as the basis for feedback

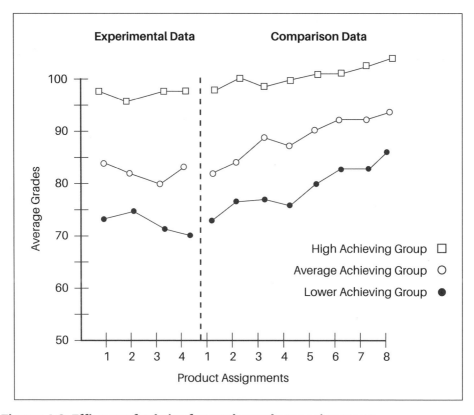

Figure 4.2: Efficacy of rubrics for each product assignment.

during those private meetings with individual lower-achieving students would continue to be necessary over the long term. In short, she was interested in the overall impact of using rubrics, and these data show that rubrics do work to help teachers provide effective, specific, and detailed feedback.

Finally, Ms. Snyder decided to share these results with the class at the end of this action research project. She took an entire class period to help the students understand and interpret this data chart. This served two educational functions: First, it helped the students to understand the decisions involved in how to state a hypothesis, measure a dependent variable, and think through the science involved in an action research project. And second, it helped these students understand "real" science. In fact, most indicated that they were glad to participate in this type of project to help Ms. Snyder understand how to better teach them.

Summary

Given the rather nonlinear nature of STEM labs, project-based learning projects, and other STEM instruction, rubrics will be a great benefit for STEM teachers in the future.

Further, even traditional science or mathematics classes will be strengthened by employing rubrics for most STEM assignments (Andrade, 2000; Hattie, 2012). While many teachers are already using this strategy, it does become more important when teachers give up some of their control of the classroom in order to foster more independent student-directed learning in STEM classes. In those cases, teachers often feel more comfortable teaching in these newly evolving, facilitator roles in the STEM class if they employ rubrics to exert some influence over the students' work. As the research has shown, using rubrics to provide effective and timely feedback does increase achievement, and both teachers and students enjoy their learning experiences more when rubrics are available for instructional and evaluation guidance. Thus, one might anticipate that STEM classes of the future will be dominated by rubric-based activities and self-reflection based on those rubrics.

STRATEGY 5

The Flipped STEM Classroom

It seems that no single instructional approach has been discussed as much by educators as the flipped learning approach (Flipped Learning Network, 2014; Flipped Learning Network & Sophia, 2014; Hamdan, McKnight, McKnight, & Arfstrom, 2013; Tucker, 2012). In the flipped classroom, the traditional lesson plan is "flipped," such that teacher-led initial instruction that is usually completed in class becomes homework, while homework becomes classwork (Bergmann & Sams, 2014; Green, 2012, 2014; Sparks, 2011). In flipped classes, the initial instruction is usually made available as homework via videotaped minilessons on the content that are published on a school or class website or simply found on a video provider such as YouTube or TeacherTube.

The Flipped-Class Strategy

This teaching strategy has not yet been included in any of the meta-analysis reviews of effective teaching strategies, so neither Marzano nor Hattie has yet addressed this strategy (Hattie, 2012; Marzano, 2009a; Toppo, 2011). In fact, the concept of flipped learning was first articulated in 2006 (Bergmann & Sams, 2014) and came to national attention as recently as 2010, but today, many teachers in the United States and around the world are "flipping the class." Those teachers are reversing the traditional order of instruction and assigning students to do initial instruction on brand-new topics as independent study work at home, prior to covering those specific topics in class.

In the context of project-based STEM instruction, students taking responsibility for their own initial instruction is an absolute requirement, because so much time in those STEM classes is spent on Internet-based research. In fact, in most PBL classes, teachers do very limited initial instruction, if any at all, and it is assumed that students will frequently be able to learn new content on their own. Therefore, few teaching strategies complement project-based STEM instruction as well as the flipped-class strategy.

> Flipped classroom—instruction in which the traditional lesson plan is "flipped" such that teacher-led initial instruction becomes homework, and homework is done during class time.

It is interesting to note that this instructional strategy was developed by two practicing teachers, Jonathan Bergmann and Aaron Sams (Bergmann & Sams, 2014). These teachers were reflectively considering how to find time to reteach topics when students didn't seem to grasp the content. They decided to record and annotate their lessons and put that content on the class website. They then noted that two groups of students were using that online content: students who didn't get the lesson, and those who simply needed more time to process the new content (Tucker, 2012). In their ongoing discussions, these two teachers determined that when the initial instruction was delivered in class, students tended to be much less attentive than when they were completing initial instruction work themselves. Further, they decided that their presence as teachers was more valuable to individual students when students were doing applications of lessons, with the teacher there to immediately assist and offer feedback. Thus, they decided to flip the traditional lesson plan by using online lesson content and requiring students to learn their material at home. They then used the class time that would usually have been taken for initial instruction to do more applications activities in which students actually apply their knowledge.

Four Pillars of Flipped Learning

Today, many teachers are experimenting with flipping the classroom, and in order to help provide leadership on this concept, Bergmann and Sams (2014) helped devise a conceptual foundation for the flipped class movement. Their Four Pillars of Flipped Learning are presented in the following box.

> **Four Pillars of Flipped Learning**
>
> • **Flexible Environments:** Educators in the flipped class will often physically rearrange their learning space to accommodate the lesson or unit, which may involve

group work or independent study. Educators are also flexible in their expectations of student timelines for learning and in how they assess students.

- **Learning Culture:** There is a deliberate shift from a teacher-centered classroom to a student-centered approach in the flipped class, where in-class time is meant for exploring topics in greater depth and creating richer learning opportunities through various student-centered pedagogies. Students are actively involved in their own learning in a way that is personally meaningful.

- **Intentional Content:** Educators believe the flipped-class model can help students gain conceptual understanding as well as procedural fluency. They evaluate what they need to teach and what materials students should explore on their own.

- **Professional Educators:** During class time, teachers observe their students, providing them with feedback relevant in the moment, and assessing their work. While professional educators remain very important, they take on less visibly prominent roles in the flipped classroom (Bergmann & Sams, 2014).

As these Four Pillars of Flipped Learning suggest, the flipped learning movement is concerned with more than merely restructuring the lesson format; it involves a richer perspective on the roles of teachers and students in the learning process, and students are viewed as more responsible for their own learning. To get a better sense of how teachers and students respond to this change, I encourage teachers to view one of the many videos on the flipped class on YouTube. Here is a brief video I recommend, featuring a flipped fifth-grade mathematics class at Lake Elmo Elementary School in Lake Elmo, Minnesota: http://www.eschoolnews.com/2012/02/09/a-first-hand-look-inside-a-flipped classroom/. This video (and many others) helps teachers see a flipped class in action, as well as get a sense of the excitement associated with flipping the class.

Classroom Example: Inside a Flipped Chemistry Class

Here is a classroom example of a flipped STEM class. Imagine a chemistry teacher beginning a unit on chemical reactions. Of course, to flip the class the teacher must provide initial instructional content to students via online video or other technologies (Flipped Learning Network, 2014; Tucker, 2012). Some teachers videotape their lectures on new content, while others find prerecorded lessons, usually through free sources such as YouTube, TeacherTube, or other video lesson archives such as Khan Academy (Khanacademy.org) or TED-Ed (http://ed.ted.com/). These video lessons are in reality minilessons that range in length from six to ten minutes, and each covers one specific type of chemical reaction.

Once an appropriate video lesson has been either created or identified, the teacher should make the assignment for students to learn that content as homework. Students might also be assigned a worksheet or brief activity to demonstrate their knowledge of the new content, to be completed at home along with the video lesson. Alternatively, the teacher might do a quick-quiz activity to begin the class the next day to determine which students mastered the content.

Following that quick-check quiz, the remaining class time would be used for application exercises in which that knowledge of chemical reactions is put to use. For that application activity, the teacher might divide the students into four teams of five students each, and present them with a series of chemical reaction problems. A reward such as extra computer time or extra time with the class robot might be offered to the team that correctly completes the problems first. Thus, no class time would be spent on initial instruction, and all team members would be quite likely to be highly engaged in the class lesson. This increased engaged time in both initial instruction and class activities is the reason flipping the class increases academic achievement (Green, 2012, 2014; Hamdan, McKnight, McKnight, & Arfstrom, 2013).

As this example shows, in a flipped classroom, students are required to use web resources and web-delivered video demonstrations as homework and undertake initial instruction of the lesson content themselves on new topics. Then their class time would be used for interesting laboratory explorations or practice activities using the new content. In this sense, the chemistry teacher has effectively flipped the learning by flipping the traditional order of instruction: initial instruction and homework are flipped (Bergmann & Sams, 2014).

A Classroom Example: A Flipped Science Class

In order to share a real-world flipped class example, I invited Ms. Jessica Shoup to share her experience. Ms. Shoup, EdM, is a veteran STEM teacher with National Board Certification. Ms. Shoup has taught middle school classes in science and mathematics for many years in both Wisconsin and North Carolina. She is now working as a teacher and professional development facilitator at Community House Middle School, in Charlotte,

North Carolina. She has been using the flipped-class model of instruction in mathematics and science for several years now:

> One of my main goals as a science teacher was to have students learn through hands-on experiences and exploration. Like many teachers, I originally felt that students couldn't be successful unless I personally taught the content through lectures, discussions, notes, and examples first. My entire opinion changed several years ago, when I worked at a project-based elementary school where students took charge of their own learning.

> We use the flipped-class approach. Flipped classrooms allow for engaging conversations and in-depth exploration of the content, and class time is no longer consumed with lecture, note taking, and repeated examples. The students are assigned a task to complete at home in order to gain background knowledge on a particular standard or topic. Gaining background can be completed in many formats such as filling in guided notes while watching a video, reading a passage and creating a graphic organizer, or answering questions after completing an online simulation. With each of these activities, students gain information on their own. In contrast, traditional copying of notes in class is mindless and students often write things down without even paying attention to the meaning of the words. When I shifted to a flipped-class model, I quickly found that my students were more likely to retain the information because they had completed the work on their own.

> After completing the background knowledge assignment on their own, students came to class already discussing the content and excited to see what they were going to do with their new information. I frequently started class with a "four-question warm-up" to review the main ideas of the concept. The warm-up was completed as a team process in a whole-class format. One student read the first question and led a discussion with classmates to arrive at the answer. Throughout the discussion, I added comments to clear up misconceptions or asked questions if they were missing necessary details. The discussion continued with remaining questions.

> The class then shifted to directions for the exploratory activity that would further student understanding of the concept. I always allowed students to work with others on these activities. There is so much that the students can learn from one another by struggling through a task and having conversations while doing so. As the students worked, I moved around the room listening to their conversations and providing input as needed. I am always amazed while listening to the students ask questions and help each other learn. Students worked through the activity at different rates. So learning continued, and extension activities were provided to the early finishers.

> At the conclusion of the activity, students shared their findings and related it to the standard being covered. This is my favorite part of a flipped lesson. Students often

argued with one another about their ideas. It is important to sit back and let the students struggle with the ideas. More is learned from these discussions than from me telling them the same information.

The class period ended with a "ticket out the door." Students had to answer questions, analyze data, write a summary, or create a list to demonstrate their understanding of the concept prior to leaving. Using that information, I was able to determine whether further teaching or enrichment should take place.

It is clear to me that my incorporation of flipped lessons has increased student engagement as well as understanding of the concepts. Moreover, my students are excited to come to class and talk about what they are learning, and that might be the best payoff of all!

Advantages of Flipping the STEM Class

There are many advantages to flipping the class (Horn, 2013; Stansbury, 2013). As discussed previously, the engaged time for most students is likely to increase both during the initial instruction completed at home and during the applications activities in class. Increasing the time that students are actually mentally engaged with the content will increase their academic performance.

Next, having lessons in a video format allows students to immediately review lesson points. Students can literally hit rewind and review content they didn't understand (Horn, 2013), or they can fast-forward through material they have already mastered. This is empowering for the students, since they themselves decide what to watch and when to review. This gives them more ownership over their learning (Horn, 2013).

Next, immediate feedback is increased in the flipped-class approach. Specifically, in traditional homework, the students probably completed drill and practice work on some type of worksheet—work which everyone would agree is not highly motivating. Should a student need help with a problem while doing that work, he or she would have to wait until the next class period on the next day to ask the teacher a question. However, in the flipped-class approach, the drill and practice applications of knowledge activities take place in the classroom, and if a student needs help, the teacher is available to respond to students, offer feedback immediately, and guide students as they apply what they have learned online. With a teacher present to answer questions and watch over how students are doing, the immediate feedback will boost learning.

Finally, because flipped learning does empower students to learn for themselves and take ownership of learning, flipping the class can lead to a more robust lifelong learning perspective. In the flipped classroom, students learn that it is their job to learn what they need, and schools will become much more effective if every student exits with that understanding of his or her role. Simply put, it is the student's job to learn what they need to accomplish their task, and that is a very healthy lifelong learning attitude to take into the 21st century workplace.

Research on the Efficacy of Flipped Learning

Research on the flipped-class strategy is still somewhat limited, but existing anecdotal evidence does provide considerable support for the flipped-class model (Bergmann & Sams, 2014; Flipped Learning Network, 2014; Green, 2012, 2014; Horn, 2013; Stansbury, 2013; Tucker, 2012). In one widely discussed example, Greg Green (2012), principal of Clintondale High School, reported his school's success with the flipped-class strategy. Clintondale is a financially challenged school in Detroit, and with failure rates "through the roof," teachers chose to improve student academic performance across the curriculum by flipping their classes. Thus, teachers videotaped shorter versions of their own lectures on new content and posted those videos to the school website. Students were then required to access that content as the initial instructional phase of the lesson when they began a new unit of instruction. The class periods in each subject then became a laboratory for practice with that content, in which students could request specific help on the content as they practiced and applied that new knowledge.

Within eighteen months, failure rates in many core subjects had gone down drastically (Green, 2012, 2014). Specifically, Principal Green reported failure rates in the flipped instruction classes dropped as follows: English failure rates dropped from 52 percent to 19 percent; mathematics, from 44 percent to 13 percent; science, from 41 percent to 19 percent; and social studies, from 28 percent to 9 percent.

As these impressive data from Clintondale High School indicate, flipping these classes produced a very positive impact on student achievement across the board (Green, 2014). Further, in a wide variety of other schools, student achievement has increased as a result of flipping the class (Flipped Learning Network & Sophia, 2014; Horn, 2013; Stansbury, 2013). While research is ongoing, there is sufficient anecdotal evidence supportive of flipped learning to encourage STEM teachers to explore this exciting new instructional strategy.

Steps for Flipping Your STEM Class

Create or select video lessons. When deciding to try flipped learning, teachers must identify a specific topic and either create or select a video-based lesson on that content. As indicated previously, some teachers merely videotape themselves when delivering the content in class and place that video on the class or school website. However, I urge teachers to first explore what lessons exist that can be used by the students to learn the targeted topic. With the advent of high-quality, web-based teaching resources, teachers in many STEM areas do not have to self-record their instructional content because many demonstration videos are already available. For example, prior to taking the time to create a video on solving one-variable equations (e.g., $5x + 4 = 20$), teachers can easily find a short video that already exists explaining exactly that. Sources such as YouTube, Khan Academy, TeacherTube, and TED-Ed all provide many videos on this and similar topics.

Teachers must ensure that the video they select is appropriate for a flipped lesson. Proponents of flipped learning suggest that these videos should be brief—perhaps six to ten minutes in length—and highly focused on only one topic: perhaps one type of math problem, a single scientific experiment, or a single historical event (Bender, 2012; Bergmann & Sams, 2014).

Ensure availability of the initial instruction content. Next, teachers must ensure availability of the online lesson content. Not all schools are Wi-Fi capable, and not all students have Internet capability at home. Teachers who wish to try flipping the class must therefore ensure that all students have the capability to see the initial instruction lesson. In most cases, students do have Wi-Fi options and computers (or tablets or smartphones, etc.) at home, and accessing these web-based lessons is not a problem. For other students, opportunities to review and study the lesson content must be provided in a school media center or in the teacher's class. This is a critical issue that must be addressed prior to the teacher assigning a video lesson as initial instruction.

Devise a quick-check tactic. Veteran teachers quickly realize that some students will use the video or online lesson to complete the initial instruction at home, whereas some won't. Therefore, proponents of the flipped class suggest following every flipped lesson with some required product or quick-check quiz by which students can demonstrate their understanding (Bergmann & Sams, 2014; Horn, 2013). Thus, students should be required to do some brief follow-up homework after watching the video, and present that work to the teacher the following day. Alternatively, the teacher may follow such lessons with a quick-check quiz at the beginning of class the next day. Bergmann indicated he always required some type of work from students to demonstrate their understanding, rather than merely taking their word that they had done their homework (Horn, 2013).

Develop engaging in-class activities. One rationale for doing flipped learning is to develop deeper understanding of the content through richer practice and more realistic application of knowledge. Therefore, teachers must develop engaging and content-rich learning activities for the class to complete. These can typically be somewhat longer than activities in traditional lessons, since little or no class time will be invested in initial instruction in the flipped-class model. Project-based learning projects certainly provide one option for these content-rich activities, but team-based investigations and even makerspace-type creative activities can also be highly effective content-rich instructional options for the flipped class.

Differentiate in-class assignments. If the quick-check quiz indicates that some students in the class have either not done the initial instruction work at home or have not understood the content, those students will need time at the beginning of class to redo that online initial instruction activity. In contrast, most of the class will have completed the initial instruction at home and will be ready for an exciting application-type activity to extend their understanding. Thus, the teacher will, of necessity, differentiate the lesson for those students. If six to eight computers are available in the rear of the classroom, the teacher might merely assign the students who didn't understand the lesson to complete it again on those computers, while the teacher begins a project-based activity with the rest of the class. This differentiation will ensure that each student is receiving what he or she needs. Further, practitioners of flipped learning have asserted that, as students get used to this learning strategy, the number of students who complete the online lesson increases to a point where noncompletion of the lesson is virtually eliminated (Bergmann & Sams, 2014).

Document the efficacy of the flipped class. When flipping the class, teachers are undertaking a new and different instructional strategy, and the effects of such experimentation should be carefully documented. I suggest that teachers devise some type of plan for documenting the impact of flipped learning. One option would be a before-and-after comparison of student performance on unit test grades or unit products, similar to that discussed in the case study for the rubrics strategy (see Strategy 4).

For example, the teacher might average student grades on unit tests for several units in which lessons were not flipped, and compare those scores with average scores from several lessons in which students did their own initial instruction via the flipped-class strategy. This would document the efficacy of flipping the class in each teacher's specific situation.

Summary

Flipping the class has become much more common, and many teachers are seeing the success of this instructional strategy (Bergmann & Sams, 2014; Flipped Learning Network, 2014). For that reason, I suggest that all STEM teachers try this instructional strategy. If the goal of STEM is a more highly engaged, self-directed group of students solving problems collectively, then those students will need to become adept at learning new content on their own. Further, the promise of flipped learning is that all students might one day leave schools as highly experienced, self-directed lifelong learners, and in order to achieve that lofty goal, many of their school activities and most of their in-school time should be dedicated to encouraging them to take direct responsibility for their own learning. The flipped learning strategy does exactly that.

From another perspective, the idea that knowledge should be spoon-fed to students, working under the immediate supervision of the teacher, is a relic of the past. In contrast, flipped learning represents the instructional strategy of the future, and thus flipped learning warrants every teacher's attention.

Section II

Technology in STEM Classes

Technology has long been utilized in classrooms around the world, and it is not surprising that model STEM instruction tends to emphasize technology for all classes. Of course, many books have been written on the latest or next technology trend in education, and no teacher can possibly keep up with all available technologies. The changes and developments in technologies for teaching are simply overwhelming.

With that noted, in this section I present an array of innovative instructional strategies to support STEM instruction across the grade levels. I have chosen to stress technologies that are used in classrooms, and in particular, technologies that tend to foster higher engagement in STEM classes. These include tech-rich teaching, coding and robotics, animation/cartooning, gaming and simulations, and augmented reality.

STRATEGY 6

Tech-Rich Teaching

Modern STEM classes tend to be enriched by technology. While some STEM classes may still be characterized predominately by lecture and student inactivity, the areas of science, engineering, and mathematics have, in most districts, been among the first to differentiate instruction using numerous technological innovations. This is not surprising because technology is a major emphasis across the board in STEM programs. With that said, it is also true, as noted previously, that no teacher can possibly use all available technological innovations. For virtually anyone, including we educators who strive doggedly to keep up with the latest in technology, the application of all technologies proves impossible.

Noting that limitation, this tech-rich instructional strategy section presents an array of tech strategies that have proven useful in STEM courses. A list of selected strategies is provided in the following box, along with specific suggestions on using these tools in a STEM approach for social studies and other subjects.

A Sampling of Tech-Rich Instructional Innovations

- **Blogger** (www.blogger.com): Blogging on topics covered in class will increase student interest and understanding. When considering what STEM might mean in nonscience classes (e.g., English or social studies), this tool (and several others below) can help infuse technology into the class. Teachers might want to review the tutorial "How to Use Blogger" at www.teachertrainingvideos.com/blogger/index.html.

continued →

- **Dropbox** (www.dropbox.com): Dropbox is a "save" spot for digital information, and teachers can communicate with students by dropping virtually any digital file into the Dropbox. Files are saved to your computer and online, and can be accessed with any mobile device.

- **Gliffy** (www.gliffy.com): In STEM, technical drawings and diagrams can be critical. With Gliffy online diagram software, you can easily create high-quality flowcharts, diagrams, or technical drawings.

- **Glogster** (www.edu.glogster.com): This software allows teachers or students to make online posters and magazines, and to include digital video files. This is a great artifact assignment, since student creations can be published and used for future instruction.

- **Google Sites** (www.google.com/sites/help/intl/en /overview.html): Google Sites allows STEM teachers to create web pages for free. Step-by-step video tutorials are available at the site.

- **Scribd** (www.scribd.com): This allows teachers to upload documents such as class notes, PowerPoints, or pdf files to share with students. Teachers can also repost documents from the students. Students can download and print the files or get the link for the document they want. When considering what STEM might look like in nonscience courses (e.g., English, literature, social studies), this tool can help infuse tech into the class. This is a great way to publish students' written work to the world.

- **Survey Monkey** (www.teachertrainingvideos.com /monkey/index.html): This allows teachers to create surveys for the class on any topic they like. In social studies or history classes, teachers can survey to identify student perceptions of various events or sociological movements. Survey Monkey will organize all the results into a graph that can be shared with the class.

- **Poll Everywhere** (http://polleverywhere.com): This is another tool that allows teachers to poll the students, or anyone, on issues in class. It can also be used to give a digital quiz. Cell phones are used as response systems and a graph appears on the screen as students text their answers to the teacher.

- **Text-to-Speech Tools** (www.teachertrainingvideos .com/textSpeech/index.html): These tools will convert text into spoken words. This will allow students whose first language is not English to hear instructions or directions as well as read them.

The list above was excerpted from a compilation of tech-based tools found online at http://stemincubator.org/en /resources/becoming-stem-certified/stem-web-tools/.

While not all of these tech tools can be discussed at length, teachers should be aware of this array of innovative teaching tools and should implement the use of some of them (Ash, 2011; Marzano, 2009b). Moreover, I encourage teachers to select one new tech-based teaching tool from this list or elsewhere every two or three months, and experiment with it multiple times in the classroom. This is one way for teachers to keep current with tech-based teaching and not become overwhelmed with the massive innovation in this area. While no teacher will use all of these tools, all teachers should use a number of them and continually experiment with others.

Below, I present more detail on several innovative tools for the STEM class that have received widespread use. Of necessity, the first issue is one of accessibility, and then several specific technological innovations are discussed, including SMART Boards, computer-driven curricula, and Khan Academy. All of these have received research support for use in the STEM class.

Wi-Fi and Computer Access for STEM Classes

The first technology goal for many schools is making the Internet accessible for every student in every classroom. Of course, this is a school and school district issue, and not a factor that teachers generally can control. Still, Internet access and digital literacy in the modern world is the rough equivalent of a basic literacy requirement. Without routine computer and Internet access, students will be at a significant disadvantage in learning. Further, without mastering the habits of learning online, self-discipline, effective searching, and digital citizenship, students are likely to suffer at an academic deficit for life.

The good news is that schools are rushing to address availability of the Internet for instruction. Even schools that are not fully Wi-Fi capable often have some areas of the building in which students can access the Internet. For example, a media center might be made Wi-Fi accessible, even when all classrooms are not, and dedicated teachers will learn to make do until more complete access is available.

Allow me to share a moving personal example. Working in a non–Wi-Fi middle school in south Atlanta, an English teacher told me she required that all themes and major papers be sent to her in a word-processed document, online via her email address. I asked her how and why she made such a requirement, and her answer is both telling and motivational.

"Dr. Bender, I will not let the limits of this school limit the future of my kids!"

Bravo! Bravo for that teacher! Though she requested to remain nameless, I have permission to share that story, and I found that moment quite moving. I learned that day, yet again, the power of one excellent, yet demanding, teacher, a teacher who set high expectations for her students. To make that idea work in a non–Wi-Fi setting, she indicated that she provided several days for the students to turn in each assignment of that type, and as necessary, she provided class time for them to access the Wi-Fi–capable computers in the media center. Of course, that required extra work and planning from that teacher, but she did not mind that work at all! Again, bravo! This is a dedication every educator should strive to emulate.

One-to-One Computer Access

Once Wi-Fi is available, one-to-one computer availability is the next goal for schools. One-to-one programs have been initiated in many schools, and most find that when students are provided with a computer, the schoolwide achievement will increase (Ash, 2011; Green, 2012). Therefore, once Wi-Fi is available at schools, students must also have access to computing devices. In an ideal world, every student would have an Internet-capable laptop computer or tablet for all STEM and other schoolwork, and schools around the world are striving toward that goal. Of course, that is a challenging goal in an era of tight school budgets, but a lack of computer availability should not prohibit educators from moving into tech-rich instruction. However, in almost all schools, computers are available to students to some degree, perhaps in a media center or certain computer classes.

Schools have also devised other options to hit a one-to-one goal (Ash, 2011). Some districts have solicited parental support by encouraging parents to purchase laptops for their children. This is often referred to as a bring-your-own-device initiative (or BYOD). Of course, for parents who cannot afford such an expense, the schools should provide one for the students (Ash, 2011).

However, with the recent development of other types of Internet-capable devices (e.g., iPads, Kindle Fire, Android-based tablets, or smartphones), availability of a laptop for each student may become less necessary. Any of these devices can provide Internet research capability within a STEM class. Further, even with only a few Internet-capable devices per classroom, it is still fairly easy to undertake tech-rich instruction by assigning Internet research to smaller groups of students. For example, with only six to eight Internet-capable devices, an entire student team can do Internet research, while the other teams work on other assignments.

Efficacy of Wi-Fi and One-to-One Teaching

Early evidence documents that Wi-Fi and one-to-one computer availability do enhance academic performance, including performance within lower-achieving schools (Ash, 2011; Dretzin, 2010; Green, 2012; Manzo, 2010). One example on *Frontline* (Dretzin, 2010) demonstrated this effect. The faculty of a South Bronx middle school initiated a one-to-one laptop program in 2004 at their lower-achieving inner-city school in New York. The school had been characterized by student violence, poor attendance, and little academic success. Within a year, the faculty found that they could re-engage nearly all of those students in their school in meaningful learning activities, resulting in a significant schoolwide achievement increase. Academic score increases of 30 percent in reading and 40 percent in mathematics were seen once laptops were made available, and the faculty credited the laptop initiative as the basis for those improved academic scores. They also noted increased motivation and participation in class, improved attendance, and a decrease in discipline problems (Dretzin, 2010).

However, research has also shown that merely having Wi-Fi and computer capability is not enough to increase achievement (Ash, 2011; Green, 2012). Rather, teachers must integrate the computer/Internet into solid instructional assignments, and not merely allow the computer to become a new encyclopedia or writing device. Wi-Fi capability and computers are highly important instructional tools, but they are tools and must be coupled with, and complemented by, in-depth, research-proven instructional approaches in order for academic achievement to be positively impacted (Ash, 2011; Bender, 2012; Bender & Waller, 2013).

SMART Boards

SMART Boards, or interactive whiteboards, are found in many STEM classes. These are electronic digitally interfaced presentation boards that replace the older whiteboards or chalkboards, and allow presentation of digital information, such as the contents of the computer screen, on the board for the entire class to see (Hattie, 2012; Marzano, 2009b; Marzano & Haystead, 2009). Using the SMART Board, teachers or students can create interactive assignments requiring students to make choices by tapping the interactive whiteboard itself. Teachers can compile data on the opinions of class members, or students can present project artifacts to the entire class.

Like the one-to-one initiative discussed earlier, research has shown that interactive whiteboard technology leads to increased academic achievement (Hattie, 2012; Marzano, 2009b; Marzano & Haystead, 2009). For example, Marzano's research documented significant increases in academic achievement, ranging from 13 percent to 17 percent when interactive whiteboards were used as an instructional medium in the classroom (Marzano, 2009b; Marzano & Haystead, 2009). Hattie's meta-analysis (2012) indicated that interactive video methods generated effect sizes of .52, thus documenting that this was a highly effective teaching strategy.

However, as in many areas, there are several caveats concerning this research. First of all, the SMART Board research available for inclusion in the meta-analytic studies by both Marzano and Hattie (Hattie, 2012; Marzano, 2009a; Marzano & Haystead, 2009) included studies of use of the SMART Board in traditional teacher-directed instructional lessons. Those results may be different in student-driven instruction such as project-based learning or inquiry-based instruction.

Next, as noted by Marzano (2009b), rather than use the SMART Board as merely a digital chalkboard, teachers should use this technology for interactive types of instruction. For example, students might be required to select teams and touch certain areas of the board when answering complex questions, or to use the SMART Board for reporting project results with multimedia presentations. It is the interactivity of the SMART Board that effectively makes it a powerful teaching tool, and teachers should devise ways to use those interactive features. Again, the technology must be coupled with and complemented by solid, research-proven instructional strategies to be most effective.

Computer-Delivered Instruction

For several decades now, various high-quality self-directed computer-based instructional programs have been available. Programs such as SuccessMaker, Khan Academy, or Academy of Math are designed as individualized curricular programs in science, mathematics, or other subjects. In these self-instructional programs, a student's academic skills are accurately diagnosed, and the student is placed in a specific spot within the curriculum. Then the computer program delivers the instruction and monitors students' progress under teacher direction. Of course, many such programs are available, and I've presented some information on several of the most widely used programs in the following box:

Computer-Driven Self-Study Curricula

- SuccessMaker Math and/or SuccessMaker Science is one of a number of commercially available instructional programs (K–8) that has received widespread research support: http://www.pearsonschool.com /index.cfm?locator=PS2qJ3&acornRdt=1&DCSext .w_psvaniturl=http%3A%2F%2Fwww%2Epearson school%2Ecom%2Fsuccessmaker. This is a comprehensive standards-based program that is partnered with online curriculum in reading/ language arts and English language development/ ESL curriculum. Delivered online, SuccessMaker uses adaptive software to adjust the difficulty level automatically in response to the student's answers, thereby providing a series of questions at exactly the correct level. Reporting and assessment components ensure that the student is placed in the correct level and help to monitor progress.

- Academy of Mathematics is a well-designed, well-researched commercially available curriculum (grades 2–12) that delivers significant academic progress: http://eps.schoolspecialty.com/ products/online-programs/academy-of-math/ about-the-program_. This web-based intervention program includes assessment and progress-monitoring components, and provides a self-paced, personalized curriculum for each student, depending on their exact needs. It has helped many students struggling in mathematics via various scaffolded, intensive, well-sequenced lessons targeted to the individual student's deficits.

continued →

- SAS Curriculum Pathways (sascurriculumpathways
  .com) provides extensive free online curricula
  with materials and instructional activities in
  English, language arts, science, social studies,
  mathematics, and Spanish. While this is not a self-
  directed curriculum, it is a high-quality supportive
  curriculum that will enhance any STEM classroom.
  These materials were developed by content experts
  in various subject areas, and they include high-
  quality graphic designs in 3-D presentations. The
  lesson activities herein are designed around the
  Common Core State Standards and are appropriate
  for grades 6 through 12. The curriculum is free and
  teachers need only log in to access the material. A
  brief tutorial video is available free of charge at the
  website above. This is a free option that all teachers
  in these curricular areas and grades should consider.

I jokingly call these the "fire-and-forget missiles," since once a student is placed, the computer leads the instruction and the teacher has the freedom to move on to other instruction with other students in the class. Of course, I would never suggest that teachers leave any student completely unmonitored during his or her work, even work that is computer driven. However, I use that "fire-and-forget" phrase to point out a subtle yet critical advantage to having one or more of these programs available in every STEM class. With these curricula available on several computers within each class, the teachers in those project-based STEM classes can much more easily address the needs of students who are not functioning on grade level and at the same time include them in much of the project-based learning teamwork.

Specifically, these high-quality programs include diagnostic assessments that will place a student at his or her appropriate instructional level, such that a student in a sixth-grade mathematics class can receive both his core mathematics instruction at the sixth-grade level and some instruction targeted on certain fourth- or fifth-grade skills that have not been mastered. By having students like this participate in most class activities, and also finding time for the student to do twenty minutes of individualized computer instruction two or three times per week at his or her grade level, the teacher can use these programs to remediate and also keep the student involved in most of the PBL activities on grade level.

In short, I do recommend use of one of these self-directed curricula in virtually all STEM classes. Below, I've chosen to discuss one self-directed program that is available free of charge to teachers in order to show how these programs may be used.

Khan Academy

Khan Academy has received a great deal of international attention recently (www. khanacademy.org). Khan Academy is a free set of online curricular materials and videos for specific problems in mathematics, chemistry, and physics, with some content in other subject areas such as astronomy, earth sciences, history, and health. This program is housed in the cloud so students can access it anywhere, and thus, Khan represents anytime-anywhere learning for students worldwide (Sparks, 2011; Toppo, 2011). As of 2015, the Khan Academy instructional videos had been viewed 365 million times worldwide, suggesting the widespread use of this program.

Khan Academy can be considered a nearly comprehensive mathematics curriculum, stressing all types of mathematical problems ranging from kindergarten up through algebra. The program was developed by Mr. Sal Khan and the academy is structured as a nonprofit organization, receiving funding from a variety of foundations. Organizations such as Bank of America, the Bill and Melinda Gates Foundation, and Google have all provided support in order to ramp up the service capabilities and make Khan available at no cost to students and teachers worldwide (Sparks, 2011).

> Khan Academy is a free online mathematics, chemistry, and physics curriculum, with some content in other areas, that is housed in the cloud and represents anytime-anywhere learning.

Components of Khan Academy

Khan Academy includes three major components, as well as some pedagogical tools. The major components of this program are game-based online exercises, video demonstrations of specific content, and an individual knowledge map for each student. First, there are thousands of online learning exercises and game-based activities in mathematics, physics, and chemistry as well as academic content in other areas, and these provide the basis of Khan Academy. In mathematics, these exercises focus on one specific type of mathematics problem (e.g., level one linear equations: $5x + 4 = ?$). Students are presented with a number of examples of this one type of problem, and they are expected to solve them successfully. Rewards in the form of merit badges are presented for successful problem solution.

Next, the website presents video demonstrations that are partnered with each type of math problem. The videos show an interactive whiteboard where the various steps of the problem appear, as a disembodied voice guides the students through the problem while explaining the necessary steps. While the steps in the problem are discussed, the narrator explains the reasons for various steps and mathematics operations. When the online exercises are coupled with the support video demonstrations, this curriculum can function as initial instruction on that type of mathematics problem.

Over 3,700 videos are included in Khan Academy, presenting demonstrations of particular problems or other content on which students might need help, and more are added each month. Each video is a single chunk of topical information and is not over ten minutes in length.

If a student attempts two or more examples of a problem without success, he or she can review the accompanying video and learn how to solve that type of problem. Thus, the videos support the online exercises. I should note a concern here. Many teachers utilize these videos as demo videos in their classes, and some of those teachers may even believe they are using Khan Academy to the fullest. While there is certainly nothing wrong with such usage, Khan Academy is primarily intended as a self-instruction curriculum. Therefore, the exercises online and other aspects of Khan should be employed to realize the maximum benefit from this tool (Sparks, 2011; Toppo, 2011).

Further, the most important aspect of Khan Academy is the third component: a structuring component for each individual student, called the knowledge map. The knowledge map for a student presents something resembling a "star chart" that monitors each individual student's progress and suggests the next skills the student should attempt. When a student earns a merit badge, that badge appears on the knowledge map for that student, documenting that the student has mastered that skill. Generally, students are highly motivated by the "gaming" and reward aspect of the online exercises. They seem to love the opportunity to add badges to their knowledge map. The more students challenge themselves, the more they achieve, and the more badges they earn on their map. While some badges can be earned by successful completion of one or two exercises, other badges take many months or even years to earn.

Teacher Tools in Khan Academy

While Khan Academy is intended as a self-study curriculum, it does include certain tools for students' "coaches." Parents, teachers, or others can serve as student coaches, and follow groups of students in Khan. For example, teachers can place their entire class on a class profile in Khan and begin a knowledge map for every student. Because the individual student work and map is housed in the cloud, teachers (or other coaches) can assess each student's knowledge map as long as they have that student's password. Teachers can then ensure that students are following a logical order in their online work (though the knowledge map itself will certainly foster a logical progression of work as well) and determine how students might proceed.

Also, students' performance data are presented as an X/Y axis chart showing individual student growth over time. Using these teaching tools within Khan, teachers will know immediately if a particular student is having difficulty and can assign other remedial work on that content or work directly with the student. Further, all of these data are saved over time so that teachers can review students' progress and make determinations about students' rates of progress relative to stated goals.

Research on Khan Academy

Early evidence suggests that Khan Academy is an effective self-instructional curriculum that students can use as a self-directed learning tool, or that both students and teachers can use together (Sparks, 2011; SRI, 2014; Toppo, 2011). The website www. Khanacademy.org presents a number of research results and several testimonials as anecdotal evidence of efficacy, including examples from Spain, Ireland, Poland, and the United States. All of those testimonials provide support for using Khan.

In a more detailed study, SRI International investigated use of Khan Academy in a number of different schools across the grade levels (SRI, 2014). Their results demonstrated that when Khan Academy was used as a supplement to in-class instruction, the students showed improved attitudes toward mathematics, increased engaged time, and increased math achievement. Students also reported that they enjoyed their "Khan time" more than traditional mathematics classes. Further, the majority of teachers were happy with their Khan Academy experience and believed this program helped them support students of varying ability more effectively (SRI, 2014). Mathematics self-concept also improved while math anxiety decreased when Khan Academy was implemented.

While this is not a large body of research, it does suggest the overall efficacy of Khan Academy when the program is used in mathematics classes. No doubt additional research will be forthcoming on applications of Khan Academy as both a self-study curriculum and a support curriculum in the STEM classroom.

Other Advantages to Using Khan Academy

There are a number of additional advantages to using Khan Academy in STEM classes. First, a great deal of scientific and mathematical information is available, and students can access these problems on a need-to-know-now basis. If students are working on a class project and need to apply an algorithm, teachers can direct them to Khan Academy and then help them individually as necessary. Next, self-directed curricula such as Khan are more motivating for some students than more traditional teacher-directed instruction, and in some cases, students will work on student-directed work when they show little desire to participate in traditional math or science classes.

Next, Khan Academy, like all of the self-directed curricula, can be used in a PBL class to help remediate students' deficits. Again, as most students work on PBL projects, individual students working alone on computers in the back of the class can receive the remediation they need on skills that are below their current grade level. This is also an advantage for highly advanced students. Because Khan Academy allows students to progress at their own pace, advanced students will certainly explore content that is beyond their current grade level! Teachers have reported that Khan Academy has helped them differentiate their mathematics instruction for both low-achieving and high-achieving students (SRI, 2014).

Finally, an even subtler advantage is the message that a self-directed curriculum such as Khan Academy sends to students: "It is your job to learn!" While schools have historically force-fed the curriculum to groups of students of the same age, covering content at the same time for all, self-directed instruction in STEM classes offers an alternative opportunity—student-driven learning. I would love to believe that every student graduating next year from high school would graduate knowing that, if he or she needed to know something, they could find that information on the web and learn it themselves! That is a potent message—that your learning is your responsibility—and this provides a compelling reason for implementing Khan Academy or another self-directed learning curriculum. Using Khan Academy systematically and regularly for all students will foster that insight, and thus systematic use of Khan Academy holds many positive implications for lifelong learning for the 21st century.

Problems With Khan Academy

While I am a strong advocate of using Khan Academy in virtually all mathematics classes and many science classes, there are valid criticisms of this program. First, while the gaming aspect of Khan Academy is highly motivational for most students, the video demonstrations are much less compelling. In fact, the videos are not interactive in any fashion and represent an approximation of 20th century instruction. Specifically, in the video demonstrations, the student sees a mathematics problem being completed on the board, in a step-by-step fashion while a disembodied teacher's voice discusses each step. This type of instruction has been done with chalkboards since the early 1900s.

Next, content coverage in Khan Academy is quite spotty in many subject areas, including some of the sciences, though the area of mathematics is developed enough to be considered comprehensive. While all STEM teachers should explore using Khan Academy, mathematics teachers will find it more useful, simply because of content coverage.

Finally, in an era when deep conceptual understanding is being stressed with the Common Core curriculum, Khan Academy is almost exclusively procedural in nature. The curriculum emphasizes step-by-step problem solution, with only one solution strategy presented. Also, each type of problem is presented in isolation with little emphasis on when students might use that specific mathematics skill in real-world scenarios. In contrast, modern math instruction stresses finding alternative correct ways to solve the problem, in an effort to develop deeper mathematical understanding.

With these advantages and concerns noted, I do advocate use of Khan Academy in STEM classes, and particularly in mathematics. Because this is a free option, and will help students in procedural processes, Khan Academy is a curriculum that every mathematics teacher should at least explore. Again, I've used Khan Academy as the step-by-step example herein, but teachers should remember that most of the implementation steps below will work with other self-instructional programs such as SuccessMaker or Academy of Math.

Steps in Implementing Khan Academy

Familiarize yourself with Khan Academy. The first step in using Khan Academy is to become familiar with it. Typically, a teacher should play around on the website for thirty minutes or so and look at the resources for teachers. Carefully consider the fit between Khan Academy coverage of content and terminology and the terminology used in your math or science curriculum. Also consider the knowledge map and possible use of that in your class. The website presents many tools for coaches to use as they guide students through the Khan Academy learning experiences.

Sign your students in. Khan Academy is most effective when teachers and students use it in a comprehensive fashion. Ultimately teachers should register their entire class, including students who have no computer or Internet access at home, and encourage students to use all the main components of Khan. Working at home, students can then use the gaming online exercises to study and practice any particular type of problem, while referring to the support videos as necessary. Also, each problem in the game-based practice sessions is broken down into simple step-by-step instructions, and feedback is immediate in Khan, should any student experience difficulty with a particular type of problem. Once they demonstrate their ability to do that type of problem on several specific problems, a merit badge appears on their knowledge map!

Use Khan Academy in class. While Khan Academy is structured as a stand-alone teaching tool, having students access and use it in the classroom two or three times initially is recommended, because in those in-class sessions, teachers can troubleshoot any issues that arise. Teachers should place students at the level of material they need to master, even if it is several years below grade level. This usually results in a fairly wide range of skills when Khan is used in most math classes, but it does address individual students' needs. I usually recommend that teachers use Khan Academy in class two or three times for twenty minutes or so, to ensure students are comfortable with it. During those initial sessions, teachers should point out how the components, online exercises, videos, and knowledge map all fit together.

As an alternative in-class implementation idea, teachers can refer students to a Khan Academy video when that student asks a question in class. This will help get students into the habit of seeking answers for themselves using this resource. Viewing these videos is also a great partner activity in class.

Share Khan Academy with parents. Khan Academy is a great tool to help parents work with their children in mathematics. Some parents may fear math, since they may not have done well in mathematics themselves, and in those situations, Khan Academy can help parents feel more comfortable helping with homework. I have often recommended it to parents in that regard.

Consider class time for Khan Academy. Some teachers provide 20 percent of their class time for Khan Academy individual work, while others do this for thirty minutes twice a week. Of course, the more time students spend with Khan Academy, the more useful it will be. However, I often recommend an alternative that takes no class time after the initial two or three in-class sessions. In that scenario, teachers can stop using class time for Khan Academy after these initial in-class sessions. For many students, Khan Academy is rewarding enough that they will continue to use it outside of class, and teachers who don't spend class time using this tool can still offer daily reinforcement for outside use of Khan Academy.

For example, teachers might ask, "Who earned a merit badge in Khan Academy this past weekend? Great! Let's Give Billy, Kanesha, and Tamal a round of applause!" Another option is the use of more structured reinforcement. Teachers might say, "OK. Every Monday you guys earn ten minutes of computer game time if the class as a whole has earned at least twenty-five merit badges! Let's count off and see how we've done!" Many teachers have stated that this will keep many students quite motivated to earn merit badges on their own. Thus, a little verbal reinforcement or class applause can help keep students moving through Khan Academy even when no class time is devoted to it.

Continually check students' knowledge maps. The individual students' knowledge maps are the key to student achievement in Khan Academy. Because all of the students' work is cloud based, both teachers and students can access a student's knowledge map and track progress. Further, anecdotal testimonies indicate that perhaps 10 percent of the class will begin to work on skills that are beyond their grade level (Bender, 2012; SRI, 2014; Toppo, 2011), and while these will typically be the highly skilled students, one can only imagine what this would do to the average achievement scores in mathematics for the class or the school. It is the knowledge map within Khan Academy that will make this possible (Toppo, 2011). Clearly, earning these badges and seeing them appear on their individual knowledge map is quite motivating for most students. For students who do excel, additional classroom or schoolwide recognition is always recommended.

Try a flipped lesson. Using Khan Academy, teachers might wish to try flipping a class or two. Merely pick a topic and assign the appropriate Khan Academy video. Teachers can then have students engage in a class project or knowledge application type of activity for the entire class period. Coupling the flipped-class idea with Khan Academy has proven to be a winning strategy in many mathematics classes and more than a few science classes.

Ultimately, each teacher's goals in using Khan Academy should be both increasing academic achievement and instilling in all students the belief that they can seek out, find, and master difficult academic content on their own. In fact, those are excellent goals for all educational endeavors in the 21st century.

Summary

Computing technology in the classroom dates from the use of the Apple II computers of the early 1980s, and following the many transitions since then, one can only stand in awe of these instructional technologies. Free, worldwide programs such as Khan Academy and the regular use of SMART Boards in the classroom represent technologies previously only dreamed of, and more change is coming. While schools still struggle to become fully Wi-Fi capable and to establish one-to-one computer availability for students, so many changes are taking place that it is quite difficult to imagine what classrooms will look like in another ten years.

Suffice it to say that the technologies presented herein for the tech-rich teaching strategy represent only the tip of the proverbial iceberg. Much more is coming below in the discussions of the software and hardware options for STEM instruction. Teachers should, of course, employ every option available to them in the classroom, because all educators may rest assured, schools in other developed countries are quickly rushing to implement these technologies in preparing their students for the world economy. No country should allow itself to be left behind on this important and ever-changing frontier.

Further, I'd suggest that all science and mathematics teachers implement Khan Academy or one of the other self-directed learning options. Making students independent, self-directed learners through constant use of a self-directed curriculum is perhaps one of the most important gifts that we, as educators, can bestow on our students. As one might expect, the current climate on school change in the United States suggests that STEM teachers will lead the way in that effort.

STRATEGY 7

Coding and Robotics in STEM

Coding and robotics are among the newest tools in the STEM arsenal, and as this book was being written, coding and robotics were still finding their way into classrooms at all grade levels (Bloom, 2015; Dredge, 2014; Fears & Patsalides, 2012; Powel, 2014; Schwartz, 2014; Yohana, 2014). Thus, STEM teachers are only beginning the exciting exploration of coding and robotics in STEM instruction (Pressly, 2014; Schwartz, 2014). In fact, it is probably true that many teachers do not yet realize exactly what coding is, and the use of robots in the STEM classroom has previously been limited by costs. For these reasons, even the most recent books on STEM instruction have not included discussions of coding or robotics (Myers & Berkowicz, 2015; Slavin, 2014); these teaching strategies are simply too new.

However, STEM teachers should make no mistake: coding and robotics are likely to define the STEM classroom in the very near future, even as they are already redefining the modern workplace. Thus, some exploration of these instructional strategies is essential.

By way of background, coding involves teaching students computer programming, using simple programming languages that are intended for younger students (Gardiner, 2014). Coding is basically learning to tell a computer or other machine (such as a robot) what to do. Anyone who has ever programmed a modern smartphone is familiar to some degree with the problem of coding, and students increasingly consider this type of digital communication to be a fundamental birthright! Schools simply must get ahead of this curve in order to keep up, not only with demands of the modern workplace, but also with many of our students.

It is important to note that proponents of coding instruction are not advocating such instruction in order to make everyone a computer programmer; rather these proponents see coding as one way to help students learn to love learning and build pathways to other critical skills, such as problem solving and collaborative work (Gardiner, 2014).

> Coding involves teaching students computer programming, using simple programming languages that are intended for younger students. Coding is learning to tell a computer or machine what to do.

Schools in the United States are just starting to gear up for these topics, and in 2015, only about 10 percent of schools were teaching coding, though that number is increasing quickly. However, many students around the world in all grade levels are already coding and using those codes to program computers and/or robots (Dredge, 2014; Gardiner, 2014). For example, all students in England are being taught coding from the age of five (Dredge, 2014). Students in Estonia are learning to program in order to create computer games in the first grade, and students in Singapore began coding in elementary school in 2016 (Gardiner, 2014). These foreign students with this level of sophisticated training represent the talented, disciplined minds that American, Australian, and Canadian students will compete against in the global marketplace of the future. Students left behind in this arena will find their future to be quite limited, and no developed nation can allow that.

While there are many good reasons for teaching coding as a stand-alone subject in the schools, in the STEM context coding is frequently coupled with robotics. Many STEM educators see coding and robotics as intertwined, and at the very least, all STEM teachers should be exploring these technology applications. One may rest assured, almost all of our students are already exploring them!

Coding in the Classroom

Coding Alternatives

As stated above, coding is the use of specified language or code to tell a computer or a robot what to do. Some codes require reading, while others are based primarily on pictures or icons, and these can help younger students or nonreaders grasp the concepts of coding. A variety of coding languages may be found online, some of which are free. Several of these are described in the following box.

Coding Languages

- **RobotBASIC:** This is a free robot control programming language with advanced graphics and free animation. It is among the most powerful programming languages available, with over 800 commands and functions (http://robotbasic.org/). Intended for use by all ages, this language includes not only simple commands, but also highly complex tasks (floating point math, multidimensional arrays, matrix algebra, and statistical functions). Teachers from kindergarten through high school find this language useful, and there is some advantage to selecting a coding language that doesn't change from one grade level to the next. Robots can be represented on screen and programmed using this language (see the video demo: https://www.youtube.com/watch?v=27Gt3IgdcMc&feature=share&list=UUixBQVQIGJ8ja-pLLm3NSjg).

- **Scratch:** Many schools use a programming language called Scratch, a free programming language developed by MIT that teachers and students can easily download (http://scratch.mit.edu). In order to understand coding, I urge educators to review a brief tutorial on Scratch, and consider the skills that are taught in the coding instructional process (https://search.yahoo.com/search?fr=mcafee&type=C211US662D20141212&p=Scratch). For teachers of younger students, there is also a Scratch Jr. (http://www.scratchjr.org/).

- **Code Studio:** Code Studio (www.code.org) is another option for teachers to consider for the classroom. This programming language is fairly simple, and the associated website allows students to sign up for a wide variety of tutorials on coding,

continued ➜

to explore environments using movie characters or to write their own computer games. Courses on coding and programming for ages four through eighteen are available, and skills such as real-life algorithms, mazes, create a story, and debugging are taught. With an assessment component built in, this option is certainly one for teachers to consider, from kindergarten through high school.

- **The Foos:** A coding language from codeSpark (www.thefoos.com) for preschool students and nonreading students. This language teaches the basics of coding skill, including sequencing, pattern recognition, and conditional logic (i.e., if/then statements). This language is aimed at students as young as five, and has been downloaded 700,000 times by teachers in over 150 countries.

A quick review of these coding tools will demonstrate that teaching coding involves much more than merely learning a coding language or a set of symbols (Bloom, 2015). In order to code, students have to identify a problem, break the problem into steps, logically order the steps, identify a solution to the problem given that sequence of steps, and then tell the robot how to proceed in terms of what to do and when (Gardiner, 2014). Thus, skills such as planning, problem solving, deconstructing a problem, identification of steps in a problem solution, sequencing those steps, finding errors in the program (called debugging), and then programming those steps, are all stressed in the coding instructional process. The payoff comes for the students at the end of the process when a coded program works. Students are then rewarded by seeing their task accomplished either in the digital realm, or in the real world, as a robot performs the programmed tasks.

Of course, coding instruction for young children is such a recent development that little peer-reviewed research exists on the efficacy of coding. However, anecdotal testimonies from those who have had students code is impressive (Gardiner, 2014). For example, Roxanne Emadi works with Code.org, a Seattle-based advocacy group to foster the use of coding and technology in schools. She has indicated that students are highly engaged when coding is included in the curriculum. She describes coding instruction as highly motivating and a must for modern schools. "Kids these days are all stuck to their phones, their tablets, and are constantly using technology, but very few of them are learning how to create it. Even if it's something simple, like a kid programming a maze or programming a robot, when you can see your work brought to life, that's where light bulbs go off. Teachers are using [coding] like candy: 'If you finish your work, we can do 10 minutes of the computer science tutorials at the end of class as a treat'" (Roxanne Emadi, as quoted in Gardiner, 2014). Clearly, coding can be a powerful motivator in STEM classes. Every veteran teacher can only envy the desirability of using coding work in the science tutorials mentioned above as a "treat" at the end of class!

A Classroom Example: First-Time Coding in Grade 1

Mrs. Eleanor Ivester is a veteran of twenty-eight years in the classroom in grades ranging from kindergarten through grade 4. She holds an undergraduate degree from West Georgia College and an EdM in Elementary Education from Clemson University. She teaches grade 1 at Liberty Elementary School in Georgia. While bots have been included in several technology classes at the middle school in her district, neither she nor her first-grade students have utilized robots in the classroom as yet.

> *I decided to implement coding and robot instruction in conjunction with a thematic unit focused on the students' place in their environment. I obtained a Bee-Bot and a Mat (i.e., a grid pattern floor map that serves as a backdrop for Bee-Bot's movements). Bee-Bot is a simple robot for preschool and primary grades. It looks like a Bumble Bee with seven "coding" buttons on the top, to create different movements or actions (a forward arrow, a backward arrow, a right turn arrow, a left turn arrow, a pause button, a "clear commands" button, and a "go" button to tell the bot to execute the sequenced commands). Pushing a code button once either moves the Bee-Bot one space across the grid, or causes the bot to turn.*

> *I used the bot in conjunction with a book called* Me on the Map *(by Joan Sweeney; 1998; Dragonfly Books). In that unit, we focused on where my students lived. The book includes pictures with captions (e.g., "This is me and my room. This is me in my house. This is me on my street, or me in my town, me and my state, me and my country"). In conjunction with that study, I created labels for the Mat so that different grid locations on the Mat would represent locations in the school (i.e., my classroom, library, lunchroom, and the school office). On the first day, I placed the bot on the floor with the class sitting around it, and I asked the class, "How do you think we might make Bee-Bot go?" One student suggested pushing the arrow button that means "go forward," but the Bee-Bot didn't move. They tried that idea several more times, and then realized that they had to push the "forward" arrow, and then tell the bot to "Go" (by pushing the Go button that means "Execute the command").*

> *Once the students learned that several commands could be "programed" at once, prior to having Bee-Bot execute the commands, they began to actually "code" various movement sequences. Initially, I asked what the bot needed to do to move from one*

area of our "building" to another, with the various rooms represented by blocks on the Mat. Then I began to give assignments like, "Take Bee-Bot to the lunchroom."

In response, the students might say that "Bee-Bot needs to move forward two times, turn right, and then move forward one more time." At that point, they were actually developing a coding sequence! On the first day, I wrote the code myself when the students gave the instructions, but the students watched me several times, and then took over that coding task as well. In our class, code is written by listing the code or the signs for the movements vertically on a sheet of paper. Thus, the code instructions for the movement above would be:

↑

↑

→

↑

Go!

Simple coding of this nature became relatively easy for the majority of the class after only a week or so, and that really surprised me. I thought it would take more time before they learned to code, particularly for the longer coding sequences. Still, in short order, the sequenced commands grew to multiple destinations (e.g., "Today, we'll go first to the office, and then to the lunchroom"). Bee-Bot can accept up to forty code commands in any one sequence, providing plenty of options to move the bot around the Mat for younger students.

One difficulty I noted with this group of students is that they could not orient themselves without some degree of practice. For example, if the Mat or Bee-Bot was turned in a different direction than the day before, or if they simply sat on a different side of the Mat than previously, the students occasionally had some difficulty understanding how to program the desired movements. They tended to program based on how they were sitting rather than where Bee-Bot was or where Bee-Bot was facing. In some cases they executed a left turn when a right was needed, or made other orientation mistakes. However, when Bee-Bot didn't get to the desired destination, the mistakes were clear, and they soon began to help each other to check and correct the code. After a few days, if I merely told them they'd be using the Bee-Bot, they got excited, grabbed a clipboard, and began to write code.

Overall, my kids loved it! They were all highly engaged whenever we were doing assignments with Bee-Bot. In fact, they enjoyed this experience so much that after a time I actually used the opportunity to play with Bee-Bot as a reward for work at the end of class. If the students collectively earned a "smiley face" for good participation and behavior, they got to use Bee-Bot late in the day. One of the brightest children in my class always gets really excited and helps all of the others with their coding, particularly when a mistake is made. He loves the challenge of coding and wants to send Bee-Bot everywhere in the school!

I like the fact that this helps students with problem solving, planning a course of action, sequencing, and correcting the code when the bot doesn't get to the assigned location. They are working cooperatively with others frequently, whenever I place them in pairs to code together. I always have students help each other to correct their code. At this point I'll be using Bee-Bot for the rest of the year, to continue their growth in coding skill. I'm planning on ordering more support materials, particularly different Mats for Bee-Bot to use! We'll be studying the continents soon, based on our social studies standards, so I might relabel the Mat to represent the continents!

Robotics in STEM

Coupled with a growing emphasis on coding in STEM classes across the grade levels is the equally recent emphasis on robotics (Fears & Patsalides, 2012; Powel, 2014; Pressly, 2014). In particular, the increased interest in STEM has fostered an increase in robotic products intended for the STEM classroom. For example, one kit that is being used frequently is the WeDo robotics kit. This is a LEGO-based robotics program, focused specifically on STEM instruction that is intended for grades 2 through 5. The program incorporates LEGOs, digital learning, cognitive learning, and fine motor skills to help students construct simple machines in the classroom (see the website: https://education.lego.com/en-us/lesi/elementary/lego-education-wedo/getting-started-with-wedo). Using a simple icon-based coding language within the accompanying software, and the LEGO bricks, students are shown how to create a variety of machines that include working motors, sensors, and a simple program to actually build movable, controllable robots. Even kindergarten students can build simple working robots and other simple machines in the classroom.

Teachers in higher grades may prefer the RobotsLab. This tool provides teachers with a robotics kit, including a drone quadcopter, a tablet, a robotic arm, a spherical robot, a circular robot, and a set of lesson plans (http://shop.robotslab.com/products/robotslab-box). Because this kit is preprogrammed, teachers do not need coding or programming skills to use this teaching tool in the classroom for demonstrating different STEM concepts. Finally, there are many other robotics products that teachers should consider for their class, and several popular robots for STEM instruction are described in the following box.

Robots for the Classroom

- **Dash and Dot:** These are small, blue, circular robots designed to help students as young as kindergarten begin the coding/robotics curriculum (from Wonderworkshop: www.makewonder.com). Students use an icon-based coding language to program these robots for a variety of tasks, so nonreaders can do programming. Robots can be programmed to travel, turn, detect objects, light up, make sounds, and interact with each other. These robots range from $169, and kits and accessories range from $39 to $299. A brief video shares the opportunities these inexpensive robots provide in the kindergarten classroom (https://www.make wonder.com/robots/dashanddot). Also, a variety of lesson plans are available for these bots (https:// teachers.makewonder.com/lessons).

- **Bee-Bot:** Bee-Bot is an exciting robot that looks like a bumblebee and is designed specifically for younger children from preschool up through grade 2. This bot can teach many early learning skills such as sequencing, simple mathematical concepts, estimation, early problem solving, and collaborative skills. Students not only learn a bit of coding (up to forty commands) while enjoying their play with the bot, but the Bee-Bot blinks and beeps as each command is completed, providing rewards for the young learners. This bot can also reinforce less tangible skills such as perseverance and collaboration (Yohana, 2014), and sells for just under $100.

- **EZ-Robot:** EZ-Robot is a new company that provides a variety of robots for STEM education that may be used across the grade levels. The Adventurebot is a small circular robot for beginners that sells for $149, whereas the J. D. Humanoid is a more complex humanoid robot listed at $429. Beginners learn logic, construction and soldering, electronics, and modular design while creating the robot, turning a toy shell into a personalized robot (Pressly, 2014; Yohana, 2014). This looks like a very promising product for schools, but there have been some shipping and supply problems. It seems to speak well of them that they cannot build the robots fast enough.

- **Nao:** The Nao Next Gen is a small humanoid bot made by RobotsLab (http://www.robotslab.com /About.aspx#gsc.tab=0). This is one of the more common bots in its price range found in schools. It was designed with STEM instruction in mind and has won endorsements from *EdTech Digest* and the Edison Awards. Students often respond better to humanoid robots, and Nao comes with many lesson options across the grade levels. Teachers might consider this when purchasing a robotics package. Nao allows for all the functions one would expect, and sells for $9,500, though certain discounts are available to educators. The same company also produces the RobotsLab Box, which includes a STEM curriculum aligned with the Common Core State Standards, as well as a tablet that allows the teacher to control the robot.

Why Teach Robotics?

There are a number of reasons to explore coding and robotics within the shift to STEM-based teaching. First, coding and robotics represent the future of much of STEM instruction. While many schools have not yet started with coding and robotics education, educators may safely conclude that all STEM schools, and eventually all schools, will be moving in this direction. This shift will be driven by the demands of industry worldwide.

It is a fact that coding and robotics represent the future of technology in many work environments, and that trend will only increase in the future (Fears & Patsalides, 2012; Powell, 2014; Pressly, 2014; Schwartz, 2014; Yohana, 2014).

Of course, in many manufacturing jobs (e.g., the assembly lines in automotive plants or furniture construction), robots have long played a role, and with the imminent increase in 3-D printing technology, this trend will grow dramatically over the next decade. We might note that one of the 3-D printers described in the former "Build Something" strategy section was a self-described robot (i.e., the Makerbot). In short, for anyone who wants to work in the future, coding and robotics are likely to be involved, and our science, technology, engineering, and mathematics courses must prepare students for that world. For students to compete nationally and internationally, coding and robotics simply have to be stressed in the STEM classroom.

Next, these instructional strategies are highly motivating for students (Nugent, Barker, & Grandgenett, 2012). Because these curricula emphases seem to most students to represent their experience of the digital world better that many hardcopy textbooks can, students are much more highly engaged in coding and robotics instruction (Fears & Patsalides, 2012; Nugent, Barker, & Grandgenett, 2012; Powell, 2014; Pressly, 2014) than in traditional science or mathematics instruction. Further, their increased interest level translates into higher levels of learning (Gardiner, 2014; Nugent, Barker, & Grandgenett, 2012; Schwartz, 2014; Yohana, 2014).

Another positive impact of coding and robotics instruction is the fact that these strategies seemingly involve young girls much more in the STEM process than more traditional instruction (Gardiner, 2014; Nugent, Barker, & Grandgenett, 2012; Schwartz, 2014). In fact, coding is actually empowering for students in the 21st century, since students who code are not eliminated from computer careers by artificial barriers. While young boys have always enjoyed computer science and simple engineering types of class assignments, these authors have reported that young girls, who have not been traditionally drawn to mathematics and science, do become more involved in coding and robotics and get quite turned on to these subject areas. In fact, Schwartz (2014) indicated that robot manufacturers are beginning to understand how to design the look of their robots (e.g., fewer external wires, wheels, or motors, and more curves for a softer appearance) in order to make them more attractive to girls.

Finally, and perhaps most importantly, teaching with robots demonstrates for future generations the potential for robotics. Imagine for a moment the potential of a robot controlled merely by one's thoughts! At the University of Minnesota, that robot already exists, and it is truly incredible to watch in action at https://www.youtube.com/watch?v=-h3kiws4I54. By developing a mind/robot interface that literally reads one's brain waves, these scientists have developed a mind-controlled flying robot that can negotiate an obstacle course of balloons scattered around the room. This flying bot is controlled by a student wearing a skullcap with sixty-four brain-wave-reading sensors. The student simply thinks of making a fist with his right hand, and a computer reads the student's brain waves in his muscle cortex, while translating that command into the code for the robot that means "turn right." At that point, the flying bot turns right. When the student thinks of making two fists, the bot climbs straight up. This holds nearly unlimited potential for our future, when we consider the uses of that robotics/brain interface for quadriplegic students or students with other disabilities.

There is only one major disadvantage to coding and robotics instruction that has been noted in the literature: like many technology innovations for instruction, these teaching tools can be expensive. For example, the RobotsLab described above costs approximately $4,000, and that is more than many schools' budgets can allow for a single robot in a single classroom. However, while many robots continue to be somewhat expensive, there are some that are not. Specifically, some robots for primary classes fall into the $50 range, and others with a similar cost can be found in many elementary classrooms. Typically, the more expensive robots, ranging from $500 to $20,000, are found in middle and/or high school STEM courses (Schwartz, 2014).

What Do I Do With a Class Robot?

The answer to this question is simple; a robot will do virtually anything you tell it to do, given the obvious limitations of computing power, size, strength, and the onboard sensors available. Thus, robots can help teach almost anything! Further, some of the concern behind this question can be laid to rest by the curricula and lesson plans that teachers can easily access. There is no shortage of predesigned STEM lesson plans covering many content standards available on the Internet for all grade levels, and the scope of those materials will only grow in the future. In fact, many proponents foresee a day when virtually all concepts taught in STEM classes can be represented with robotics lessons (Powell, 2014; Pressly, 2014; Schwartz, 2014; Yohana, 2014).

Here is a higher level mathematics example of what a robot can demonstrate: In one RobotsLab lesson, quadratic functions are taught using a drone quadcopter robot to demonstrate what the mathematical equation means in a real-world example. The camera attached to the flying robot correlates the area viewed on camera with the mathematical algorithm and the associated graph. Specifically, when the robot is programmed with a quadratic equation, the quadcopter rises to specific designated heights, demonstrating the visible relationship between the hovering robot and the area captured by the camera. As this example indicates, virtually anything that can be programmed into a robot (and virtually everything can) will provide content options for a lesson, not only in STEM subjects, but in many others as well.

Robots as Teachers

Given this relatively unlimited possibility, some have asked the question, "Will high-level robots replace teachers?" (Powell, 2014; Yohana, 2014). This question is not as far-fetched as it sounds, and one may well remember that only a decade or so ago, educators were asking the same question about computers. At this point, the answer seems to be a tentative "maybe, but not yet." Here are several examples from the literature, showing both the promise and programming concerns with the use of robots as teachers.

In some remote villages in South Korea, robots are being used to replace teachers entirely in teaching English. English teachers are in high demand, and few can be found in rural areas, so robots became a possible solution. These robots operate under supervision, and really represent virtual-presence devices, but they can be programmed for independent instruction as well. The goal is for the robot to eventually lead the instruction entirely within a very few years (Powell, 2014; Yohana, 2014).

Education in remote regions of Alaska has always been challenging, and the state has always used distance-learning options to address the need for high-level courses in less populated areas. Thus, it should come as no surprise that robots are being used to "staff" distance-learning locations for some classes (Yohana, 2014). Bob Whicker, director of the Consortium for Digital Learning at the Association of Alaska School Boards, envisions a day when educators will be able to "roll into their distance classrooms on two wheels" (Yohana, 2014)!

Robots can be a virtual presence in the classroom for students with severe illnesses (Yohana, 2014). A robot created by VGo Communications might soon roll into your class, while it is controlled by a sick student at home. The bot would include a webcam and some type of communications option (voice options via phone connections, or perhaps Skype). Yohana indicated that about thirty students were using this device in the United States by 2014.

Gretchen Robinson, a second-grade teacher using a Nao robot in her class in Onslow County, North Carolina, has some concerns with the "robots replacing teachers" idea. She has programmed her Nao to answer questions, read a student's poetry, or call out vocabulary words, and she reported that students will often engage with the bot more than with a teacher (Schwartz, 2014). However, she suggested that actually having a bot teach an entire lesson would involve many hundreds of hours of programming time. Ms. Robinson did indicate, however, that students wanted to "work with the robot for as long as possible. Every time their lesson is done they're disappointed." She also found that students do develop a good grasp of the content in robot-led lessons (Schwartz, 2014).

Clearly, robots are finding a variety of useful applications in STEM instruction, though replacement of teachers with robots seems to be far in the future, if such a replacement can take place at all. Rather than worry about that concern, I suggest that STEM teachers begin their journey in the use of coding and robotics immediately, and allow the student energy thus generated to become the motivating factor for further use of coding and bots in the classroom.

Efficacy of Coding and Robotics

As the discussion thus far has indicated, only limited scientific evidence is available on the efficacy of coding and robotics instruction in STEM classrooms, but that evidence is supportive (Nugent, Barker, & Grandgenett, 2012; Schwartz, 2014; Yohana, 2014). Also, a great deal of additional anecdotal evidence is available that is supportive of these innovations (Bloom, 2015; Dredge, 2014; Fears & Patsalides, 2012; Powell, 2014; Pressly, 2014; Schwartz, 2014; Yohana, 2014). Of course, with educational innovations, it is often the case that experimental evidence on efficacy lags behind anecdotal and/or testimonial evidence, and when the anecdotal evidence is strong, teachers should not hesitate to explore the new instructional options. Schwartz (2014), for example, indicated that "students universally enjoy the robotic lessons, and respond very positively, often wishing to continue the lesson long after the lesson time has run out." Further, the extant literature presents no real downside (other than expense) to coding and robotics in STEM classes (Bloom, 2015; Dredge, 2014; Fears & Patsalides, 2012; Powell, 2014; Pressly, 2014; Schwartz, 2014; Yohana, 2014).

Jerry Moldenhauer's positive teaching experiences with bots is typical (Schwartz, 2014). Moldenhauer has been using robots in his engineering classes at Eastside Memorial High School in Austin, Texas, for several years, and reports that the bots boost engagement and help students grasp challenging concepts. "Kids are calculating the velocity of the robot without realizing they're using algebra. It really makes the connection better for them." Moldenhauer also suggests that the robot is especially useful for explaining the math behind more advanced engineering topics (Schwartz, 2014).

Steps for Teaching Coding/Robotics

As indicated above, only about 10 percent of schools were teaching coding in 2015, and while a higher percentage was teaching robotics in one form or another, it is a safe assumption that many STEM teachers are still new to both of these areas. Thus, the steps below will assist those who are beginning to teach coding and robotics in the STEM class.

Partner up. Partner with another teacher or two in your school, and discuss how coding and robotics might fit into your teaching, with consideration on using these newly evolving tools in the Common Core standards or your state's standards. Also investigate schools that your students might attend next. If you are in the elementary grades, find out what coding/robotics instruction is taking place in the middle school, and consider using the same coding and robotics options they are using. Also, by partnering up, you might find that you can afford a more sophisticated effort, and this will help when you request school funds to purchase a robot, as recommended below.

Try coding. For preschool and primary grades, codes are typically supplied with the robots, as was the code for Bee-Bot described above. For elementary and higher grade teachers, I suggest that teachers download Scratch (or another free coding language) and just play with it. A variety of interesting tutorials are available free for Scratch on YouTube, and with a free coding language and good tutorials, virtually every teacher across the grade levels can gear up for this STEM instructional strategy.

Seek school and district support. As teachers begin to explore new instructional methods in STEM, I suggest that they approach both their school principal and the science and mathematics coordinators at the central office for support. While school budgets always seem to be limited, perhaps funds can be found for a small bot or for attendance at a STEM conference on teaching coding and robotics, particularly if pairs of teachers show an interest together.

Pick up a bot. At some point, teachers should purchase a simple, lower-end robot, and explore its use in their classes. Even in higher grades, these inexpensive robots can capture students' attention, and motivate them to explore coding and robotics. I do urge teachers to explore bots described here, as well as others, since many options are available. Again, find out if others in the district are using specific coding languages and/or bots, and seek their advice.

Explore the curriculum. Most bots come with some curricular lessons for various STEM classes. These should provide a good first step for teachers in consideration of how to use coding and robotics in class. Further, the Internet is loaded with lesson plans teachers should explore. These websites can provide a place to start: http://robotics.usc.edu/~agents/k-12/curricular.php, https://www.raspberrypi.org/, and https://www.pinterest.com/weareteachers/stemsteam-lessons-activities-and-ideas/.

Dive in. Teachers should not wait to become experts in coding and robotics prior to trying both in the classroom. Rather, after three or four hours of initial exploration to complete the steps above, teachers should dive in! You will have found plenty of lesson plan options for use in your subject and grade level, and the novelty of coding and robotics instruction will so engage the students that you will wonder why you didn't try this sooner.

Summary

As this discussion makes clear, the twin instructional strategies of coding and robotics are soon coming to a STEM class near you, and all STEM teachers should begin their explorations of how these tools may help in their subject area and grade level. The only real limitations seem to be expense and teachers' imaginative use of these tools, and the field suggests a positive outlook on both. As bots become more ingrained in STEM instruction, prices will come down (as they did for computers), and with many millions of teachers joining the STEM revolution, there is no shortage of brainpower exploring how to move forward with robotics in the classroom in the foreseeable future.

STRATEGY 8

Animation in STEM Classes

Animation is a teaching strategy that can reach many students who are otherwise uninterested in STEM subjects (Bender & Waller, 2013). Not only are animations attention grabbers that make content come alive, but with animated cartoon characters in virtually any subject, they also enrich the visual representations associated with subject content and can enhance long-term memory (Moreno, 2009; Stansbury, 2013; Zimmerman, 2014).

Classroom Animation in STEM

Teachers have long recognized that learning involves not only focused attention, but also concentration on the content and long-term memory, and animation is a teaching tool that enhances each of these aspects of learning (Kuchimanchi, 2013). In short, animation can make dull subject matter come to life by incorporating movement, illustrating processes over time, and showing relationships, while focusing concentration and enhancing memory of the content. This will increase academic achievement (Moreno, 2009; Stansbury, 2013; Zimmerman, 2014).

As an example, one might imagine the difference between hanging a breeze-activated mobile of the solar system over a child's crib versus hanging a printed picture of planets orbiting the sun. Which of these will engage the child's attention faster? Further, because of the movement of the mobile, children will concentrate on the mobile for long periods of time. Like the mobile, animation is one way to represent processes involving movement.

> Animations—attention-grabbing cartoon characters that make content come alive in virtually any subject and enrich the visual representations associated with subject content.

Classroom tools are available that allow both teachers and students across the grade levels to animate the content under study, and animation of content is a powerful tool (Hatten, 2014; Kuchimanchi, 2013; Moreno, 2009; Stansbury, 2013). Stansbury (2013), for example, suggested that animations should be considered a universal language that reaches virtually all students, including lower-achieving students or others with varying backgrounds, languages, or academic strengths. In addition, allowing students to learn through animation lowers the intimidation aspect of the STEM classroom and provides an avenue for learning in a nonthreatening environment. Finally, many teachers have reported that students are more engaged and retain more content material when they are able to creatively express themselves through animation ("Detroit Schools," 2011; Stansbury, 2013).

Animation can be quite personalized for classroom use. For example, many students use animation to create personal avatars. An avatar is an animated digital character that might represent the teacher, the student, or a scientist or historical figure. When appropriate dialogue is provided, the avatar comes to life and presents that dialogue, and thus, can be used in a variety of classroom instructional activities (Bender & Waller, 2013; Hatten, 2014; Moreno, 2009; Stansbury, 2013). Several examples are provided below.

> Avatar—an animated digital character that can represent oneself or other figure, and can be made to engage in prerecorded dialogue.

How Can I Use Animation?

Some teachers inexperienced with animation might wonder how such animations might be used in the STEM class. There is no one answer to that question, since avatars and animated characters may be used in a wide variety of ways (Bender & Waller, 2013; Stansbury, 2013). For example, students can use their avatar to present their oral reports, book reviews, or presentations of theme papers. In that fashion, shy and reluctant students can be encouraged to present in a much more entertaining fashion. Student or teacher animations can be added to PowerPoint presentations, and animations can be developed by students at virtually every grade level. Students might create avatars and appropriate scripts to practice development of their persuasive arguments, to present research findings, or simply to introduce themselves at the beginning of the year.

Further, animations can be saved over time, such that reports from students' avatars might be uploaded to class wikis or blogs, for use or reference by other students. Students might create a portfolio of their avatar presentations and share that with parents or other teachers. Students can also access their peers' avatars to review content material throughout the year. Here are some other ideas:

Use animation to help manage the class. Within some of these animation websites, teachers are presented with various instructional options. For example, as a part of the Voki Classroom, teachers can outline an assignment on the website for students to complete: http://www.voki.com. Once they have completed their assignment with their avatar, the teacher can go online, access the avatar, and evaluate the work. Teachers will be able to manage several different classrooms on the account, as well as different lessons and assignments.

Use animation to teach processes in science. Various scientific processes are best illustrated with movement over time. Therefore, animations (cartoons that move) can be critical in understanding processes such as planet rotation, life cycles, collecting solar energy, moon phases, erosion, or even genetics across multiple generations. Animation can make these processes easier to understand (Hatten, 2014).

Teach patterns and relationships in mathematics. Various math concepts can be illustrated with moving animations, including skip counting, the relationship between addition and multiplication, or creation of algorithms. In this sense, animation lends itself to the effort to teach the deeper relationships that are emphasized in Common Core mathematics.

Use student avatars for proofreading. Students can check their papers and reports by having their avatar read it. As students hear their avatar speaking, they can read along, and this partner reading process makes errors more obvious. Students can then make corrections based on the avatar's speaking, by adding a period or rewriting the text a bit (Bender & Waller, 2013).

Use introduction avatars. In the lower grades, students might create an avatar that introduces them to their classmates at the beginning of the year, and continue to use that digital self throughout the year. This can assist withdrawn or shy students, and sometimes make the first days of school easier.

Use avatars for recitation. Some students are shy about reading in front of the class, or reciting their own written assignments such as poems or stories. Avatars can be used to do that type of assignment and alleviate that problem. It will also help struggling readers, who can practice the recording of voice for the avatar several times to get it exactly right, prior to the class recitation.

Use animation to practice reading fluency. For struggling students, teachers should have them record themselves via their avatar while reading particular texts. Students and teachers can then jointly analyze their fluency rates. The avatars can also be used for repeated readings of the same text.

Use animations to develop automaticity with math facts. Teachers might encourage students to recite math facts using their avatar. These recitations can be uploaded to a class wiki so that there is a bank of facts for the entire class to use as a study guide. Students can also use their avatars to explain any tips and tricks that they know for their number (Bender & Waller, 2013).

Use avatars to represent scientists or historical figures. Have students choose a historic figure and produce an avatar to represent that figure and explain why that historical figure acted in a certain fashion. For example, an animated Pythagoras might explain his theorem to the class, or several members of the Continental Congress might debate conflicting perspectives during a virtual session of the Congress itself.

As this list indicates, animation can be used in a limitless number of ways in the STEM classroom. Also, creative teachers and students together are likely to find additional uses for their avatars. Finally, as these instructional avenues are explored more fully, students get excited about animation. Thus, empowering students with animation tools is one method of engaging them more deeply with the STEM content.

Which Animation Option Should I Explore?

A variety of animation options are available, and the following box presents several of the more commonly used animation options for the classroom. Some of these offer free-use options for teachers, while others offer both free and fee-for-service options. I generally suggest that teachers explore two or more of these animation programs using perhaps twenty minutes per website and then select one option. However, if a teacher in your building is using a particular animation tool, I recommend giving special attention to that tool, since use of the same animation program would essentially mean the novice teacher would have some in-school support in the initial animation efforts!

Animation Tools for Teachers

- **PowToon** (www.powtoon.com/blog/how-teachers -and-students-are-using-powtoon-to-flip-the-classroom): This is a free website that allows teachers and students to create brief animations. An ebook guide "The Power of Cartoon Making" is available free to get teachers started.

- **GoAnimate** (http://goanimate.com): This site offers various free and fee-for-service plans, and provides backgrounds and a selection of characters for student creation of animated videos. This site is recommended for middle and high school students for PBL and STEM use, since it is more sophisticated than some other animation options. Here, teachers can make their first free video in under five minutes! To further explore this site, teachers should dive right in. They might wish to create a video lesson plan, an announcement for their class using one of these animated characters, or a political debate (Zimmerman, 2014).

- **Bararosa** (http://babarosa-gif-animator.download -420-33521.programsbase.com/): This is a free animator option that allows students and teachers to create animations using individual student-drawn images. These drawings can then be saved, uploaded, and brought to life!

- **Anim8or** (www.anim8or.com/index.html): This animation site allows students to use algebraic and even calculus functions to create 3-D animations, while teaching an array of computer skills. A downloadable guide is provided, so even novice students and teachers can use this in STEM classes.

continued →

- **Pencil** (http://pencil.evolus.vn/): This is a free option with some online support. This option is somewhat less well developed than others, but can be useful in the classroom. Students draw using various tools, while learning the basics of both animation and graphics design (Zimmerman, 2014).

- **DoInk.com:** This animation website allows students to create an animation and then clone it to place it in a sequence of scenes. Thus, this is a great site for creation of larger project-based learning assignments focused on specific content.

- **Xtranormal** (www.xtranormal.com): This site allows teachers or students to build avatars, environments, and then make the avatars speak. Different camera angles can be used, along with many other features, to make a movie. The ability to use different languages is available.

- **Voki** (www.voki.com): This site helps students customize an avatar and make it speak. It provides a free option (funded by pop-up advertising), or a fee-for-service option with no ads. Different languages are available. Avatars can be used to make announcements, hold journal posts, or other activities. There is also a database for teachers to check out other educators' lesson plans using Voki (www.voki.com/lesson_plans.php). Those lesson plans can be searched by grade level and subject.

Below, I present more detailed information on one animation option called Voki. This site provides excellent support for teachers, and there is a YouTube video that presents this teaching option for second-grade through high school students. Teachers may wish to view that video to get additional ideas on using animation (http://www.youtube.com/embed/304rQXcBrp4).

Voki in STEM Classes

For teachers who have not yet explored this teaching strategy in STEM classes, the mere thought of creating animated movies or presentations can seem daunting. However, animation tools such as Voki make this task easier across the grade levels (www.voki.com). Voki is an animation site that allows teachers or students to create avatars for various uses. Once created, the avatar (called a voki in this program), can be used in multiple tasks and stored for reuse on future content. While basic voki creation is free (i.e., funded by occasional pop-up adds), use of the service for the entire class is priced on a reasonable fee-for-service basis.

When using Voki, teachers or students first create their own avatar and then write dialogue for their avatar to speak. Once created, these speaking avatars and their created dialogue can be posted on student or teacher blogs or websites, or even shared through email. Avatars can be created to look like historical figures, or important scientists or mathematicians from the past, or merely like lovable cartoon characters.

Voki Classroom is a subscription service available for educators at a price of around $2.50 a month. In this service, a teacher is given access to all standard Voki features as well as a system to manage vokis created by all members of the class. Teachers can then create student accounts, manage assignments, receive unlimited tech support through the Voki website, and set a range of privacy settings. Again, a variety of introductory videos are available on Voki (e.g., http://www.youtube.com/embed/ao9KQltMkPO), and teachers who wish to explore animation in STEM classes should review those.

How to Get Started With Animation

Websites for animation vary in complexity and ease of use, but the ones discussed in this book, listed previously, have all been used by teachers who were beginners. None of these are highly complex, and the following steps are reasonably universal.

Complete several tutorials. Teachers should spend an hour on several tutorials for Voki or any other alternative they choose. All of these animation websites include videos from the creators and most include videos created by teachers using that animation option. After considering several animation options, teachers should pick the one they feel most comfortable with.

Create an initial avatar or animation. Next, teachers should spend some time and create an animation or avatar for themselves. This will help them understand the process, and note any limitations of that animation site.

Select your level of service. Most animation websites offer a minimal service free of charge and more expanded fee-based options. For example, the Voki Classroom fee-based service is $29.95 per year for one class. Teachers should experiment with the free service for a while prior to jumping into the subscription service.

Create your avatar. Once you have signed up for an animation service, you will be able to create or select a long-term avatar. Teachers should go through this process before opening up this animation site for their students, but students as young as first grade have successfully created stories using animations or avatars for themselves. When creating an avatar, you can typically customize the avatar's style, looks, voice, and background. When students are customizing their avatars, teachers should set a definite time limit to the process in order to avoid having students endlessly copy each other's style.

Select a background. Animations take place somewhere, and avatars have to have an environment. Thus, students will typically need to choose a background for the avatar. At this point, it can be helpful to discuss the subject theme and content with students. If students plan to use an avatar to depict a scientist from the 1700s, they should choose or create a background reflective of that time period. If they wish to use the avatar for an oral report in a foreign language, have them select a background that resembles the chosen culture. Thinking about and selecting appropriate background customization gives students an extra focus on the content material.

Create animation content. Development of information or "content" for an animated video or an avatar represents the creative aspect when using animation for teaching. Even for the simplest, briefest animations, students will need to create some vocal content or dialogue, and they should carefully check that the content is relevant and is presented accurately and in depth. For more complex animated content or longer animations, students will need to understand storyboarding, sequencing of content, and the development of additional details that support the content. This process will become more complex in the upper grade levels, and complexity increases when multiple avatars are presented in one presentation. The level of interaction of the avatars results in increased complexity.

Select a voice option. Once a storyboard has been developed and content is complete, the presentation voice must be selected or developed. Voice and dialogue are what bring the animation to life, and provide the animation with subject content. Some animation sites allow multiple options for avatar or animated voices. In Voki, for example, there are four options for giving the avatar a voice. Students can call in to the Voki website and record their voice through the phone. They can type text content at the website, and Voki will turn the text into speech. Next, students can speak into a microphone or simply upload an audio file. Typing is, by far, the most commonly used method, but using a student's actual voice can be quite engaging for many students.

Publish the animation! Animations are student creations of which students are quite proud. Therefore, they should be published and saved for future use. Students will respond more positively to animation in the STEM process and will devote more time to animation when they know the work will be broadly published. For some animation options, the student might simply click a "Publish" icon, and the website will provide the teacher and student a code that can be emailed or uploaded to a class blog or wiki. For others, saving the animation on a class or school website can make it available for the class and others, such as parents, who may wish to look over the work.

Research on Animation

Peer-reviewed research on use of animation in the classroom is somewhat limited, but the existing research shows that animations in science, math, and other subjects do increase retention and academic achievement (Detroit Schools, 2011; Hatten, 2014; Kuchimanchi, 2013; Moreno, 2009; O'Day, 2007; Stansbury, 2013). O'Day (2007), as one example, directly compared the efficacy of animation versus presentation of static information supplemented with high-quality, hard-copy graphics on retention of information in a biology class. The results showed increased engagement and retention when animations were used to present the same content, compared to the graphics informational text.

Also, the available anecdotal reports show that teachers using animation enjoy this teaching strategy (Hatten, 2014; Kuchimanchi, 2013; Moreno, 2009; Stansbury, 2013). Increased student engagement is frequently reported by teachers using animations, along with increased achievement when animation is incorporated into the teaching/learning process (Bender & Waller, 2013). This limited research has not yet allowed the animation strategy to be placed in meta-analytic research designs, since such research requires multiple studies on the same strategy. However, the extant research on the efficacy of animation supports teachers moving forward with the use of animation in STEM classes across the grade levels.

Summary

In some ways, animation may be one of the more important strategies presented in this book. When one considers the fear many students have of science or mathematics classes, a tool such as animation seems increasingly important because animation does more than merely present information in a highly engaging manner. Animation can actually help the most shy or reluctant learners succeed in the very subjects that terrify them. For this reason, I urge all STEM teachers to consider use of animation in the class in one fashion or another.

If time to develop animations is a concern (and teacher time is ALWAYS a concern), teachers can merely use an animation tool only long enough to become familiar with it, and then present that as an option to the students. From that point on, the students will be doing almost all of the animations for the class, and teacher time will not be involved. Still, the class will have access to this powerful teaching and communication tool and will find themselves more deeply engaged with STEM content.

STRATEGY 9

Gaming and Simulations

Gaming and simulations have become increasingly important components in many STEM classes around the world. In fact, since 2010, educational gaming has come into its own as a viable STEM instructional strategy (Maton, 2011; Schwartz, 2015, 2014; Wolpert-Gawron, 2015). While teachers have used both stand-alone board games and technology-based games for decades, students on occasion actually create games for teaching content.

Games and Gaming in Education

Clearly, gaming has become an important instructional component in many STEM classrooms, rather than merely an afterthought or reward for other work. In fact, the use of games seems to be increasing exponentially, for a variety of reasons.

First, the commercial video gaming market continues to reach new sales heights nearly every year. Billions are spent on commercial games yearly, and this enthusiasm carries over into education. Next, educators have noted the excitement many students show for gaming or simulation scenarios and have harnessed this powerful tool for motivational purposes (Miller, 2012; Shapiro, 2014). Most importantly, the early data suggest that gaming and/or simulation scenarios are highly effective STEM instructional tools (Ash, 2011; Hattie, 2012; ISTE, 2010; Maton, 2011; Miller, 2012; Short, 2012).

Stand-Alone Gaming

Teachers have become very familiar with many commercial, digital games that include an educational component. Computer-based games, such as the Age of Empires,

Civilization, or SimCity have long been used to teach how civilizations come into existence and developed over time, or how cities might be organized (Bender & Waller, 2013). The decades-old Oregon Trail taught recent generations of Americans what the settlers of the western frontier faced as they traveled across the continent in the 1800s. Both educational games and simulations, as well as many other games that were originally developed for personal entertainment, are being used in STEM classes. For example, one teacher has used a popular game called Angry Birds to teach physics principles, while others have used popular commercially available games such as SimCity to teach how complex systems interact (Sheely, 2011).

These games are generally considered stand-alone game applications when used in the classroom, and such stand-alone games represent the simplest class of games used in education. These are simple games or apps that can generally be played individually, often in one sitting, while teaching specific predesignated content. While students make choices in these games, there is less creativity required for most of them than in the games discussed later in this section. Of course, some stand-alone games do allow multiple players, so several players might work together to accomplish the game objectives, while mastering various targeted STEM content. Many, if not most, teachers across the grade levels are familiar with gaming sites such as BrainPop, Pemdas Blaster (for teaching the order of operations), and Algebra Meltdown (www.mangahigh.com). These stand-alone games and associated websites grow in popularity among educators each year (Bender & Waller, 2013; Shapiro, 2014; Short, 2012; Wolpert-Gawron, 2015).

For a better understanding on the use of games for learning in STEM, teachers might wish to view a brief video on gaming in the classroom from Edutopia.org (http://www.edutopia.org/blog/games-for-learning-community-resources-andrew-miller). The following box presents additional information on several of the more popular gaming websites for stand-alone educational games.

Educational Gaming Sites for STEM Instruction

- **BrainPop** (http://educators.brainpop.com/about/): This is one of the most popular stand-alone gaming sites and is used in over 20 percent of schools in the United States (http://educators.brainpop.com /about/). They feature many games in various STEM topics across the primary and elementary grade levels in science, mathematics, technology, engineering, social studies, health, and many other core courses. These games work well on computers, tablets, and other mobile devices, and this site offers animation options for the classroom. This site is also home to GameUp, an educational portal for the classroom, and Make-a-Map, a map generation tool for the classroom that can be very useful in geology, history, or social studies. Teachers can customize assessments or participate in professional development. For many teachers, this is the first website they explore for educational games. At this site, teachers may wish to explore the many videos of how other teachers are using games in STEM instruction (http://educators.brainpop.com /whygames/).

- **Public Broadcasting System** (www.pbs.org): Many mathematics and science games can be found at PBS. At that site, parents or teachers can pick an age range from kindergarten through upper elementary, and look at a variety of free games for children and elementary students.

- **Mangahigh.com:** The games at this site are targeted for students ranging in age from seven to sixteen. The games all stipulate a goal for students to achieve by repeatedly practicing the core learning concept, and teachers can track the progress of their students using their own login and passwords. Teachers report anecdotally that these games result in students playing their math games long after school is over and sometimes well into the night (see the website www.mangahigh.com for several teacher reviews). Certainly any mathematics teacher should take advantage of this website to access some educational games that will motive most students.

continued →

- **BrainWare Safari** (www.mybrainware.com/how
-it-works): This is a set of game scenarios that are
intended to strengthen certain cognitive skills,
including skills in the areas of attention, memory,
visual and auditory processing, thinking, and sensory
integration. This educational software program is
being used by teachers and homeschooling parents
alike (Shah, 2012). The game is a cloud-based
program (i.e., user performance data is stored on
computers of the publisher) and operates like a video
game. Over twenty different games are included,
and each offers many levels of play and focuses on
multiple skills. These games are sequenced and
intended to help the student develop automaticity
in the targeted cognitive skills. The developers
recommend that students access the games three to
five times weekly, and spend thirty to sixty minutes
on the game each time they play in order to improve
those targeted cognitive skills.

Gaming Versus Gamification

As teachers explore this rich teaching strategy, they quickly come to understand the
difference between use of games and "gamification." While teachers have long used games
and simulations for drill and practice of curricular content, gamification typically refers
to use of various game attributes such as competition, rewards, and accumulation of
points to turn all or most of the curricular activities into some type of competitive game
or simulation, including even the initial instruction activities for new subject-area content. Thus, gamification might involve using predeveloped games in the class or creating
competitive practice activities. Gamification may even involve teachers or students actually authoring digital games or creating virtual-world learning experiences for teachers.

Gamification refers to use of various game aspects
such as competition, rewards, or the accumulation of
points to turn most of the curricular activities into some
type of game or simulation, including even the initial
instruction activities for new subject-area content.

In that creative sense, gamification becomes much more complex and time-consuming. When teachers or students author games, there are many rich creative options, but most teachers do not explore authoring or student authoring simply because of the time commitment involved. Also, a full exploration of gamification would take many volumes. For these reasons, this book will focus primarily on using games or virtual-world simulations in the curriculum. However, one section below does explore Minecraft and Second Life as cutting-edge gaming options that are being used in classrooms around the world for STEM subjects.

A Classroom Example: Gaming in Mathematics

Stephanie Bowling is a five-year veteran of the classroom who teaches mathematics at Scott Middle School in Denison, Texas. She has seen the benefits of gaming in the STEM classroom:

> *I believe that if the students aren't having a positive experience in class, then they will not be as engaged, so I try to make mathematics as fun as possible. I don't use games every day, and also try to "gamify" other exercises. I try to create ways for students to practice concepts while having fun at the same time. For example, I often have them practice their work in either teams or with partners, in a friendly competition.*

> *One idea is to incorporate whiteboards into the lesson. I often split the class into teams of two, three, or four students. Each student will use a whiteboard, an erasable pen, and an eraser. I also print out a worksheet that all students can use on an individual basis, or I project the problems on the board. Next, I call out the number of one of the problems on the page, and they get to work solving that problem. They have to work together to get the correct answer before the time is up, and the time allowed varies with the difficulty of the problem. To create a game environment in the class, I use an online timer, downloaded to my desktop (www.online-stopwatch. com). That is easy to use and has several different timer options. The team with the first correct solution wins!*

> *One game that I have used came from the Secondary Math Activities Middle School Math Workshop by Susan Scott (www.secondarymathactivites.com). Ms. Scott presents many awesome ideas that can help every teacher find ways to incorporate games of all types in the classroom. One of my favorites is "Pin the ghost on the graveyard" (or "Pin the arrow on the heart"). Basically, the teacher prints out ghosts, arrows, or pumpkins, based on the holiday that is closest, along with the "board" (graveyard or heart, etc.). The graveyards have a hidden prize underneath. Teachers also need task cards presenting the concept or problems under study. Then the teacher hands one card out to each group and they all work the problem on the*

card individually. They then must show all their work, and they raise their hand when everyone on the team is finished. The teacher then checks the cards, and if they have them all right, they get to get a ghost for the group. They put their group number on the ghost and pin or tape it to the graveyard. The team with the most ghosts on the graveyard wins that prize at the end of the game. My students absolutely love this game!

For all of the games in my class, I use the same ground rules, including: (1) everyone has to do the problem, (2) everyone has to show their work, (3) everyone has to have the correct answer to get points, (4) when the timer goes off I say "three, two, one" and when that countdown ends, everyone must raise their boards in order to earn their points, and (5) everyone must show good sportsmanship. In that sense, my games are teaching the content but also emphasizing good citizenship. Also, I often award prizes for these games, but I've discovered that middle school students will work just as hard and be just as engaged without prizes.

Finally, it is exciting for me to teach this way. During the games, I see my students talking math, working together to get the right answer, and helping each other succeed. I think that is the most rewarding part. While we don't necessarily complete thirty math problems, like we would had I merely used a practice worksheet, the fact is, using games, every single student is participating and gets something from the experience.

ARGs and Virtual Worlds for STEM Instruction

One type of complex educational game is the alternative reality game (sometimes called an ARG or a virtual world), in which students explore, interact with, and/or create an alternative digital world while in the process of learning STEM content (Ash, 2011; Rapp, 2008; Shapiro, 2014; Short, 2012; Wolpert-Gawron, 2015). ARGs typically offer either the option of using these virtual worlds as games or actually creating content within a virtual world; thus, they represent both gaming and gamification options. These are multiple-player games or "worlds" and are often used over a long period of time, with students accessing the ARG space many times over a school year.

As one example, Kevin Ballestrini developed an ARG for his Latin class that placed the students' avatars in the alternative virtual world of ancient Rome in order to teach them Latin (Maton, 2011). The students' avatars (i.e., their digital selves) were required to work in the ancient city, wandering the streets of Rome and interacting with others in Latin. To successfully play, the students had to plan, act, create, and write like a Roman citizen, and during the game the students helped to rebuild the city of Pompeii. Students sought inscriptions on stones and solved mysteries during that process, thus learning the language and applying their knowledge in ways that are simply not possible in standard Latin classes. That particular ARG is being used experimentally in thirty classrooms across the United States, and the latest version can even be played using Internet-capable cell phones (Maton, 2011).

> Alternative reality game (ARG)—a technology-based game in which students create, explore, or interact within an alternative digitally created reality on a single computer or online.

As this indicates, ARGs are among the most complex games and can be used for high-level instruction in virtually any subject. In an ARG environment, students can tour the inside of a nuclear reactor, look one mile deep in the Earth along a fault line during an earthquake, travel inside a volcano, fly inside a hurricane, or travel inside the human body. The possibilities are limitless, and that is one reason educators have become so enamored with virtual world instruction.

Below, I describe several of the most popular options used in education, and teachers might wish to explore these options for STEM instruction. Before beginning, I would urge teachers to consult with their colleagues in their own school or school district to see what gaming sites or virtual worlds others are using. Also, teachers should note that these ARGs typically take more time to master than stand-alone games or apps, and time constraints should be considered prior to using an ARG for instruction.

Minecraft

One ARG that has captured the imagination of educators worldwide for use in many STEM areas is Minecraft: https://minecraft.net/ (Schwartz, 2015; Sheely, 2011; Short, 2012). This is one of the most popular ARGs, with over 30 million players worldwide. In this game, students either explore existing content within a precreated world, or they use blocks of various resources to construct a virtual world with which they then interact. Mathematics, in particular, is stressed in Minecraft, since construction requires placement of blocks on a grid pattern continuously (Schwartz, 2015), but Minecraft can be used across the curriculum. For example, students might construct a pirate ship that includes various details which document the life of male and female pirates from the golden age of piracy along the eastern coast of the Americas. The city of London might be re-created as it stood in the days of the Black Plague, in order to explore the spread of disease, or a Mars colony might be created to depict how early explorers might support themselves in a Martian environment.

Both students and teachers can visit existing worlds, or as an alternative, create their own worlds in Minecraft. Students can work independently, or work together in collaborative, long-term projects. In fact, any world that one wishes to imagine and create is possible in Minecraft, and both students and teachers find this work absorbing, resulting in a total-immersion learning experience. For many students who do not respond to traditional instruction, game-based instruction using Minecraft in this fashion will reach them.

As these examples show, Minecraft has been used as a teaching tool in many subjects, but it is particularly useful in several STEM subject areas. Because virtual worlds are structured with blocks in Minecraft, the program lends itself nicely to geometry, problems dealing with volume, and even structuring equations in algebra (Schwartz, 2015). In science, teachers have used Minecraft to help students tour inside an animal cell, watch as a single DNA strand is transcribed into mRNA, or even measure gravity in a virtual world, and then transfer the discussion to the real world (Schwartz, 2015).

Educators around the world, in all subjects and virtually all grade levels, use Minecraft in order to harness the power of an ARG that students love. For example, one second-grade teacher, Joel Levin, decided to use Minecraft because he wanted his students to learn computer skills (Sheely, 2011). For his second-grade class, Levin eliminated some inappropriate game content (e.g., some of the scary monsters). However, Levin reported that his students loved the experience while they learned computer skills, online etiquette, Internet safety, and even conflict resolution in a gaming context (Sheely, 2011).

After his own use of Minecraft in the classroom, Levin later helped found MinecraftEdu http://minecraftedu.com/ (see also Levin's personal blog: http://minecraftteacher.tumblr .com/), a company that provides precreated worlds using Minecraft for teachers to utilize in the classroom. I suggest that teachers who wish to explore using Minecraft in STEM classes begin with this site rather than Minecraft itself, since much of the early creation work has been done for you.

Many other resources may be found with a simple online search to assist teachers in using Minecraft for a variety of STEM courses, and teachers interested in using Minecraft in STEM should consult not only the online sources, but teacher communities focused on Minecraft in the classroom. A simple Google search of Minecraft and your subject area will provide contacts for teachers using Minecraft in your subject, and many of those online communities share very useful information free of charge. In addition, Short (2012) provides a series of descriptions of how Minecraft is being used in various science classes at the upper levels. The following box presents several of these teaching ideas for various STEM areas. As this shows, there is no shortage of resources devoted to Minecraft as an educational tool.

Science Instruction Examples With Minecraft

- **Biology:** Minecraft maps of the human body, including the vascular system, nerve cells, and an animal cell are in development. Students are immersed in a visual 3-D environment and are able to move in all directions. Cell functions may be demonstrated by moving and placing blocks in order to mimic cellular activity. As one example, in a map designed to represent the human body, the premise of the map would be similar to the movie *Fantastic Voyage*, in that your friend is sick, and you (or the class) have to go inside his body to cure him by solving puzzles, or killing bacteria and viruses, while exploring the different aspects of the body.

- **Ecology:** Minecraft worlds can represent various biomes, including communities of plants, animals, and soil organisms. In Minecraft, biomes are created by the map generator and display different heights, temperatures, and foliage. Examples include forest, swampland, hills, desert, plains, oceans, or tundra. Trees vary in height depending on the biome in which they are located. Animals such as pigs, cows, chickens, sheep, squids, and wolves may be included. This world can even be used to document how competing human populations might deplete the existing resources, leading to depopulation.

- **Chemistry:** Students in Minecraft can literally enter into a chemical reaction when they represent particles of matter. Stephen Elford, an Australian primary school teacher, has developed a basic states-of-matter and phase-change simulation for Minecraft (e.g., solid, liquid, gas) using players as particles. A four-by-four area is bounded with wooden blocks; this area simulates the solid phase. Students enter the area and are told that they are particles of matter

continued →

with limited mobility. The area is made larger by burning (simulating an increase in temperature), leading to a phase change to a liquid state. Students have more freedom of motion in the liquid phase but are still constrained by the boundaries, which are set further away. Finally, the last boundary is removed, thus simulating the gas phase.

Second Life

While virtual worlds such as Minecraft are receiving increasing attention as instructional tools (Schwartz, 2015), others are likewise being used in the classroom. For example, another virtual world that is growing in popularity is Second Life. Second Life is an unregulated digital world that has become the largest virtual world on the Internet (Secondlife.com). In this world, users worldwide can connect, socialize with each other, and create content or "virtual islands" (virtually all content created in Second Life is created within an "island") that focus on any topic whatsoever, including STEM instructional content (Nussil & Oh, 2014; Oh & Nussil, 2014; Sequeira & Morgado, 2013). Those virtual islands and the content therein are saved in Second Life, and may be accessed at a later time. Thus, the content created in Second Life is preserved over the long term.

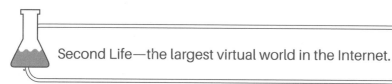

Second Life—the largest virtual world in the Internet.

Second Life can be a great source of information and an opportunity for students to create something for use by others worldwide. For example, in preparing this book, I visited Second Life, and created my own avatar. I then visited the destination for Genome Island. Once there, I clicked on several informational signs, each of which opened some scientific content. First, I stopped by a patch of flowers and clicked on the sign that said, "Test Cross." That opened a content box, which explained about the cross of red-colored flowers (the dominant gene in that example) with the white flowers. I then walked down the path a bit to select a "Mutant Beehive" sign and was presented with information on cross-breeding of bees.

There are thousands of similar locations in Second Life, and students can visit these to research various topics, or as a creative option, students or teachers can create their own island in Second Life. STEM teachers and their students can then stash information in their subject area there. Most teachers merely wish to have their students use Second Life as a research tool to seek information on various STEM topics. For less motivated students, who are less likely to participate in online or traditional hard-copy research in the media center, research in Second Life is much more engaging. Upon reflection, if this tool allows teachers to reach these otherwise disengaged students, then the effort has been worthwhile.

Also, Second Life might become a useful tool for very advanced students in STEM classes. Specifically, many higher education institutions, including Harvard University and Ohio State, as examples, are creating Second Life islands so that students worldwide can audit college-level classes (Bender & Waller, 2013; Wolpert-Gawron, 2015). Also, various public school districts are using Second Life as an educational platform in a variety of classes (Miner, 2015; Rapp, 2008; Wolpert-Gawron, 2015). For STEM, there are a number of virtual worlds in Second Life that students can experience, and numerous museums available such as museums on astronomy, technology, STEM Island, ecology, and "Spaceport." Ryan (2015) identified sixteen ways for schools to use Second Life in higher education, and many of these likewise apply in the public school classroom. Several of those instructional options are summarized in the following box. All of these resources might help keep the highly gifted students engaged in study of complex STEM topics.

Ways to Use Second Life in the Classroom

- **Add a visual element:** Virtual worlds such as Second Life are highly graphical in nature, and any user can create 3-D objects. Thus, teachers can create examples such as DNA strands, chemical molecules, or solar systems in visual form.

- **Create an interactive library:** While virtual worlds should be more than merely a collection of videotaped information videos, such videos can be placed in Second Life and complemented with graphics, sound, visual images, and maps, thus enriching the content.

- **Increase connectivity:** Second Life, or any virtual world, can be a repository of material to be accessed at a later time.

continued →

- **Use for role play or simulation:** Students can be placed in various situations in Second Life (including some that would be dangerous in real life). For example, in Second Life, they can mix chemicals that might explode if mixed in the real world. In that sense Second Life provides a safe environment.

- **Use as a gaming platform:** Second Life is not technically a game (though it feels like one), since there is no stated goal, and no beginning or ending. Still, it is a wonderful platform for other educational games.

- **Develop social skills:** Second Life does require certain social skills, and other avatars (Remember, most of the avatars in Second Life are real people!) will caution your students if they are behaving inappropriately.

- **Take virtual field trips:** Second Life is an excellent platform for virtual field trips, and many virtual worlds useful in STEM classes already exist there.

- **Create anonymity:** In some cases, students might desire anonymity, and Second Life allows for that. For example, students may critique each other's work in Second Life, with others not knowing who is doing that critique. In this case, the teacher should be fully aware of which avatars represent which students, in order to closely monitor student behavior.

- **Create virtual worlds:** Creation of digital virtual worlds requires planning, organization, and structuring, all of which can easily be taught using Second Life.

- **Build for the sake of building:** As discussed in Strategy 2, STEM requires building or creation, and Second Life (or other virtual worlds) facilitates that. This will enhance students' understanding of 3-D creation, scripting, spatial relationships, animations, and database and grid management.

Cautions in Virtual Worlds

Second Life has received much attention from educators (Rapp, 2008; Wolpert-Gawron, 2015) because it is the largest virtual world on the Internet. While this can be an important tool for STEM instruction, teachers must realize that, like much of the Internet, Second Life is completely unregulated (Rapp, 2008; Wolpert-Gawron, 2015). Students using these virtual world sites are therefore completely unprotected. Moreover, some locations within Second Life are specifically developed for hookups (i.e., meeting others for virtual-world sexual interactions), and these are clearly not appropriate for students. Also, almost every avatar on that site is actually a real person, interacting simultaneously with everyone else at the same Second Life location. Thus, various avatars on that site can be literally anyone on Earth, including a number of persons that teachers would not want interacting with students in the public school classroom.

For these reasons I recommend use of Second Life or other unregulated virtual worlds in education only when students are mature, experienced digital citizens, and when teachers can carefully monitor their participation. I also advocate strong digital citizenship policies, such as a signed Internet usage contract between the teacher and students, stating that students will avoid inappropriate online content. Most such contracts further state that should a student accidently find himself or herself in such an inappropriate online location, they will immediately leave and let the teacher know of their mistake. Bender and Waller (2013) provide an example of a digital citizenship contract that includes these provisions. Contracts of this nature not only make students responsible for themselves, but they help students develop safe and healthy Internet usage habits over time. Of course, another option is the use of more controlled virtual worlds and games, and the next section presents several examples of more regulated virtual environments.

There is one additional caution on using games, simulations, and virtual worlds in the classroom: the possibility of "gaming addiction" (e School News, 2012; Shah, 2012). In Japan, games have become much more entrenched than they are in the United States, and some educators have cautioned that digital gaming might be addictive to young minds (Shah, 2012). Of course, that concern is focused on commercial games that are played strictly for personal enjoyment and might very well be overstated when it comes to educational gaming. To date, there is no evidence of that problem for educational games or ARGs, so teachers can proceed with explorations of these tools for STEM teaching, while being aware of this possible concern.

Other Virtual Worlds

Given the concern for student safety in unregulated virtual worlds, some educators have chosen to use other virtual worlds for STEM instruction rather than Second Life. The only problem is that in many alternatives, the content in a particular area may not be as deep or rich as in Second Life. For example, sixth-grade students at Nature Hill Intermediate School in Wisconsin studied history and English in a virtual world called Quest Atlantis (Game-Based Learning, 2012). In that multiuser 3-D game space, students direct avatars in various missions, while interacting via chat functions with other students' avatars about the content under study. Also, the material written by students must be evaluated and accepted by the "Council" (who is, in reality, the teacher), so virtually all written material is checked and evaluated for accuracy.

As another example, schools in a suburb of Atlanta are using the OpenSim virtual-world platform (http://opensimulator.org/wiki/Main_Page). This open-source software allows educators to create virtual worlds related to their class content (Georgia District, 2012), and likewise allows educators to engage students in authentic problem solving within the virtual world. Role playing is used and students act out their lesson content in science, social studies, mathematics, or other content areas (Georgia District, 2012).

Research on the Efficacy of Games in STEM

Research has shown many advantages to teaching with games and virtual realities in STEM classes. Perhaps the most important advantage is the motivational impact of games (ISTE, 2010; Miller, 2012). For many students in mathematics or science classes, gaming is a preferred after-school activity, and building on this desire, teachers can have students play games to get them more highly engaged with their tasks in STEM classes. The research data on gaming or virtual realities in the classroom suggest that games and educational simulations are effective instructional tools (Ash, 2011; Hattie, 2012; ISTE, 2010; Maton, 2011). Hattie's (2012) meta-analytic research, for example, shows that simulation-based instruction yields an effect size of .33, which documents the efficacy of simulation-based instruction.

Games and simulations can teach content in exciting ways, and these tech tools have the advantage of actually putting the student into the situation or event under study (Miner, 2015; Rapp, 2008). This "immersion" advantage alone has already motivated many educators to explore game- and simulation-based instruction, and proponents of gaming in STEM classes view this as the future of STEM instruction. Short (2012), as one example, called Minecraft a "game changer in the field of science instruction."

In addition to this research, many teachers have anecdotally reported that their students enjoyed learning in technology-based gaming formats (Ash, 2011; Maton, 2011), and that they saw benefits from these games in terms of students' achievement overall. Also, gaming fits well within a project-based STEM classroom (Wolpert-Gawron, 2015). For these reasons, many STEM curricula include games.

In addition to being highly interactive, games and simulation offer cross-cultural options within the STEM class. Depending on the game or virtual world used, competition between students within a class, or with classes anywhere in the real world, is possible. One might imagine the impact of having American students, German students, and students in Great Britain consider the spread of the Spanish flu of 1918. That pandemic killed many millions of people worldwide and was spread largely by troops returning home at the end of World War I. Interactions such as these with other students in a gaming scenario are very motivating for students, and while such options can be difficult to arrange, instructional gaming provides this option.

Steps for Beginning Gaming

Start with what you know. Several authors have presented suggestions for how to begin gaming in the classroom (Bender & Waller, 2013; Shapiro, 2014). First, teachers should begin with what they know. If you have personally never played an educational game, don't jump into the most difficult ones initially. Specifically, teachers who have never played Minecraft or explored Second Life should not dive into them expecting to use them the next day in science class. Rather, those teachers should carefully select one or two websites that provide simpler stand-alone games focused on specific instructional content. Many of those games are quite engaging and can be used the next day, after an initial teacher exploration. Teachers might then assign several students to play it.

Match games / virtual worlds with your content and instructional purpose. While many teachers use the Common Core State Standards, other teachers may have standards unique to their state. When considering a game for STEM use, teachers must ensure that the game content is consistent with the appropriate curricular standards. Of course, games created for educational purposes typically are developed with standards in mind, but games or virtual worlds developed for entertainment purposes are not. While gaming is a great activity that students are supposed to enjoy, teachers must select games to maximize student learning in the STEM class, and some games have much richer, deeper content than others. Also, teachers must consider their use of the game. Is the game to be used for initial instruction, or practice of previously learned content? Different intended uses can inform which games or ARGs teachers might use in the classroom.

Preview the game. Teachers should preview any game or ARG selected for classroom use, and for most stand-alone games, this involves playing the game at least once (Shapiro, 2014). This preview will allow the teacher to determine possible uses of the game and, in many cases, to set up differentiated levels of game play for students at various academic levels.

Relate game themes to nongame content. Games, ARGs, and virtual worlds in the classroom are most effective as educational tools when the relationship between game content and activities and the content in the instructional unit is highlighted. While students can learn content from games, it is ultimately the teacher's role to demonstrate for the students the relationship between the game content and the subject matter, and this can typically be done with a well-planned postgame activity that reinforces the instructional content.

Teach digital citizenship. As the previously presented cautions state, instructional games, and in particular, real-time virtual worlds, can be unsafe online environments, and that is the perfect time for teachers to teach cyber safety and appropriate use of the Internet. Because gaming is likely to be a significant part of STEM instruction in the future, student safety should always be paramount. Most school districts have Internet use policies and guidelines, and there are plenty of published guidelines, strategies, and curricular materials for this instruction (Bender & Waller, 2013).

Do not limit game usage. One mistake many teachers make is unintentionally limiting what students might accomplish with educational games and virtual realities. Thus, while teachers must set parameters relative to their expectations for students' use of the game, teachers must likewise take care to not let their assignments limit what students can accomplish in gaming formats. For ARGs in particular, teachers should make specific assignments, complete with general rubrics, without killing any opportunity for creativity in creation of the virtual world.

Play, quiz, and repeat. With the previous steps accomplished, teachers should assign several students to play the game, and then report back to the teacher. Teachers may wish to follow most gaming sessions with a quick-check quiz to ensure that students are picking up the content as anticipated. If students don't do well, the teacher may assign them the game again, once they see the types of learning expected of them.

Summary

Virtual-world ARGs, games, and other simulations are likely to be a definitive element of STEM instruction in the next decade, and teachers are well advised to get ahead of their personal learning curve, as quickly as possible. Many teachers are just beginning to explore this gaming/virtual-world instructional option, and the creation of virtual worlds for instructional purposes in Minecraft or Second Life involves a set of skills that many teachers do not yet possess. However, research has shown the validity of gaming and ARGs in education, and teachers should launch themselves into exploration of what these teaching tools have to offer in the STEM classroom.

STRATEGY 10

Augmented Reality in STEM Classes

The gaming/virtual worlds described previously involve a hard barrier between reality and the digitally constructed world. In contrast, augmented reality (AR) involves the use of modern computer and communications technologies to augment or supplement the real world, and this technology holds the potential to make classroom learning in STEM subjects much more interactive and engaging (Burns, 2014; Politis, 2015). In most educational settings, AR (not to be confused with ARG) involves using one of several apps on a mobile device to read a digital overlay of information marked or triggered on a real-world object, image, or location (Walsh, 2012). In that sense, each image or object becomes a "tutor" for further information (Bharti, 2014; Dunleavy, Deed, & Mitchell, 2009; Holland, 2014; Klopfer, 2008).

From the teacher's perspective, AR allows students access to extended and expanded information about the physical world via a virtual overlay of information. The mobile device (e.g., iPad, Android, or a smartphone) will scan a "trigger" or "marker" associated with an object, image, or location. When scanned, the device shows a new layer of information such as informative text, images, video or audio recording, or a 3-D model (Politis, 2015). For example, AR can assist students in understanding chemistry by helping them to visualize the internal structure of a molecule using a dynamic 3-D model that appears when they scan a picture of the molecule.

> Augmented reality involves using technology to overlay digital information onto real-world objects, images, or locations. In that sense, each image or object becomes a "tutor" for information on itself.

Here's another example: imagine a student pointing his or her mobile device toward a photograph of the Milky Way galaxy, and the tablet immediately provides a 3-D overlay of the galaxy with supplemental information such as the number of stars, information on galactic shapes, and the location of our own solar system. Students are using AR to make their map work interactive or to solve complex problems in mathematics (Politis, 2015). AR involves use of triggers associated with various pictures or objects, so that when students scan the image, the picture comes alive with information. Here is a video showing how AR can be used to teach students how to calculate the area of different two-dimensional shapes: https://www.youtube.com/watch?v=8Zb2spZvHFQ.

Using AR in the classroom presents the option of turning virtually anything into an interactive lesson. Textbooks, flash cards, and other educational reading material can contain embedded triggers or markers, and when those triggers are scanned by an AR device, additional information pops up on the mobile device in a variety of 3-D or multimedia formats. This allows students to actually participate interactively in simulations of historical events or scientific processes.

A more complex AR option is construction of an AR trail around the school. Imagine a history teacher who wants to utilize the STEM focus on exploratory learning while using an AR trail to teach about the building of the interstate highway system in the United States. Using an AR trigger affixed to a poster of a road construction site from the 1950s when the interstate highway system was built, the teacher can have students begin the trail at that location by holding a mobile device up to the poster. Then the trigger affixed to that poster will present the initial plan and perhaps the legislation for that highway system from the Eisenhower administration. Next, the information associated with that first trigger should give instructions to "follow the interstate to the door!"

At that location, by holding the mobile device on the class doorframe, students will see more information presented, perhaps in the form of a video news story from 1956 showing a work crew on the interstate highway system. The final information at that site might suggest that students "follow the highway" down the hallway to the media center doorframe, where another trigger presents tabled information on miles of interstate built on a year-by-year basis. This AR trail can proceed throughout the building or school grounds, with more trigger locations or posters presenting additional videos, text information, or even quick quizzes that might pop up when the mobile device is held up toward the trigger (Bharti, 2014; Politis, 2015; Walsh, 2012).

Again, to get a sense of what AR can do for the STEM class, teachers should explore actual classroom video examples. Walsh (2014) provides several brief video examples of AR in STEM areas. Finally, for videos on how students are using AR in STEM classes, teachers should view one or more of the videos from this site: http://www.educators technology.com/2013/10/excellent-videos-on-the-use-of-augmented.html.

After viewing two or more of these videos, I invite every STEM teacher to professionally challenge himself/herself with the following question: "Am I preparing my students as well as those students using AR in their STEM class? Are my students being trained in this 21st century technology as well as other students around the world?" This personal reflection is usually quite motivating for teachers. The good news for STEM teachers is that a variety of options exist that allow teachers to create AR markers associated with posters in their room or images in the textbook. While some of these are aimed primarily at business, teachers are using all of the options presented in following box.

AR Options for Teachers

- **Aurasma** (www.aurasma.com/): This AR option works with either iOS or Android mobile devices allowing teachers or students to create their own 3-D overlays that will be triggered based on an image. This will greatly extend and enhance learning context. A free ebook on using Aurasma in the classroom is also available from a teacher, Paul Hamilton. His website also presents several videos on AR (http://augmentedrealityeducation.blogspot.com/).

- **Daqri** (http://daqri.com): This site, like many AR sites, is primarily devoted to the business and industrial sector but is being used by educators to create augmented reality options for the classroom. This does involve use of a "helmet" for AR rather than use of tablets or mobile devices, and for some students this might be a more engaging format for AR.

- **Layar** (www.layar.com/): This is one of the most popular AR tools used by teachers and works with both iOS and Android mobile devices. Using a drag-and-drop creative system, this site allows teachers to enhance pictures with interactive content such as photo slideshows, video, or 3-D projections. Users are offered an option of free creation for their first-time experience.

continued ➜

- **Build AR** (http://buildAR.com): This platform is for teachers and others who want to create augmented reality without the need for coding or development. Teachers and students can create AR experiences in a standard Web browser for multiple devices (including smartphones, tablets, or even wearable devices like Google Glass).

- **Bounce Pages**: Pearson Education is a leader in the commercial STEM education market, and they are working quickly to bring AR to every classroom. For example, Pearson's Bounce Pages app presents engaging animations that bring any text page to life, with enhanced information, animation, and video (http://www.pearsoned.com/news/new-app-makes-print-textbook-pages-come-to-life-on-a-mobile-device/). These Bounce Pages even include brief practice items for students to demonstrate the skill they just learned.

- **LangAR** (http://labs.pearson.com/prototypes /langar-augmented-reality-talking-phrasebook/): This is an app that can overlay a picture of any city with information desired by a traveler, such as hotels nearby, restaurants, or other locations of interest. It will also provide phrases in any foreign language that might be used in that selected AR environment (an order for coffee, for example). This is an excellent way to enrich any foreign language class.

Beginning AR in Your STEM Classroom

View several AR tutorials. Teachers might begin their AR experience by viewing videos that are provided on several of the websites in the previous box. These can give teachers a sense of what the process is when setting up AR triggers for objects or posters in the classroom. However, teachers should remember that the flashiest video portrayal of an AR option does not necessarily mean that teachers will find that option easy to use. Also, cost is a factor, and while some AR sites offer a free option for initial AR development, others do not. Prior to making a final selection, teachers should view a number of videos and then consider the other selection factors.

Select the platform. This initial exploration will take some time, but after viewing several videos, and prior to using AR, teachers should consider cost factors, ease of use by students, what other teachers in the school might be using, and what seems to feel most comfortable for the teacher. Based on several hours of video viewing and exploration of the websites above, teachers can make their selection of an AR platform.

Select initial objects for triggers. Teachers should consider what items they might wish to use as trigger options. These might include posters in the class, pictures in the text, or simply a location in the classroom. For example, a physical science class might have a poster of the solar system, or a biology class might have a picture or diagram presenting the parts of a cell. Each of those posters would be a great location for a marker. Also, a teacher may wish to designate a copy of the text and associate a marker with pictures throughout that book. Of course, this does not mean that all texts in the class would be marked, but the marked copy could be circulated among the students during class, to best utilize the AR content.

I urge teachers to remember that even five or ten triggers around the classroom can greatly enhance an instructional unit; so the initial goal is not to mark every picture or poster, but to have a few AR options for each planned topic. Further, those markers can be permanently associated with the objects or locations, and used again the following year.

Select the AR content for each trigger object. For each trigger around the class, the teacher must determine what supplemental information to provide to make the trigger come alive. While text material or table material provides additional information, video and 3-D presentations are typically much more engaging for the students. Using YouTube, TeacherTube, and other similar open resources, teachers can often find excellent video clips for use with AR triggers. You should select video clips that range from a minute to three or four minutes for these AR locations. Also, knowing what content you have to present will help determine where you might wish to place the triggers around the class. Therefore, this content selection step and the previous step on trigger location are often undertaken together.

As noted previously, an excellent, highly engaging option for AR is an AR trail, sometimes referred to as "progressive AR content." In this application of AR, the final information presented with one triggered object must include either specific travel instructions or at least hints for where students might find additional content hidden with other objects in the class. This AR trail concept effectively turns the AR content into a game.

Surprise the students. I encourage teachers to surprise the students the first time they use AR content in the class. By merely suggesting that students hold their mobile device near a poster, suddenly students may find additional, highly engaging information on the topic under study, and this can motivate students to further explore the class, seeking additional triggers for content.

Hand the AR responsibility to students. Teachers in many STEM classes are having students develop the markers in selected topics, with teacher approval (Klopfer & Sheldon, 2010; Noonoo, 2012). In fact, using students to develop additional AR content in the classroom not only enriches the classroom for future classes, but also prepares the students with a high-level 21st century communications skill that they can take with them long after that particular STEM class is over.

Research on the Efficacy of AR in the Classroom

AR in the educational setting is relatively new, and research is ongoing. However, the available research shows a number of benefits in using AR in the classroom (Bharti, 2014; Dunleavy, Deed, & Mitchell, 2009; Holland, 2014; Klopfer, 2008). For example, Dunleavy, Deed, and Mitchell (2009) conducted case studies of AR implementation in classes in two middle schools and one high school to investigate teachers' and students' reactions to AR implementation. Both teachers and students reported that they found AR to be highly engaging, particularly for students who had previously presented behavioral and academic challenges. Teachers indicated AR potentially held "transformative value" for middle and high school teaching.

Several researchers report that students enjoy working with AR and even creating AR options in the classroom (Klopfer, 2008; Klopfer & Sheldon, 2010; Noonoo, 2012). Noonoo (2012), for example, indicates that during AR implementation, students were highly aware that teachers were as new to AR as they themselves were, and this caused the students to consider themselves as "co-researchers" in the AR transformation. Students were often suggesting to teachers what objects or locations might be enhanced with AR. Clearly that level of engagement would be hard to top for any STEM teacher.

With these research findings noted, solid evidence on improved academic skills resulting from AR implementation is not available to date. Of course, many universities are exploring AR implementation in the classroom, and one might well anticipate that, with students reporting much higher engagement with the science or math content, achievement will increase. Teachers should proceed with their explorations of how AR might benefit them while carefully watching for additional research on overall efficacy.

Summary

Like the gaming simulation strategy presented previously, it is very difficult to guess how AR technologies might impact the STEM classroom over the next decade. This enhanced reality allows students to experience science, engineering models, or mathematics algorithms from the inside out, in a very profound way, and it is quite likely that the increased engagement resulting from this teaching strategy will generate increased achievement. Also, the creative options involved when students themselves are creating AR science or mathematics content are staggering. In one sense, all a teacher has to do is complete enough AR generation to understand the process, and then turn this process over to the students! This is clearly a teaching strategy that all teachers should soon begin to explore, if they are not already using it.

Section III

Collaborative and Cooperative Learning in STEM

Collaborative and cooperative work environments are, and will continue to be, a hallmark of the modern workplace, and therefore cooperative work should become a hallmark of the modern STEM classroom. For that reason, cooperative learning is one instructional approach that virtually all proponents of STEM instruction emphasize (Myers & Berkowicz, 2015; Slavin, 2014; Vega, 2012). Of course, collaborative and cooperative learning have also been stressed repeatedly with the implementation of the recent Common Core standards in education, so many educators are exploring various cooperative learning practices in an effort to implement them in their STEM classes. However, the cooperative learning practices of a decade ago represent only one approach to cooperative and collaborative learning that is being utilized in the STEM classroom. In fact, important collaborative instructional tools that have developed only within the last ten to fifteen years are being widely applied in science, mathematics, and engineering classes, including many tech tools such as wiki-based instruction and use of social learning networks.

This section begins with a description of the more traditional approaches to cooperative learning, and then continues to explore some of the more recent innovations in this broad instructional area. Strategies 11 through 16 provide teachers with several options for increasing collaborative instruction in the STEM classroom. These specific strategies include cooperative learning, social learning networks, teaching with wikis, mindfulness in STEM classes, classwide peer tutoring, and reciprocal teaching.

STRATEGY 11

Cooperative Learning

Cooperative learning strategies may seem like an old friend for many STEM teachers, as these instructional approaches have been around for many decades (Johnson, 2009; Kagan, 1994; Marzano, 2009a, 2007; Marzano, Pickering, & Pollock, 2004; Schul, 2012). While somewhat more frequent in elementary classes than in middle or high school classes, cooperative learning procedures such as jigsaw or student-teams achievement divisions are commonly used. Nevertheless, these strategies are receiving increased attention, not only because they work so well (Alstad, 2014; Brown & Ciuffetelli, 2009; Giles & Adrian, 2003; Hattie, 2012; Sharan, 2010), but because the concept of collaboration has received increased emphasis in all areas of education.

Cooperative Learning in STEM Classes

In simple terms, the reason for this renewed emphasis on cooperative learning involves changes in educational reform efforts. When STEM education, like all educational endeavors, is placed in the context of preparing students for the workplace of the 21st century, it becomes clear that schools need to do much more to prepare students for cooperative and collaborative tasks in industry than has previously been the case (National Research Council, 2011; National Science Board, 2012). The Common Core standards, for example, stress collaborative learning efforts as one of the main thrusts. For these reasons, cooperative learning is highlighted among proponents of STEM as one of the instructional strategies that should be evident in virtually every STEM class (Slavin, 2014).

However, collaboration and cooperative learning have become much broader topics than they previously were. In addition to the traditional cooperative learning procedures, the STEM instructional practices recommended in this book provide both teachers and students with much richer collaborative possibilities (Alstad, 2014; Brown & Ciuffetelli, 2009; Sharan, 2010). For example, multiplayer gaming, as discussed previously, is becoming a major activity in STEM classes, and with technology, such cooperative learning options can involve students in only one class or students in any class around the world. Moreover, beyond merely playing games while learning content, students are creating games and/or virtual worlds in their learning processes. Clearly, the creative options presented by game creation or generation of virtual worlds provide many new and highly engaging opportunities for collaborative work, and such collaborative creation closely resembles the actual work required in the 21st century marketplace. Finally, the remaining instructional strategies discussed in later sections of this book give teachers and students many options for cooperative learning endeavors.

Jigsaw: A Traditional Approach

STEM teachers who have not yet explored cooperative learning can take heart from the fact that the majority of cooperative learning strategies follow the same general procedures. A brief instruction to one of the original cooperative learning approaches is a great starting point.

In a jigsaw cooperative learning procedure, students are initially presented with only partial information on a topic, which they have to master, and subsequently they must put that information together with other information, as is required in a jigsaw puzzle. To begin, each student in the class is placed into two groups for initial instruction (Johnson, 2009; Johnson & Johnson, 1994; Kagan, 1994). First, students team up—usually teams of four to six students—and thus everyone becomes a member of a "home group." In that home group, students are each assigned to learn a particular part or portion of a broader topic. Group formation and topical assignments should be relatively quick, taking at most three to five minutes at the beginning of class.

Next, after each student has been assigned a topic, the teacher calls for the students to switch: students leave their home group and go to a second group, called the "expert topic group." Those expert topic groups are composed of students from the various home groups that are assigned the same content to study and master. In the expert topic groups, students work together for fifteen to twenty-five minutes to explore and discuss the assigned material, and then the teacher calls for another switch, at which point students return to their home group. Once there, each student must teach their partial knowledge (i.e., their portion of the jigsaw) to others in their home group. That typically takes another fifteen to twenty-five minutes. In this fashion, every member of every group both learns and presents to others in both the home and the expert topic groups.

Jigsaw was one of the earlier cooperative learning procedures developed, and while other procedures quickly followed, most are similar. Of course, other cooperative learning procedures do involve other implementation steps, and in order to assist teachers in exploring alternatives, the steps for several common procedures are briefly described in abridged fashion in the following box.

Common Approaches to Cooperative Learning

- **Think-Pair-Share:** In this procedure, teachers might pose an open-ended discussion question to the class and have the students think about it for two to three minutes (Kagan, 1994). Then, students pair up to exchange thoughts and ideas. Finally, the student pairs can share their responses with their team, other pairs of students, or the whole class (Alstad, 2014).

- **Jigsaw II:** Jigsaw II is a variation of jigsaw in which members of the home group are assigned the same material to learn, but focus on separate portions of the material. Each member must become an "expert" on his or her assigned portion and then teaches the other members of the home group (Alstad, 2014).

- **Reverse Jigsaw:** This variation, created by Hedeen (2003), differs from the original jigsaw during the teaching portion of the activity. In the reverse jigsaw technique, students in the expert groups teach the whole class rather than return to their home groups to teach the content.

- **Inside Out:** In this procedure, students form two concentric circles. Students in the inside circle face students in the outside circle and discuss possible answers to the teacher's questions. Then the circles move one place in opposite directions, resulting in each student facing another partner for a similar discussion. This is a good method for brainstorming and generating novel ideas.

continued ➜

> • **Student-Teams Achievement Divisions (STAD):**
> In this procedure, students are placed in small teams, and all teams are presented with a lesson. Next, the students are assessed on the content. Individual students are graded on the team's overall performance, so students are motivated to work together to improve the overall performance of the group.

As this discussion of jigsaw and other strategies shows, most cooperative learning procedures are based on formation of cooperative learning teams, generally four to six students, and all procedures involve students learning from each other. Further, cooperative learning procedures often involve the same instructional practices as those found in PBL, such as brainstorming, joint research, time-lining, and sharing information. The teacher in cooperative learning, rather than instructional leader, becomes an instructional facilitator, which is also similar to PBL practices. Thus, cooperative learning is a great procedure for initial instruction and minilessons during collaborative PBL projects.

Given that many teachers are quite familiar with cooperative learning procedures and that different cooperative learning procedures do use different rules, this section will not present specific steps for implementation. The discussion above will generally be sufficient for most teachers to implement these practices, even if they have not undertaken these strategies previously.

Classroom Example: Cooperative Learning in Mathematics

I did want to share a teacher's experience with cooperative learning in a STEM class. Once again, I've asked Stephanie Bowling, a teacher in mathematics who wrote about using games in the STEM class, to discuss her use of cooperative learning.

> *Cooperative learning and how to implement it was a struggle for me and many other educators. We might wonder if it's effective, are we doing it correctly, or if there is a better way. I don't have it figured out completely by any means, but it works in my class. I set up my desks in groups for cooperative activities. Sometimes I use groups of four students while at other times I use student partners, depending on the lesson plan for that particular day.*
>
> *I've found that the more you change the environment, the more they seem to be interested in what's happening that day. At the beginning of the year, I talk about group expectations and guidelines, because I wanted to make sure my students*

understand the type of atmosphere that is needed in a productive cooperative learning classroom. We go over my list of expectations for cooperative group activities:

1) Understand that those who work, learn.

2) Be a part of the solution and not the problem.

3) Three questions burns up your opportunity. (In my group work they get three questions only—a rule by which I try to eliminate silly questions such as "Do we have to show our work?")

4) Participate actively with a low inside voice.

5) Give 100 percent effort.

6) Share and challenge ideas.

I also use specific student roles (I call them group jobs), so that each student has a role in order to make everyone accountable for work done inside the group. The team captain keeps the group on task, reminds about noise level, and is the substitute for any other student's job, if a student is absent. The supply manager takes responsibility for collecting supplies for the group work and returning them at the end of class. The recorder's role is to write, if the group is turning in one paper, and also to make sure everyone else has the correct notes. The speaker will present group information to the class, request help from the teacher, as necessary, and help clean up before the end of class. Everyone is expected to participate in each activity regardless of their job, and I allow no sitting around waiting for someone to complete the work.

I don't use cooperative groups every day. A lot of the time I have my desks in rows and will have students push desks together to work in pairs on practice problems. It takes only 30 seconds or so for them to arrange their desks and get to work. Other times, I will count them off and they will gather ones with ones, twos with twos, etc. I try to give them an opportunity to talk each day. I've also used the Kagan strategy called "Think-Pair-Share" to help students discuss a particular math problem. I encourage them to use "math only" talk, and to help, I gave them a list of accountable talk questions that they keep in their journal. (I found that list on Pinterest, a site I consider an educator's dream!)

I agree with ___ because....

I sort of disagree with ___ because....

Why do you think that?

Where can I find that in the book?

So, what you're saying is... Couldn't it also be that ...

Can you explain what you mean? Can you tell me more?

Can you give me an example?

I also use games in cooperative settings. For example, I found a game online called Equation Race Game by The Enlightened Elephant. Basically, from that website (https://www.teacherspayteachers.com/Store/The-Enlightened-Elephant), the teacher gets worksheets with a set number of problems (alternatively the teacher can use a page protector). Setup for this game is easy. Next, you put students with partners with only one writing utensil and one die (dice). The object of the game is to complete all the problems on the page. While one student is working the problems, showing all their work, the other student is trying to roll a one on the die. Once a one is rolled, the students switch roles, resulting in the other student is working the problems while the other is rolling. Results were amazing! They were completely engaged! In fact, I've never seen my students work so hard without any outside motivation. There were no prizes and no grades, but they worked together all class period!

In general, cooperative learning is a great tool for teachers! I've learned so much from different cooperative learning workshops and from other educators about how to do this, but my motivation to continue using cooperative learning is what I see in my classroom; my students are engaged. I see them talking math, explaining the concept in language that is familiar to them, and helping their friends learn the content. I also believe that the more they use these types of collaborative skills, the more successful they will be in the real world. Life is hard and so is math, but by working together, my students learn that they can do anything!

Case Study: Cooperative Learning in STEM

Teachers are widely encouraged to conduct action research in the classroom and with cooperative learning, teachers can easily implement an in-class experiment on the efficacy of this procedure. In STEM classes in particular, showing students that they are actually participating in a real experiment can be of great benefit. The case study below provides a model for such action research.

Ms. Lovorn taught a seventh-grade earth science class, and as a part of her personal professional development plan she wanted to conduct action research on the efficacy of using jigsaw in her teaching. In her instructional units, she typically did a two-day emphasis at the first of the unit which she called "20 Essentials." For each unit, she identified twenty statements, definitions, or concepts that were essential to the unit, and that material served as the subject matter for initial instruction in that unit. For each unit, she shared a written copy of her 20 Essentials with the class and then used videos, lecture, and group discussions to teach those 20 Essentials for two days. At the end of day two in that unit, she conducted a quick quiz on those facts and concepts. For the rest of her unit, she used those quiz grades to guide her in planning additional activities to cover the gaps in student understanding. Thus, she had a ready-made set of curricular content, and an assessment that she could easily use in her action research project.

First, Ms. Lovorn identified two dependent variables for her action research. She initially returned to her gradebook and averaged the quick-check quiz grades for the class for each of the previous two instructional units. That provided her one variable for her research, along with a three-data-point baseline. Next, as a second dependent variable, she counted the actual number of students who scored below 80 on each quick-check quiz for those two instructional units. That raw score provided her with a second dependent variable that was not based on a grade-averaging procedure. She knew that averaging scores sometimes masked important information, and she wanted a raw score that dealt directly with how cooperative learning might help her students overall. She also wanted to summarize those data on one chart, so she generated a data chart with two labels for the x-axis (average achievement and raw score number of students scoring below 80 on the assignment). That raw score count showed exactly how many students failed to learn the essentials to the desired mastery level.

At that point, Ms. Lovorn began her cooperative learning intervention. For the next four instructional units, she began with her 20 Essentials identified, and on the first day of each unit, rather than use videos and lecture, she put students in teams and used a jigsaw procedure. On the second day, she taught with video and lecture on those essentials, and then administered the quick-check assessment. Data for each dependent variable are presented in baseline and intervention phases in figure 11.1.

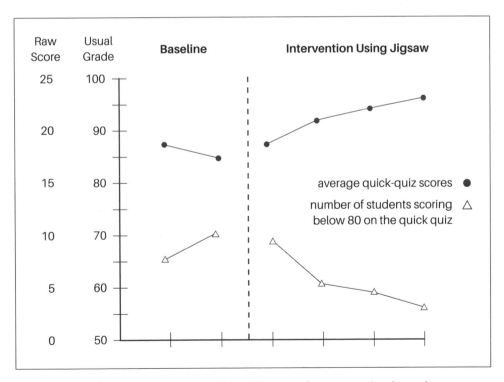

Figure 11.1: Action research on the efficacy of cooperative learning.

As the data show, Ms. Lovorn's action research demonstrated the academic impact of cooperative learning in her STEM class. The average quiz scores increased in the units in which cooperative learning was used. Also, the number of students who did not master the material was reduced over time when cooperative instruction was implemented. Finally, anecdotal comments made by the students suggested to Ms. Lovorn that the students, by and large, enjoyed the cooperative learning classes more so than the other, more traditional, instructional practices.

Of course, the dependent variables in this action research did not address other potential positive effects that might result from cooperative learning. For example, cooperative learning more closely resembles how work gets done in the real world. In the real world, colleagues divide up various tasks, work on them, and then share the results with coworkers, and that is exactly the set of skills fostered in cooperative learning. In short, cooperative learning parallels the real world much more so than traditional instruction. For that reason, STEM teachers are well advised to implement cooperative learning in their classes.

Research on the Efficacy of Cooperative Learning

Research on cooperative learning strategies over the years has shown this to be a very effective instructional strategy (Alstad, 2014; Brown & Ciuffetelli, 2009; Gilles & Adrian, 2003; Hattie, 2012; Johnson, 2009; Johnson & Johnson, 1994; Marzano, 2009a; Marzano, Pickering, & Pollock, 2004; Schul, 2012; Sharan, 2010). Research has shown that students enjoy cooperative learning procedures and achieve consistently higher academic scores across the grade levels when cooperative learning is part of the instructional process (Johnson & Johnson, 1994; Schul, 2012). This procedure works in every subject in the school curriculum and even works well for students of all ability levels (Johnson, 2009; Schul, 2012). Students using cooperative learning procedures not only achieved more, but also reasoned better, gained higher self-esteem, and enjoyed more social support than in traditional classrooms (Johnson, 2009; Schul, 2012).

Interestingly, John Hattie and Robert Marzano, the two gurus of meta-analyses that are focused on instructional strategies, both present evidence on the efficacy and importance of cooperative learning strategies (Hattie, 2012; Marzano, 2009a; Marzano, Pickering, & Pollock, 2004). Hattie (2012) for example presented a meta-analysis in which cooperative learning generated an effect size of .59, indicating that use of this strategy increased achievement by over half a standard deviation, compared to traditional, individualist instruction. Likewise, Marzano's research (Marzano, 2009a; Marzano, Pickering, &

Pollock, 2004) showed similar findings, though somewhat less dramatic—a 23 percent gain in academic achievement when cooperative learning was used in the classroom.

Clearly, with research support that is this demonstrative, coupled with demands for increased collaborative skills among future U.S. graduates (National Research Council, 2011), STEM teachers must begin to employ cooperative learning strategies if they are not already doing so. Simply put, these two factors form a "perfect storm" of demand for collaborative skills in the future workforce. This is the reason, as stated in the introduction of this book, that virtually every proponent of STEM instruction identified cooperative and collaborative learning as one major focus of STEM.

Summary

Many teachers are already using cooperative learning procedures in their classes, and for those teachers, an exploration of other cooperative learning procedures would certainly expand their instructional repertoire. The efficacy research presents a compelling reason for exploring many versions of this instructional strategy, and among teachers who are already using one or more of the traditional approaches to cooperative learning, the following sections in this book will provide some new collaborative learning options to consider.

STRATEGY 12

Social Learning Networks
for STEM Instruction

Social networking is a fact of life for many people around the globe, and educators worldwide are exploring options for using social network platforms in the classroom by forming "collaborative learning networks" among their students (Curtis, 2015; Ferriter & Garry, 2010; Grisham, 2014; Walsh, 2011; Watters, 2011). It is difficult to find a middle or high school student who does not use one or more social networking sites, so this exploration makes sense. In fact, teachers, often to their dismay, have seen students using these social networks in the middle of class, and thus providing no end of frustration for many educators! Data show that at least 95 percent of teens have consistent online access, and 81 percent of them indicate that they use social networking frequently (Grisham, 2014). Why not use this tool in the classroom?

> Data show that at least 95 percent of teens have consistent online access, and 81 percent of them indicate that they use social networking frequently. Why not use this tool in the classroom?

Rather than fight this trend, educators are beginning to embrace social networking as a powerful teaching option (Grisham, 2014; Madge, Meek, Wellens, & Hooley, 2009). Clearly students are highly motivated to "connect" with their peers, and if that motivation can be directed toward discussions of class content, the possibilities seem endless. In fact, several of the larger networking sites, Facebook and Twitter, for example, have been discussed as educational options, though others (e.g., Snapchat, MySpace, Flickr, LinkedIn, Tumbler, GamerDNA, Google+) have not been widely used by teachers as yet.

Facebook is the most popular social networking site, used by over 1.2 billion students and adults worldwide. In contrast, Twitter, the second most popular social networking site, has 650 million users. Also, 77 percent of teens report using Facebook while only 24 percent use Twitter (Grisham, 2014). These data suggest that either Facebook or Twitter could be profoundly powerful teaching tools, since so many students and teachers are using these communications technologies by choice. Further, there are several other social networking options that tend to be much more private than the largest of the social networks, including Edmodo and Ning. These are described below.

Facebook is the most popular social networking site, used by over a billion students and adults worldwide.

I typically recommend use of Facebook as a social learning network tool in the classroom for students in middle and high school, since students and teachers are already likely to be familiar with it. For that reason, this chapter will be primarily focused on Facebook. However, Facebook is limited to students who are thirteen years and older, so for lower grades, there are other options to consider. For example, Edmodo is a free social networking option at which teachers and students engage in a Facebook-type fashion (http://www.edmodo.com). Teachers can store links to information, assignments, videos, and class calendars, and teachers and students alike can create and respond to information posted by others (Bender & Waller, 2013). Once teachers create their free account, they invite their students to join, and the students sign up using a teacher-generated code that specifically assigns them to that teacher's class. Teachers can post to their class or privately to students (e.g., for awarding grades). Also, this site includes a set of reinforcement badges, which teachers can award to students for individual work.

Ning is another social network option available to educators free of charge (List & Bryant, 2009). Ning (http://www.ning.com) was originally designed on a fee-for-service basis as a social/business networking platform for business, but Ning Mini offers a free option for up to 150 individuals associated with an individual teacher's class, as a result of a partnership between Ning and Pearson Education. Teachers need to visit the Pearson sign-up page to create a free Ning network (http://go.ning.com/pearsonsponsorship/). This will provide a somewhat more secure platform for social networking in the classroom. However, millions of students are already using Facebook and that is not the case for the Ning or Edmodo options.

Twitter (twitter.com) is another highly popular social networking option. This is a microblogging site, at which students, parents, and teachers can post pictures and up to 140 characters of text. There is no age limitation associated with Twitter as there is on some other social network sites, making this useful at various ages. Also, many educators are using this option for personal communications with parents or to set up personal learning networks to discuss professional educational topics. I have personally found this to be a great way to keep in touch with new teaching ideas and tactics for the classroom. Readers are invited to connect with me in this networking site. (You can follow me if you'd like on Twitter @williambender1.)

With these options noted, for the purposes of this book I will discuss primarily the use of Facebook in the classroom as a social networking and cooperative learning tool. However, teachers may rest assured that the issues and guidelines presented below generally apply for the use of any social network as a teaching strategy.

Using Facebook for Teaching

Social networking in the classroom does increase students' engagement and helps students collaboratively explore a topic (Curtis, 2015; Ferriter & Garry, 2010), and for those reasons, many teachers are using Facebook as a teaching strategy to increase collaborative activities in STEM instruction. Once a class Facebook page or a Facebook group is established by the teacher, students use this network to share information, websites, and ask questions of each other any time during the day. The social network allows all users in that network to see those interactions on the topic under study. Note that these educationally based social networks are not primarily intended for social exchange; rather, these networks typically present information about the topic under study, including teacher's notes, reminders, or student-created posts on the topic of study.

In Facebook, teachers typically establish a Facebook page for their class, and invite all the students to likewise create a separate individual page including very limited personal information or no personal information at all. Students can then use those pages to follow the class Facebook page (Walsh, 2011). In that sense these Facebook pages are dedicated exclusively to networking on the STEM topic under study. In fact, most school districts prohibit teachers from using personal Facebook pages for teacher/student communications, in order to prohibit inappropriate communications.

As another option, teachers can establish a Facebook page and then use the "groups" function to invite students to join the class group. This provides essentially the same privacy options as having students create separate pages (Curtis, 2015).

On the class Facebook page, teachers can post text, thoughts, questions, reminders for assignments, videos, pictures of class activities, specific assignments, hints to help with student research, or a written paragraph on the class topic (Curtis, 2015; Ferriter & Garry, 2010). Other types of uses go beyond merely information sharing and represent collaborative interaction focused on the subject content. For example, class polls can be taken on topics under study, or students can work together during homework on brief (three- to four-paragraph) written assignments.

Once information is on the Facebook page, anyone else on that Facebook network can read those entries. There are some controls that individuals can exercise to limit the information available about them. In most cases, teachers limit the class Facebook page to students in the classroom and their parents, and perhaps one or more school administrators, and that means that any of those participants can post to the class Facebook page. Of course, teachers typically request that parents not post to the page, but merely use it to monitor their own children's work, as they choose.

Here is an explanation from a student of how Facebook was used in her classroom. This student described her work in a history course, after she and the class joined the class Facebook page (Walsh, 2011).

> We'd finish our reading for class and then get online and write a paragraph about what we'd read, focusing our comments on the specific course aims created for the class. We would then go to class and note the ways in which we'd covered the material well. (Walsh, 2011)

As these ideas suggest, there are many uses for Facebook or other social networking tools in the classroom, and teachers who are considering this strategy should investigate other options that can be found on the Internet. I suggest that teachers begin with a YouTube video by John Bunker, Facebook for Your Classroom in 7 Minutes (www.youtube.com/watch?v=8aO9aVRC8bs). Also, a simple Google search or search of the YouTube site will result in many other videos teachers might wish to review on using Facebook or other social networks in the classroom.

While Facebook alone will provide an intensive social networking option, I also recommend that teachers consider using a supportive Facebook app called Hoot.me (http://hoot.me/about/). This app connects students from the same school or class that happen to be studying the same content at exactly the same time at home (Watters, 2011). Specifically, this application will seek out other students with a Facebook account from the same school or class who are likewise working on that topic at that moment (Watters, 2011), and then suggest that those students chat with each other about that academic content. Thus the application is effectively pairing students together for additional collaborative study opportunities.

Steps to Using Facebook in STEM

It takes very little time to begin using Facebook or other social networking options in the classroom, simply because many teachers are already quite familiar with Facebook. For this reason, many teachers are using this tool. Further, because many STEM classes already involve small group work on a fairly regular basis (e.g., lab partners in science classes), this tool is certainly something teachers should consider. Here are some initial steps for beginning Facebook in the classroom.

Investigate school policies on learning networks. Different schools and districts have different policies on use of social networks, and of course, teachers should always follow district policy. With that noted, most administrators recognize the amazing advantages in student engagement to be tapped by using a social network as a learning network in the class, so district policy roadblocks are less common than they were in the past. If Facebook and Twitter are not options, perhaps Edmodo or Ning are allowed by your district. Teachers may begin with their principal and then explore using social networks with the instructional technology person at the school district.

Set up a class Facebook page. The class page should include information on the class such as the grade level, school, and intended purposes, which may include student or parent communications or both. Teachers can go to the Facebook website (www.facebook.com) to complete this process. The website requires an email address and age verification. The process for establishing a Twitter, Ning, or Edmodo account is similar and is explained at those respective websites, but regardless of the tool selected, some basic information on the class should be posted.

Create initial content. Next the teachers should create the initial content for the class page, including photos, projects, and other things that make the page interesting. Teachers might periodically upload a brief paragraph on the unit under study and, if appropriate, ask students their opinions on one of the major issues or concepts within that unit. This initial question will let parents know how the page might be utilized and will often be the catalyst for an exciting in-depth discussion of that issue or topic.

Next, teachers might upload short videos on the first topic under study. Teachers might seek out short videos at YouTube, TeacherTube, or Khan Academy. Of course, teachers should always preview the video carefully prior to putting it on the Facebook page. Alternatively, teachers might include links to those videos. Finally, pictures and videos of students doing projects are essential for the Facebook page. Most schools obtain a "blanket" permission to post pictures and/or videos of students doing school activities, and these postings are very likely to motivate parents to occasionally check the class Facebook page.

Inform parents. Parents may have fears associated with Internet or social network usage in the schools, and educators must be sensitive to those fears (Bender & Waller, 2013). In fact, parents expressing such concerns are advocating for their child's safety, so these concerns are understandable, realistic, and should be carefully considered and compellingly addressed. Once a teacher determines to use Facebook or another network, the teacher should inform the parents about their intended use of that social network for school studies, and of the safeguards that will be used. Support from the school administrator should be documented in the letter to the parents.

Also, the initial letter to parents about using a social networking site should convince them that safety is of paramount concern. For example, parents should be assured that neither students nor teachers should use their personal Facebook page for instruction and that both students and teachers will set up separate pages to be used only for the class (Grisham, 2014; Walsh, 2011). Certainly, no personal information need be shared on those "class" Facebook pages, and no personal addresses, phone numbers, or location information should ever be shared. Finally, all the parents and at least one school administrator should be participants on the Facebook page for monitoring purposes.

I also encourage teachers to let parents know that specific lessons on Internet safety and appropriate social network and/or Internet usage will be facilitated by using a social network for the class. Teaching students how to be responsible for their own digital safety in the modern world can be a factor that motivates parents to allow their children to participate. Many guidelines on digital safety and digital citizenship are available, including specific guidelines for using Facebook safely in the classroom (e.g., http://www .heppell.net/facebook_in_school/). Also, Bender and Waller (2013) provided guidelines for appropriate Internet and social network usages in schools.

Finally, the Facebook site has some guidelines on the safety of Facebook when used in the classroom, called "Teaching Digital Kids" (https://www.facebook.com/safety/groups/ teachers/).

Teachers should certainly look at that site. Attention to these resources, plus attention to the safety issues above, should assure parents of the safety of this social network instructional usage.

Invite students to join. Walsh (2011) suggests, as noted previously, that students should set up a Facebook page to use for class interactions that is separate from their personal page. Others have set up a Facebook "group" for class interaction. Also, as noted above, social network options like Edmodo and Ning offer networking options that are not as accessible as Facebook. At any rate, all students should join the social networking class page, to ensure classwide communications and collaboration.

Post daily. Teachers should post something on the class Facebook page daily in order to ensure that students are checking the page. Teachers might post reminders of homework that is due, quiz questions that might be used in class, notes on interesting things for students to explore, or a suggestion to check out local or national news items related to class content. Daily postings will foster higher student engagement and will lead to richer collaborative discussions (Watters, 2011).

However, rather than using the page as merely a digital textbook for information sharing, teachers should plan their postings to encourage students to explore topics and collaboratively research topics. Posting hints on where to find information can lead to richer learning than merely posting websites to investigate, and while the class Facebook page will probably include both types of information, teachers should focus on building a learning community among the students, suggesting research options, and encouraging collaboration. In that regard, complimenting students' individual and group work is recommended. Teachers can also recommend that other students attend to excellent assignments from their peers.

Research on Social Networking in the Classroom

Use of social networks in schools, like many topics in this book, is very new, and efficacy research is very limited. Further, because of the limited research base, none of the meta-analysis studies undertaken on instructional strategies to date have included social networking as an instructional option. With that noted, there is some anecdotal research and a few case studies that do consistently show that students and teachers prefer use of social networking for learning (Curtis, 2015; Ferriter & Garry, 2010; Madge, Meek, Wellens, & Hooley, 2009; Prescott, 2014; Walsh, 2011). These studies and case studies show that students and teachers tend to use social networking more for communications than for building a true learning community, so the true power of using social learning networks for instruction has not yet been explored. Further, most of the available support for social networking comes in the form of specific examples or case studies in higher education (Curtis, 2015; Madge, Meek, Wellens, & Hooley, 2009). For example, Curtis (2015) presents several case studies on the use of Facebook in college classes, and in each case, student excitement about the content under study increased. Prescott (2014) reported that professors' use of Facebook did enhance communication between the teacher and students and that shy students, in particular, preferred this type of interaction.

Summary

As this shows, there is very limited research support for using social networking in the public school classroom. However, this is not uncommon for any teaching strategy that is less than five to ten years old (depending on the social networking site). It is clear that teachers are increasingly exploring this application for social networking, and the existing anecdotal research does show that students and teachers alike respond positively to this effort. At the very least, use of a social network can help engage the shy students a bit more while at the same time keeping parents more informed, via postings of class assignments, expectations, and activities (Curtis, 2015). On that basis, and given the relative ease of implementing this strategy, STEM teachers should consider setting up a social network, or more accurately, a social learning network for their class.

STRATEGY 13

Wikis for STEM Instructional Units

Using this simple teaching tool, STEM teachers can immediately create endless collaborative instructional options for any instructional unit, and with wikis, the students do most of the work! Using any of the free wiki sites, teachers can establish what is essentially a private website for their own class (Pappas, 2013; Richardson, 2010; Tomaszewski, 2012). They can create such a site for each instructional unit or one for the entire year, on which teachers and students post collaborative or individual work, share web links, post videos, or compile group presentations. Teachers can invite parents, grandparents, or other teachers to review the work done on the wiki for their STEM class or even have experts in science or engineering in the field comment directly on students' work in the wiki!

The Basics of Wikis

A wiki is essentially an editable webpage or set of pages that selected persons can edit, and this allows students to collaboratively write, create presentations, or post any digital files such as digital photos, audio, or video files (Pappas, 2013). There is limitless collaborative flexibility in wikis because any student can edit, add to, or reflect on every other student's work. Most wikis allow teachers to follow every entry to see who has posted which edits, and also to identify students who are not participating. This facilitates immediate, individual feedback within the wiki from both teachers and other students.

> A wiki is an editable webpage or set of pages that selected persons can edit, which allows students to collaboratively create and post written work or digital files, such as digital photos or even digital video.

Teachers Use Classroom Wikis

Wiki usage is becoming more prevalent in schools, although wikis have been used in some classrooms since about 1995 (Richardson, 2010). As schools increase Internet connectivity and more tablets and computers reach the classroom, wikis are a teaching tool that every STEM teacher should consider (Bender & Waller, 2013; Richardson, 2010). Teachers not familiar with wikis might wish to think of a wiki as a digital unit syllabus combined with daily instructional activities that students complete online. Should a teacher choose, any student or student team can edit any work done by others, making this one of the most collaborative of the recent technology options available for teachers. When a student group is working together on a class presentation, video, mathematics problem, or science experiment, any student who wishes to contribute a thought or idea merely gets into the wiki and makes a comment or edits/extends the work done previously by others (Pappas, 2013). Thus, the student's new idea is embedded directly in the original work. This interactive and collaborative functionality makes the wiki an excellent tool for increasing the types of collaboration and social learning that students expect and enjoy.

Some teachers and students do virtually all of their instruction within a class wiki because wikis are so very versatile. Teachers can post a link to YouTube videos, or other presentations, or post any report, digital file, presentation, theme paper, or group project. All can be embedded within a class wiki, as well as virtually any other type of class assignment teachers might imagine. Further, almost every student from grade 3 and up is familiar with at least one wiki—Wikipedia. Most students use Wikipedia as their go-to research tool, so this format is quite familiar.

Parker and Chao (2007) provide a comprehensive discussion of wiki usage in education that teachers might wish to review. Also, teachers should view a YouTube video by Vickie Davis. Some teachers might recognize that name, since Ms. Davis is the "Coolcatteacher." Her teaching blog of that name is one of the most popular educational blogs in the United States. In this twenty-seven-minute video, Ms. Davis explains her use of a wiki in her computer tech class (http://www.youtube.com/watch?v=-3MTJ5rz8Cc). Of course, any Google search on classroom wikis will also provide additional videos for you to consider, including brief tutorial videos on how to set up a wiki. Finally, teachers might wish to look at one or more "class wikis" developed and used by other teachers. Here are several options:

- http://maggilit.wikispaces.com/home—a teacher-created wiki for literature

- http://dino.wikia.com/wiki/Main_Page—a created wiki anyone can use

- https://grade7wiki.wikispaces.com/—a nice teacher-created wiki including math, science, and other STEM topics, including PowerPoint presentations that can be used in your class

Students' Response to Wikis

Wikis are used in many ways in the classroom. Teachers may organize a STEM instructional unit (discussed at length below) or assign groups of students to create their own wiki on a specific topic. Either type of wiki (teacher or student created) encourages students to publish their own work, as well as collaboratively critique anyone else's content. Thus, over time, wiki usage leads to an online collaborative community of information providers, and because of the constant editing, most inaccuracies within the content on a wiki are quickly corrected by later users. Using wikis for instruction will motivate your students and is likely to increase their participation.

In developing written or video content for the wiki, students learn how to work together, sort through information, evaluate information using other sources, create newly synthesized information, and make contributions to the content already on the wiki. All of these clearly represent skills that 21st century learners will need throughout life (Richardson, 2010). Further, wikis are powerful platforms to teach students to evaluate information from others. Students are inundated with information, so each teacher must teach students how to interpret, evaluate, and sift through information. This is the essence of online research, and wikis provide an excellent medium for teaching those skills (Richardson, 2010).

Finally, wikis are a great tool for teaching subject-area vocabulary, while saving time in the process! Within a wiki for a particular instructional unit, teachers should merely list the vocabulary terms and assign students to provide definitions and/or examples. In many cases, students will pick up the definitions for each term as they work through the wiki for that unit, and teachers will not have to spend initial instruction time teaching those terms.

A Classroom Example: Wikis in Mathematics

In this example, Jessica Shoup shares her experience using wikis. You may recall that Ms. Shoup shared a contribution previously in this book, dealing with the flipped classroom (Strategy 5). Again, Ms. Shoup, EdM, is a veteran STEM teacher with National

Board certification, having taught in middle school for many years. She is now working as a teacher and professional development facilitator at Community House Middle School, in Charlotte, North Carolina.

Teaching STEM classes comes with a challenging task of motivating students and keeping them engaged in rigorous activities that allow for high levels of success. When used properly, technology in the classroom will achieve this task. While technology should never be used as a substitute for the teacher, technology tools, such as wikis, can be used to enhance lessons and provide learning opportunities that a teacher may not be able to provide.

While teaching middle school science, I used Wikispaces in my classroom. Our district required every teacher to have a wiki page. When I first created mine, it had my course syllabus, a calendar that listed activities we had done in class, links to important class documents, and links to videos and websites that related to the content. I was proud of what I had done until I learned how much more wiki pages had to offer, and how my website could be a learning tool for students. Wikis not only can provide information, but when structured appropriately, they can help students interact with one another, collaborate to arrive at joint answers, or to complete an activity.

At the beginning of each unit, I typically add an essential question to the wiki page. My students knew that it was their "job" to find the answer to the question during the unit of study. As they found facts or pieces of evidence to answer the question, they posted it to the class wiki. Students were expected to not only add facts, but to respond to those posted by other students. We discussed etiquette for responding politely and for offering constructive criticism if necessary. All students, especially the introverts, were included in the conversation and were learning from one another. While reading those student posts, I added comments to clear up misconceptions or asked questions to guide them in the right direction.

For a few years, I made detailed reading the focus of my wiki. To encourage my students to read closely, the wiki page was used as a debate platform. Articles were chosen on a topic that clearly had two sides, such as genetically modified foods. As the students read the articles, they gathered evidence to build a strong case either for or against genetically modified foods. The evidence was used to build a powerful opening statement that would make everyone agree with their perspective. Comments were then added by other students to either agree or politely disagree. After a certain period of time, a vote was cast and a team was chosen as the wiki debate winner!

Virtual labs and virtual field trips were also added to my wiki page. As students explored the field trip location, data tables were completed, observations were noted, and student questions were answered. Students were able to discuss their findings with one another while working, using the wiki, and each student was able to work on their own device while collaborating with others in the room. With each lab/field trip, students were to post their "gem," i.e., the biggest "take away" that they had from the experience. They were also asked to comment on the gems of others.

My favorite part of using wikis was the immediate feedback that students received from their peers. Many students were more comfortable sharing on a computer than in an open class discussion. We had a "no judgment rule" for our wiki work, and that made everyone feel that what they had to say was important and that it was valued by the other readers. Students often posted work to the wiki page and peer evaluations were completed on the page as well. The evaluations came in different forms, such as rubrics or posting one wow and one wonder. I noticed an increase of pride among the students for the work completed on the wiki.

So many educators use wiki pages today, and like me, these pages may not be meeting the full interactive-teaching potential. I would encourage all STEM teachers to look at these ideas, and others, for interactive wiki work. I strongly feel that students' STEM discussions should not end with the class bell. Instead, wiki pages will keep the STEM discussion alive outside of school, and students will love it!

Which Wiki Should I Use?

For novice teachers, setting up a wiki takes thirty minutes to an hour, and several websites provide the option of free wiki development for teachers, along with their more functional fee-per-service options. Teachers should initially select a free wiki option, and the sites below offer that option. Also, each of these sites provides instructions for teachers, and setup procedures are very similar across the sites. However, if a teacher in your building is using a wiki site that he or she recommends, you should certainly consider using that website, because of the possibility of in-school assistance from that teacher. Here are several wiki site options:

- www.wikispaces.com
- www.wikisineducation.wetpaint.com
- www.wikia.com/Wikia
- www.plans.pbworks.com/signup/edubasic20

Setting Up a Class Wiki

Select a wiki site. Personally, I agree with Ms. Shoup in the classroom example above. I prefer wikispaces.com, a site used by over seven million educators, so I'll use that in the sample steps below. Teachers should begin with a review of videos from the Wikispaces home page (http://www.wikispaces.com/content/wiki-tour). While many demonstration videos are found there, the first two are called "Introduction" and "Creating Educational Wikis." These are very brief and will help in the creation of your wiki.

Create the wiki. Next, teachers should go to the Wikispaces website (http://www.wiki spaces.com/site/for/teachers). Teachers will be asked to select a username, a password, and a wiki name. Then teachers should click on the option on the lower right to create a free wiki. Next, teachers should select the "Private" wiki option. That is a free option and allows only class members to participate. As teachers begin to get comfortable with their wiki, they can choose a more public wiki option later. However, within the "Private" option, teachers should put an administrator's name (perhaps the principal or assistant principal), as a "child" in the class. That will allow the administrator to carefully monitor the wiki content.

Create a wiki home page. The home page is the first page of the wiki. This page introduces the instructional unit and should include a unit title and a paragraph about the unit under study. When writing that title and paragraph content, remember that the goal is to hook the interest of the students, so include some high-interest information and a few questions.

To create the title, you type in an appropriate descriptive title and highlight it in the text box. Next, click on the "Heading" function at the top of the page, and select "Level One Heading." That will place the title in bold and increase the size. Then, below that, write a general introduction paragraph that will generate interest. Perhaps you can highlight controversial areas within the topic or challenge the students to find answers to various questions.

Add videos or digital photos. Pictures and/or videos enrich the home page and will help generate interest. Teachers should add a picture or two and perhaps a link to a video about the topic. If there are several videos, teachers may wish to create a second heading a bit lower on the home page (using the same procedure as creating the title above), and call that "Recommended Videos." Below that heading, list two or three websites that present brief introductory videos on the topic. Teachers can find interesting content-rich videos anywhere, and should begin with sites they already use, such as YouTube, TeacherTube, PBS.org, Discovery Channel, NASA, or the Nova Channel.

Teachers should remember that the home page is designed to heighten interest, and not teach content in depth, so shorter videos are recommended for this page. Later pages may involve presentation of a longer, content-rich video on one aspect of the unit under study, along with an activity for students to complete based on that video. Those video links should be placed on subsequent pages rather than the home page. Of course, teachers should always review any video they list. Finally, for each video, teachers might wish to add a brief study guide (three to four questions, or points to consider).

For longer instructional units, teachers might add on the home page a schedule of activities that includes dates and specific assignments students should undertake that day. This will help students navigate the wiki, and should a teacher be absent, a substitute can get into the wiki (the students can help with that) and continue the planned activities for any particular day.

Create a navigation option. Students will need a way to navigate within the wiki. While only one page (the home page) has been created up to this point, others will be created, and each one will need a navigation tool that moves the student to other pages. Thus, teachers will need to add a navigation tool to each page of the wiki.

To create a navigation option, teachers should click the "Wedgets" button in the edit bar at the top of the page. A list of options will open, one of which is "Add the Navigation Tool." When you click that, a navigation button will be added at the bottom of the page to allow you and the students to navigate to other pages in the wiki.

Lock the home page content. The power of using wikis is the collaboration stemming from the fact that anyone can edit the content, so many pages in the wiki will be open for editing. However, the home page as described above should not allow an editing option. Thus, that page should be "locked," which means the content cannot be edited or changed by the students (the teacher, as the wiki creator, will always have an editing option). To lock a page, move the cursor to the top right of the edit bar, and click over the series of dots. That will open some options, one of which is "Lock" the content on the page. You should click that once you are completely done with your home page. For other pages that you want students to edit, you simply don't perform this "Lock the Page" step.

Create other wiki pages. Next, you should create additional wiki content pages, including activity pages for each day of the instructional unit. These pages will, for the most part, be unlocked pages, and thus will allow students to make contributions to the wiki. One content page might be a vocabulary page. Teachers should list the vocabulary for the instructional unit, but not the definitions, with the expectation that, once assigned, students will edit those pages by providing definitions and examples. Another page might be a content study page that presents a link to a longer video, or a PowerPoint presentation on one aspect of the unit, along with an extensive study guide for students to complete. Having students watch that video and do the study guide in partners is one way to increase engagement and foster some discussion of the content. This can provide an excellent initial instruction assignment on new STEM content.

Another page option involves the creation of a collaborative writing project on a wiki page. Teachers can create a wiki page that includes the beginning text for two thematic papers that students, working in teams, are required to complete. In many cases, having thematic writing that presents opposing views, and giving students a choice between them can increase student engagement and excitement about the task.

A webquest can easily be housed on a wiki page, and again, I like seeing this type of assignment done by partners or three-person teams (Bender & Waller, 2013). Teachers should develop a webquest that is more complex and involved than merely a Google search on a topic. Students should be required to research factual material up front and more conceptual content later in the webquest. Toward the end of the webquest students could be required to do something, such as create a paragraph reflecting on the new content or taking an online classwide survey on students' positions or opinions of the content. The webquest could be created as a digital word file and then pasted into a wiki page.

Tomaszewski (2012) identified a number of additional ideas for wiki-based exercises, including an online debate page, a "role reversal" page (e.g., have Copernicus argue for an Earth-centered solar system), or a newsroom page on which teachers post daily news items on the topic under study and ask for student comments. The collaborative instructional possibilities are nearly limitless, and here are several more examples of things that might be on wiki pages.

- Daily written work assignments for the unit
- Study guide questions or graphics
- Descriptions of unit-length class projects
- Scanned digital reading assignments
- List of sample questions for the unit test
- List of subject content links

As this indicates, the wiki should become not only a set of lesson plans, but an organizational outline for an entire instructional unit, complete with online work pages for students to complete. Using wikis in that fashion makes this information available for students at home via the Internet, so the distinction between classwork and homework becomes less meaningful, leading to increased student engagement. In short, most teachers, once they become wiki fluent, begin to do most of the instructional planning and development within a class wiki. This reflects the best practices for instruction in the 21st century.

Adapt the wiki. The look of the wiki can help students and teachers—once they become comfortable with wiki creation—find nearly unlimited options to create any look and feel for the class wiki they desire. Using the "Edit This Page" tab in the toolbar at the top of the page, you can manipulate text, change fonts, set colors, and set the spacing for each page. Of course there are standard default options that can be used, so teachers might not wish to adjust the look of the wiki at first. However, as you become more fluent in using wikis, you will probably begin to experiment with these features to enrich the wikis.

Include the class and parents. When the wiki is ready, you will have to either invite students to join the wiki (using the "User Creator" button) or import the class list. Teachers then need to help students walk through wiki navigation, but that can also be done with an instructional video from the wiki website. Generally, that is not terribly time consuming, and students pick up those skills quickly. At that point, the teacher merely assigns students to read through the home page, and begin their work on the vocabulary page or elsewhere.

After using a wiki for one or two instructional units, you might consider inviting parents to join the wiki as observers. This helps involve parents in the class, and generally improves the parents' perception of the class. Some teachers choose to do this, while others don't, so I suggest you make that determination after some experience in teaching with wikis.

Research on the Efficacy of Wikis

Similar to the research base for many STEM teaching tools, research on the efficacy of wikis is still somewhat limited. The available research does show that wikis are an effective strategy and lead to increased engagement and student collaboration (Benson, Brack, & Samarwickrema, 2012; Bold, 2006; De Pedro, Rieradevall, López, Sant, Piñol, Núñez, & Llobera, 2006; Deters, Cuthrell, & Sapleton, 2010; Lund, 2008). For example, Mak and Coniam (2008) showed that wiki usage did enhance collaborative writing skills among high school students, and other research has likewise documented increased collaborative work when wikis are used (Bruns & Humphreys, 2007; Churchill, 2007; Trentin, 2009).

Other research has investigated student response to the use of wikis. For example, De Pedro and his coworkers (2006) showed that wikis improved students' collaborative writing projects in a higher education course. Deters, Cuthrell, and Sapleton (2010) conducted research on students' responses to the use of wikis in college classes, and results indicated an initial hesitation on the use of wikis by the students. Overall, however, students did report a positive experience in wiki usage. Thus, these results show that wikis increase student engagement and achievement and that students prefer using this collaborative online instructional tool.

Summary

Given the emphasis within STEM for increased collaboration and cooperative learning, STEM teachers should certainly begin to set up their instructional units and project-based assignments in a digital format using a wiki. This online presence for a class is a hallmark of 21st century teaching, and using a separate wiki for each instructional unit means that students are creating content for use by other students next year and that the lesson plans for the following year are already done!

STRATEGY 14

Mindfulness in STEM Classes

Self-awareness of moods and emotions, reflective thinking, and persistence are frequently referred to as the soft skills that underlie both effective collaboration in the classroom and curricular success (Davis, L., 2015; Ryan, 2015; Symonds Elementary School, 2015). While these are not academic skills in the traditional sense of the word, educators have long realized that without self-reflection and persistence in the face of difficult tasks, students will not succeed academically. This is particularly true in certain STEM classes because scientific hypothesis testing requires honest self-reflection as a part of the scientific method. Further, persistence is critical in STEM because of the sequenced actions that are often found in mathematics proofs, science labs, or engineering projects.

Soft Skills for STEM Success

To address these soft skills, STEM teachers and many others have begun to explore mindfulness programs in order to help alleviate the student stress that is very frequently associated with certain STEM classes. In particular, many students are quite apprehensive about taking demanding mathematics classes, and research suggests that mindfulness activities might help alleviate that stress (Albrecht, Albrecht, & Cohen, 2012). For these reasons, STEM teachers, along with educators worldwide, are increasingly exploring programs that teach mindfulness (Albrecht, Albrecht, & Cohen, 2012; Bender 2016).

What Is Mindfulness?

Mindfulness is a meditative time period, in which the student reflects on his or her emotional state and level of relaxation, in an effort to boost productivity. In addition to such inner reflection, Albrecht, Albrecht, and Cohen (2012) discuss a second emphasis in mindfulness, which is more external and emphasizes the need to be deeply aware of one's surroundings, the moods and emotions of others, and events in the immediate environment. Using mindfulness exercises, educators can teach students to assess their own emotional state, calm themselves down, concentrate on one thing at a time, and reflect more deeply on their work (Albrecht, Albrecht, & Cohen, 2012; Harris, 2015). With roots in both yoga and certain Buddhist meditation practices, mindfulness has become both a disciplinary and an academic enhancement strategy in schools in the United States, the United Kingdom, Australia, and elsewhere around the world (Harris, 2015; Symonds Elementary School, 2015).

> Mindfulness is a meditative time period, in which the student reflects on his or her emotional state and level of relaxation in an effort to boost productivity.

The term mindfulness was coined by a biologist, Jon Kabat-Zinn in the 1970s, when he applied the principles of meditation in a medical setting. He developed a program, Mindfulness-Based Stress Reduction, to assist patients dealing with chronic pain. With the success of that program, he founded the Center for Mindfulness at the University of Massachusetts Medical School (Davis, L., 2015). With that background in science, various national and international organizations such as Google, the United States Army, and the Seattle Seahawks football team have all adopted mindfulness as a way to boost energy and productivity (Davis, L., 2015). With that growing emphasis on mindfulness in the last two decades, it should come as no surprise that this practice has received increasing attention among educators (Davis, L., 2015; Harris, 2015).

Many educators are practicing mindfulness with their students (Bender, 2016; Greenberg & Harris, 2012; Oaklander, 2015). As early as 2007, schools in the United Kingdom began using mindfulness, and many schools in the United States soon followed suit (Davis, L., 2015). At Symonds Elementary (2015) for example, mindfulness is part of a broader social/emotional learning effort that includes activities to help students focus attention and learn to take stock of their emotions and how those emotions might be playing out in their relationships with teachers and other students.

A Classroom Example: Mindfulness in High School

Here's an example from a high school in one of the poorest inner-city districts in New York City. Argos Gonzalez taught an English class with a mix of black and Hispanic students in the Bronx (Davis, L., 2015). When class began, Gonzalez rang a bell and said, "Today, we're going to talk about mindfulness of emotion. You guys remember what mindfulness is?" When no one spoke, Gonzalez gestured to one of the posters pasted at the back of the classroom that summarized an earlier lesson on mindfulness (Davis, L., 2015). In the earlier lesson, the students had brainstormed the meaning of "mindfulness" and listed some terms such as "Being focused," "Being aware of our surroundings," and "Being aware of our feelings and emotions."

Gonzalez continued with the following instructions: "I'm going to say a couple of words to you. You're not literally going to feel that emotion, but the word is going to trigger something; it's going to make you think of something or feel something. Try to explore it. First, sit up straight, put your feet flat on the ground. Let your eyes close."

Gonzalez then tapped the bell again (Davis, L., 2015), and the class became quiet. Then he said, "Take a deep breath into your belly. As you breathe in and breathe out, notice that your breath is going to be stronger in a certain part of your body. Maybe it's your belly, your chest, or your nose. We'll begin with trying to [silently] count to ten breaths. If you get lost in thought, it's okay. Just come back and count again. Whether you get up to ten or not doesn't really matter. It's just a way to focus [your] mind" (Davis, L., 2015). Then the students practiced that mindfulness activity for several minutes.

Of course, teachers like Gonzalez would not be spending the ten to fifteen minutes of precious class time on this type of procedure unless the benefits were clearly evident in his class (Davis, L., 2015). Teachers often report increased productivity among the students, and a better class climate when they practice mindfulness with the students (Albrecht, Albrecht, & Cohen, 2012; Greenberg & Harris, 2011; Harris, 2015). For those reasons, Bender (2016) recommended mindfulness as a preventative disciplinary technique based on the successes in various schools, including reducing behavioral problems as a result of schoolwide mindfulness implementation. Schools all across the United States and the United Kingdom (e.g., schools in New York, Kentucky, and California) are beginning to practice mindfulness daily in the classroom (Davis, L., 2015).

To get a sense of what mindfulness looks like in the classroom, readers should review a six-minute video from the actress Goldie Hawn, who is a committed proponent of mindfulness in schools (www.youtube.com/watch?v=tAo_ZSmjLJ4). Also, the following box presents several national curricula that have been developed specifically to teach mindfulness in the schools.

Programs That Teach Mindfulness in Schools

- MindUp (http://teacher.scholastic.com/products /mindup/): This fifteen-lesson research-based curriculum is available from Scholastic, and it comes in several grade-level variations (K–2; 3–5, and 6–8). This program was developed by actress Goldie Hawn, working with neurologist Judy Willis. The company claims that the program will improve both behavior and learning. Lessons are said to help students focus their attention, improve their self-regulation skills, build resilience to stress, and develop more positive attitudes. According to the company, the lessons require only minimal preparation.

- Mindful Schools: This is a California-based nonprofit company that provides training for teachers on mindfulness in the classroom (http://www.mindful schools.org). This group has produced many training options and videos on mindfulness (I'd suggest teachers review one called "Mindful Schools Testimonials from Adults and Children" www.youtube.com/watch?v=fZks0vFVwjE). By 2011, this organization had trained 11,000 students and 550 teachers, in forty-one schools. Seventy-one percent of those students were considered high risk. Another excellent video of how this program looks in the classroom is available (www.youtube.com /watch?v=MMK481p5wWM).

Teaching Mindfulness in STEM Classes

In addition to the published curricula, there are many individually developed approaches to teaching mindfulness in medical, therapeutic, and classroom settings, and various approaches stress different things. These range from intentional breathing to self-awareness to walking meditations (Nhat Hanh, 2010; Welham, 2014). Some approaches suggest that teaching of mindfulness requires more than merely reading about the technique, and some of the existing training programs for educators take a year or more to complete.

With that noted, the compilation of suggested procedures below comes from a variety of sources (Caprino, 2014; Nhat Hanh, 2010; Welham, 2014). While these are presented in no particular order, these activities do represent the types of mindfulness exercises that are being done in the classroom.

Teach about brain-based moods and emotions. Some teachers teach students a bit about the human brain and regions of the brain associated with different types of moods and emotions (e.g., the amygdala as the "emotional brain" and the frontal cortex as the "planning brain"). Students then refer to those brain regions while they explore their own moods and behavior or the moods and behavior of others (Welham, 2014). Some teachers have students keep a mood diary to discuss their feelings and moods daily.

Teach breathing exercises. This was discussed in the previous text, when Mr. Gonzalez had students count their breaths in a calm, soothing setting. Like Mr. Gonzalez, many teachers teach breathing exercises to focus students' attention, and help them relax (Davis, L., 2015).

Teach focused awareness. This involves having students focus on doing only one thing at a time (e.g., walking, looking at nature, or completing a morning reading with no distractions or outside thoughts allowed). This will help students develop task persistence and focused attention.

Teach about the senses and sensory experience. Some mindfulness trainers have the students practice focused awareness by stressing sensory stimuli. Students might be asked to chew a raisin (only one raisin) for an entire minute—chewing slowly and focusing their attention only on the sensation of chewing or on how the raisin tastes. Alternatively, students might touch different textured cloth while they concentrate on the sensations with their eyes closed.

Teach focused attention with a walking meditation. By having students walk around the classroom or the school for a time, teachers can have students continually focus on exactly what they witness at each turn in the hallway, without latching on to something that they passed previously (Nhat Hanh, 2010; Welham, 2014).

Teach mindfulness with a focus on student health and well-being. Many parents might object to mindfulness instruction if mindfulness is approached as yoga or religious instruction. However, by approaching mindfulness with a focus on stress reduction, STEM teachers can usually forestall that potential parental concern. Parents should be fully informed of this instructional focus and assured that no religious training is taking place (Welham, 2014).

Efficacy of Mindfulness

Mindfulness as an instructional strategy has not yet been "ginned" into the meta-analyses-based research by John Hattie or Bob Marzano, but reviews of research on mindfulness are available and show many positive results of mindfulness training in both the class-room and clinical settings (Albrecht, Albrecht, & Cohen, 2012; Greenberg & Harris, 2011). Part of the difficulty in conducting research on mindfulness is that mindfulness is implemented in many different ways. Also, some of the research results are ambiguous (Greenberg & Harris, 2011). To date, research does indicate that mindfulness is an effective treatment for improving behavior and attention skills of students with ADHD, anxiety, and aggressive tendencies (Davis, L., 2015; Greenberg & Harris, 2011; Harris, 2015; Ryan, 2015). In general, mindfulness also improves attention, reduces stress, and improves emotional regulation for many students without disabilities (Albrecht, Albrecht, & Cohen, 2012; Greenberg & Harris, 2011).

Most of the research to date has investigated the impact of mindfulness on increasing social-emotional health and/or decreasing behavioral problems rather than increasing achievement in STEM or other academic classes (Albrecht, Albrecht, & Cohen, 2012; Greenberg & Harris, 2011). However, improved academic scores in mathematics resulting from mindfulness training have been reported (Albrecht, Albrecht, & Cohen, 2012; Oaklander, 2015), and research is ongoing.

Summary

The extant research suggests that mindfulness should be considered for implementation in STEM classes. In particular, STEM teachers should consider the level of stress that students show relative to their particular STEM subjects, and if appropriate, those teachers might explore using mindfulness in the classroom. If mathematics anxiety or other types of anxiety and student stress can be alleviated by a series of three- to five-minute mindfulness breathing exercises, teachers would be well advised to make time for those exercises in the STEM instructional period. We may find that this instructional practice opens doors of opportunity in STEM classes more than many other instructional strategies do.

STRATEGY 15

Classwide Peer Tutoring

Peer tutoring is one of the most effective teaching strategies available (Arreaga-Meyer, 1998; Bowman-Perrott, 2009; Ginsburg-Block, Rohrbeck, & Fantuzzo, 2006; Greenwood, Tapia, Abbott, & Walton, 2003; Hattie, 2012; NEA, 2015). Moreover, research has shown this strategy to be effective in many subjects including STEM areas such as mathematics and science (Burnish, Fuchs, & Fuchs, 2005; Kunsch, Jitendra, & Sood, 2007; NEA, 2015).

Tutoring: A Proven Strategy

In many ways, this strategy serves as an effective replacement for lectures in content area classes, so many STEM teachers are exploring the use of peer tutoring in STEM instruction across the grade levels. In particular, for content-heavy classes in mathematics and science, peer tutoring provides a degree of mutual student support that will increase both the quality and the amount of instruction that students receive. In effect, peer tutoring provides immediate tutoring support as well as cooperative instructional support for mastering the difficult content in many STEM areas.

Variations in Peer Tutoring

There are many variations of peer tutoring from which teachers might choose, including cross-age tutoring, after-school tutoring, or one of the several peer tutoring options previously discussed in the cooperative learning section, such as think-pair-share and jigsaw. Two of the most popular approaches to tutoring are classwide peer tutoring and PALs. Classwide peer tutoring has proven effective in all subject areas (NEA, 2015; Greenwood et al., 2003), while PALs (a form of peer tutoring supplemented with cognitive strategy activities such as prediction and summarizing) has been shown to increase achievement particularly in mathematics (Burnish, Fuchs, & Fuchs, 2005).

The emphasis in this strategy section will be classwide peer tutoring because that tutoring approach has been applied more broadly than the several other options (Greenwood et al., 2003; Kamps, et al., 2008). Developed by Charles Greenwood and his associates over the years, many teachers have employed this strategy at the elementary level and increasingly in the middle and high schools.

A Classroom Example: Classwide Peer Tutoring in Seventh-Grade Science

In Ms. Richey's seventh-grade science class, she liked to stress factual information, new definitions, and less complex aspects of the topic for several days at the first of a two- to three-week instructional unit. These could typically be summarized as a set of factual statements, definitions, or concepts for the students, and she often presented these in a study guide on the first day. Sometimes, she prepared an answer sheet for that study guide. Upon reading about classwide peer tutoring, she realized that her study guide provided an excellent opportunity for using classwide peer tutoring, so she taught her class the tutoring procedure, as described below.

In the classwide tutoring procedure, each student must receive instruction on his or her own academic level, so Ms. Richey prepared versions of the study guide sheet at four levels of difficulty. When the students arrived, Ms. Richey handed every student his or her study guide and an answer sheet for that study guide. Next, she divided her class into two heterogeneous teams. Then she had students partner up with a member of their team for the classwide tutoring.

After getting the tutoring partners formed, Ms. Richey had the students number off as either "one" or "two." She then said that the twos would tutor first, and called, "Begin tutoring." The tutor for each pair began by calling out the first science question on the tutee's study guide, while the tutor looked at the tutee's study guide answer sheet.

If the tutee provided the right answer, the tutor said, "Correct! Good job! You earned two points for your team." The tutor then made notes of those points, and asked the next question. If a tutee responded incorrectly, the tutor said, "Incorrect. Let me share this answer and we'll talk about it." The correct answer was then shared and briefly discussed. The general guideline is to discuss the answer enough so that the tutee understands, but for no more than thirty seconds. Ms. Richey was available for any pairs of students that needed help. Then the tutor presented the same question a final time, and when the tutee answered correctly the tutor said, "Good job. You've earned one point for your team." Then the tutor recorded the point or points earned for that question and moved on to the next factual question.

After ten minutes of this tutoring, Ms. Richey called, "Time to switch. Make sure you use the correct study guide!" The students in each pair then switched roles, with the previous tutor becoming the tutee for the next ten minutes. Note that students in the same tutoring pair often worked on different versions of the study guide in order to ensure that each student was working on his specific level. At the end of the second ten-minute tutoring session, all points earned by each team were tallied, and the winning team was recognized and rewarded.

Steps in Classwide Peer Tutoring

As shown above, classwide peer tutoring is a tutoring approach whereby all students in the class form tutoring partnerships and reciprocally tutor each other. This is a procedure that requires some tutoring training for students in the class, and the steps below will guide you in implementing this in your STEM class (Arreaga-Meyer, 1998; Bowman-Perrott, 2009; Ginsburg-Block et al., 2006; Greenwood et al., 2003).

Prepare materials. Classwide peer tutoring is most effective when used for learning factual material early in the science or mathematics unit. The type of complex conceptual ideas found later in instructional units can be the content for this tutoring but should be avoided until both the teacher and the class are familiar with the tutoring process. As shown by Ms. Richey in the example above, teachers should prepare versions of a worksheet or study guide at several levels, and for each study guide, they should also prepare an answer sheet. Prior to beginning the tutoring on any particular day, teachers must ensure that each pair of students has the appropriate study guides.

Explain the procedure and point scoring. When the training begins, the teacher should first describe the tutoring procedure, the specific language for tutors to use to be both clear and supportive during the process, and the scoring procedure. Note that, even when a tutee gets an answer wrong, he or she is supported with a brief explanation and a chance to earn at least one point for his or her team. Let students know that they are serving an important role as "teachers" to each other.

Teacher models the procedure. On the first training day, the teacher should work with a cooperative student and model the classwide tutoring procedure. It will not be necessary to demonstrate the procedure for ten full minutes; a two-minute tutoring session should do. However, the initial modeling should include how tutors must respond to both a correct and an incorrect answer. Also, the teacher should model how to be supportive for incorrect answers. Next, teachers should explain how the tutor keeps a record of all points scored by the tutee. Also, this modeling should include one shift, where the tutor and tutee change roles.

Use students to model the procedure. After the teacher has modeled the procedure, two other students from the class should be called forward to model the procedure a second time. During this modeling the teacher should emphasize that those students are working with different versions of the same study guide, and stress the importance of having the right study guide for each student involved. While this may sound like a challenge, the research shows that students in the primary grades soon got used to using different study guides, under teacher supervision (Greenwood et. al., 2003). Again, for this modeling, a two-minute tutoring can be used, but students should have to model switching roles.

Have everyone in the class practice tutoring. Finally, on the first day of training every student should partner up and complete a tutoring session. This example should use a ten-minute time frame for each tutor before the teacher calls, "Switch roles," and the teacher should carefully monitor students' supportive language when incorrect answers are given.

Subsequent teaching modeling. Some teachers choose to model the procedure on a second day, whereas others choose not to do so. This may depend on the grade level of the class or academic abilities in the class as a whole. However, research shows that even students with mild disabilities can perform very well in classwide peer tutoring if effective training is provided over several days (Arreaga-Meyer, 1998; Bowman-Perrott, 2009; Ginsburg-Block et al., 2006; Greenwood et al., 2003).

Efficacy of Classwide Peer Tutoring

Research has been strongly supportive of peer tutoring in terms of positive academic results for both tutors and tutees (Bowman-Perrott, 2009; Burnish, Fuchs, & Fuchs, 2005; Ginsburg-Block, Rohrbeck, & Fantuzzo, 2006; Greenwood et al., 2003; Hattie, 2012; Kamps, et al., 2008; Kunsch, Jitendra, & Sood, 2007; NEA, 2015; Topping, 2008). Hattie's meta-analyses demonstrated that peer tutoring generated an effect size of .56, and was number 34 on his list of 150 effective instructional strategies. The research studies on classwide peer tutoring in particular are quite extensive and have demonstrated its effectiveness in many areas, including mathematics and science (Greenwood et al., 2003; Kamps, et al., 2008). Furthermore, this approach to peer tutoring has been demonstrated to be effective for students with learning disabilities and other disabilities in the general education class (Arreaga-Meyer, 2009).

However, there are advantages to classwide peer tutoring beyond increased achievement. Tutoring will increase the time-on-task for both the tutors and the tutees, which makes this strategy particularly effective for differentiating instruction. Also, implementation requires that all students be trained to be supportive of other students, and this emphasis on supportive help can improve class climate overall (Arreaga-Meyer, 1998; Bowman-Perrott, 2009; Ginsburg-Block et al., 2006; Greenwood et al., 2003).

Summary

Few strategies are as widely recommended for teachers as peer tutoring, and STEM teachers who are not already employing some peer tutoring strategy are well advised to consider this tactic. For the types of extensive factual material that seem to be present in almost all STEM instructional units, classwide peer tutoring can easily replace a lecture or two, and the increased student engagement resulting from this tactic is likely to increase student achievement overall. STEM teachers will see grades improve classwide by implementing this tactic.

STRATEGY 16

Reciprocal Teaching

Reciprocal teaching is a specialized form of peer tutoring that emphasizes teacher modeling to teach several specific instructional activities during the tutoring process. This is a research-proven strategy for helping students understand reading content that has been practiced in elementary classrooms since the 1980s (Lederer, 2000; Pilonieta & Medina, 2009; Rosenshine & Meister, 1994), and it remains one of the most recommended instructional strategies available (Frey & Fisher, 2013; Hattie, 2012). While this strategy was most frequently applied in elementary reading instruction, it can also be utilized for text-based reading in content areas such as science, engineering, and technology.

Palinscar and Brown (1984) are typically identified as the theorists who developed this technique. They focused on creating a form of structured dialogue in which the teacher begins a question-based discussion of the reading content using four different activities in the following order: predicting, question generating, summarizing, and clarifying. After the teacher models the procedure, the students themselves take turns serving as the teacher. At that point, they lead a structured discussion of the academic text using the same activities. Thus, each student becomes responsible for teaching the lesson through questions and focused dialogue (Frey & Fisher, 2013).

As this shows, reciprocal teaching is a scaffolded procedure, with the teacher providing significant modeling and instructional support early in the process, while gradually removing that support as students take over the discussion. To get a better sense, you might wish to review a video example of reciprocal teaching (https://www.youtube.com /watch?v=My68SDGeTHI).

Because this procedure has been around for a while, many teachers are familiar with it, and we will not spend a great deal of time on this strategy. However, reciprocal teaching has typically been used for reading instruction in the early grades, and not in content area reading, so I wanted to briefly explain the technique in the context of a science class, as well as provide an action research case study.

Steps in Reciprocal Teaching

Reciprocal teaching is typically done as a teacher-led, small-group activity involving four to six students. This makes for a manageable group and helps to ensure involvement of everyone in the small group. In the reciprocal teaching strategy, the common activities for each student are predicting, question generating, summarizing, and clarifying. Each of those activities must initially be taught separately. At first, the teacher will model the procedure, while discussing each of these major tasks, as he or she does them. At some point, during the first day, the teacher will ask a student to lead the discussion, using the same four activities. Other students will use the same activities and lead the discussion on subsequent days, under the direction of the teacher. In order to get the entire class up to speed on reciprocal teaching, the teacher should plan to conduct at least four small groups involving different students in the class, in which he or she models the procedures.

Predicting. Step one involves the teacher explaining the concept of prediction, and discussing the benefits of prediction as a reading strategy. For example, when looking at a chapter in a science text on the solar system, the teacher might ask that students flip through the first ten pages of the chapter, noting the major headings and the pictures. Then students would be asked to predict what those sections might include or what might come next. Prediction of text content involves the students' relevant background knowledge of the text and provides students with a reason to read further, as they try to confirm or refute their predictions. In that sense, this prediction activity involves both comprehension of material being read and self-monitoring of the material previously read.

To facilitate prediction, the teacher should consider preparing a wall chart of the various aspects of prediction. That chart should be kept in front of the class to assist students who are leading the prediction activity on any particular day. That poster might include prediction strategies such as:

> *Look at the pictures in the text. What is similar about them?*
>
> *Look at the main text headings. What might be the focus or topic under each?*
>
> *Do these text headings relate to the chapter title? How?*

Question generating. The second activity in the reciprocal teaching strategy is question generating. Question generating gives students the opportunity to identify the type of information that might be used in subsequent test questions. Emphasizing that test questions will come from the types of things that students predicted will encourage high levels of engagement for most STEM students. Also, question generation provides an occasion to discuss methods of study for various types of questions (factual questions versus questions that require synthesis of information).

Students should be encouraged to write down their predictions and questions, to help them at a later phase in the study process. After students have predicted text content and generated questions, time should be given to check the answers to those questions, and/or verify the accuracy of their predictions. In elementary reading, this step is often incorporated into the procedural steps above. However, in the context of subject-area reading, this activity takes on additional importance, and may require more time. Thus, after the question-generating step, STEM teachers should have students check the text to explore accuracy of their predictions, answer their questions, and compare their predictions and questions with others in the small group.

Summarizing. The summarizing step provides an opportunity to integrate information from different sections of the text and/or different students. Here, the teacher, or the student leading the discussion, should point out the important ideas in the text and have the students discuss them. Again, when using this technique in a subject area, students should be encouraged to take notes during this step; in contrast, note taking is not typically included in an elementary reading application of reciprocal teaching.

Clarifying. The fourth activity—clarifying—encourages students to identify the major points of the reading selection and to discuss once again any concepts that may be particularly difficult. Seeking clarification also allows students to ask questions without embarrassment because the role of the students in reciprocal teaching is specifically to question and clarify the problem areas. Again, when using this strategy in a subject-area text, the note taking should continue during this step.

Applications of Reciprocal Teaching in STEM Classes

As shown above, reciprocal teaching will be practiced somewhat differently in a subject-area class, and there are likely to be several other differences. First, in elementary reading instruction, each of the four activities of reciprocal teaching is completed in a single instructional period, but as the discussion above suggests, when using this with a science or engineering text, the steps will take more time. Thus, I suggest that for STEM applications, teachers may wish to complete two of the activities above during a given instructional period, and do the other two later, while preserving the overall order of these four activities.

Next, in STEM classes, teachers may not lead every reciprocal teaching group. While all students will need to see the teacher model these activities initially, once that is completed, the students themselves should begin to lead the reciprocal teaching discussions. Thus, after teaching this procedure in two or three instructional units at the beginning of the year, teachers can do reciprocal teaching by forming groups and letting students lead the various group discussions while the teacher "floats" between groups. In that sense, reciprocal teaching can become a whole-class strategy, based on small-group work.

Finally, as another alternative, teachers may actually assign each of the four reciprocal teaching activities as a specific teaching role to individual students in each group. One student serves as the small-group leader during the prediction phase, whereas another would serve during the question-generating phase. An example of this application can be found at http://www.readingquest.org/strat/rt.html.

Efficacy of Reciprocal Teaching

Reciprocal teaching has been widely supported by research in a variety of academic areas and a variety of grade levels (Hattie, 2012; Lederer, 2000; Marzano, 2009a; Pilonieta & Medina, 2009; Rosenshine & Meister, 1994). In Hattie's meta-analyses, reciprocal teaching compared quite favorably to traditional instruction, generating an impressive effect size of .74. On Hattie's (2012) list of 150 teaching strategies, reciprocal teaching was near the top (at number 11 on the list). Further, while Marzano (2009a, 2007) does not specifically mention reciprocal teaching as one of his nine most effective teaching strategies, he does recommend several specific components of the reciprocal teaching approach (e.g., predicting, clarifying, summarizing), and states that those teaching procedures yielded a 34 percent gain in academic achievement compared to traditional instruction. In short, research has consistently documented the efficacy of reciprocal teaching.

It is important to note that reciprocal teaching is effective for students of all ability levels, including students with disabilities (Pilonieta & Medina, 2009; Rosenshine & Meister, 1994). For example, Lederer (2000) investigated the efficacy of reciprocal teaching among students with learning disabilities in a social studies class. Using six inclusive classrooms, Lederer (2000) had several classes teach for thirty days using reciprocal teaching and compared those to students in traditionally taught classes. Fifteen students with learning disabilities were in the experimental classes, while ten students with learning disabilities were in the control group. Repeated assessments throughout the thirty-day period indicated a consistent advantage for the experimental group in each of the three dependent measures: ability to answer comprehension questions, generate questions, and summarize a reading selection.

Case Study: Reciprocal Teaching in Science

Mr. Eubanks was looking for an alternative to lecture to use in his three sections of ninth-grade biology, and he had read about reciprocal teaching. He usually taught biology using instructional units on different topics, and those units ranged from two to three weeks each. Because of a school improvement initiative, every teacher in his high school was expected to implement a new teaching approach during each semester and conduct action research to document the efficacy of that approach. Mr. Eubanks decided to try reciprocal teaching. As a dependent measure, he chose to use an average score on his unit tests, for each section of his biology class. He could, with relative ease, average those grades for students in each period for several instructional units during the fall of that academic year. That provided the baseline data found in figure 16.1 (page 198).

In order to get a reliable measure of the impact of reciprocal teaching, Mr. Eubanks determined to use a multiple baseline design and teach several instructional units using reciprocal teaching at least five different times per unit with small groups of six students in each reciprocal teaching group. Thus he replaced virtually all of his lecture-based classes in each instructional unit taught during the intervention phases, with a reciprocal teaching procedure. Also, he taught reciprocal teaching by modeling it during the first instructional unit in the intervention phase in each of his three biology classes. By doing the procedure five times in that unit, he could ensure that every student participated in at least one of his training sessions. Again, during those first small-group teaching sessions in the intervention phase, he was modeling the technique himself in order to teach what reciprocal teaching is.

As shown in figure 16.1, each time Mr. Eubanks shifted from lecture-based instruction to reciprocal-teaching-based instruction, unit test scores improved. The baseline data document a lower average unit test score than the intervention data, so Mr. Eubanks was able to summarize his action research on reciprocal teaching by stating that this strategy was a more effective teaching strategy for his biology classes.

Summary

Reciprocal teaching has been around for several decades, and many elementary teachers have used this strategy in their reading instruction. The research on that application of the strategy is solidly supportive. While there is not a large body of research on this technique in subject-area STEM classes, there is considerable research on the components of this strategy (i.e., summarization, predicting), which were discussed previously in this book. Clearly STEM teachers can and should implement this strategy with confidence, and for the middle and secondary science classes still characterized predominately by lectures, reciprocal teaching offers an excellent alternative strategy that will increase student engagement and student learning.

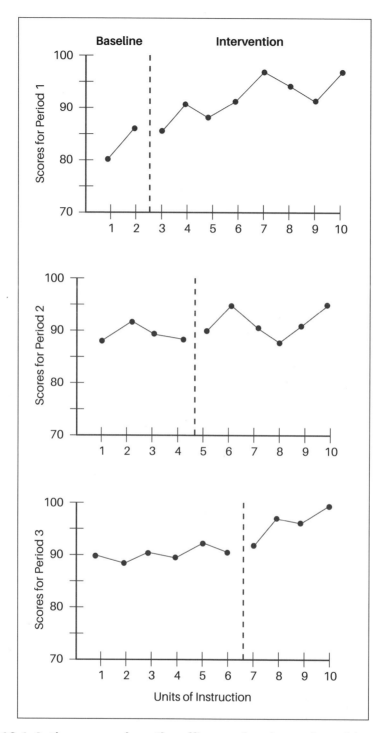

Figure 16.1: Action research on the efficacy of reciprocal teaching.

Section IV

Differentiated STEM Instruction

Differentiated instruction is a concept that is over a decade old (Tomlinson, 1999), and many teachers are familiar with it. In essence, differentiation suggests that students learn better when teachers attend to, and develop different activities for, students with different learning needs. While some proponents of differentiation emphasize various learning-style theories as the basis for differentiating instruction, others suggest that previous learning or academic achievement differences should likewise be considered. What all proponents of differentiation agree on is the proposition that learners do learn differently, and instruction is more effective when those differences are considered in instructional planning.

Several STEM proponents have stressed differentiated instruction for STEM classes in order to break away from the endless "lecture, discuss, test" paradigm that characterized so much mathematics and science instruction in the 20th century (Haldane & Smith, 2014; Myers & Berkowicz, 2015). In those discussions, a wide array of differentiation strategies have been proposed including use of rubrics, prediction/summarization strategies, formative assessment, and providing effective feedback. Some of these strategies have been presented previously, and in this section, a broad differentiated instructional strategy is presented, along with strategies for differentiated metacognitive instruction, peer evaluation and feedback, goal setting, and self-evaluation.

STRATEGY 17

Differentiated Instructional Practice

Differentiated instruction involves varying the instructional activities in the class by selecting specific types of activities for each student based on his or her individual learning characteristics and learning-style preferences (Bender, 2013a; Sousa & Tomlinson, 2011; Tomlinson, 2003, 2010). Carol Tomlinson originally developed this teaching strategy in 1999, and since then, much work has been done to further this concept, with Tomlinson herself leading this effort (Sousa & Tomlinson, 2011; Tomlinson, 2003, 2010). Over the last decade, the differentiated instructional approach has moved away from a dependence on only one learning-style theory to embrace a variety of student differences and appropriate curricular modifications (Bender, 2013a; 2013b; King & Gurian, 2006; Lee, Wehmeyer, Sookup, & Palmer, 2010). Further, the concept has been applied in a variety of subjects and a variety of ways across the grade levels (Bender, 2013a; King & Gurian, 2006).

> Differentiated instruction involves varying the instructional activities in the class by selecting specific types of activities for each student based on his or her individual learning characteristics and learning-style preferences.

Differentiating Instruction in STEM

Many educators might consider differentiated instruction as more of an overall instructional approach rather than a specific teaching strategy, since several different differentiation tactics have been identified in the literature (Bender, 2013a, 2013b; Tomlinson, 2010, 2003). However, I believe differentiation can represent a strategic modification in how STEM instruction is delivered, and with that in mind, I have chosen to include this as a strategy herein. At least four different models for differentiation have been developed and promoted (Bender, 2013a, 2013b; Tomlinson, 2010; Tomlinson, Brimijoin, & Narvaez, 2008), including: modification of a traditional lesson plan, learning centers, project-based learning, and the flipped classroom. All of these teaching approaches are in essence various ways to differentiate instruction. While other researchers may not interpret the flipped class or project-based learning as differentiated instructional models, these approaches do foster highly differentiated lesson activities and allow students to use their preferred learning style to maximum effect, so I have discussed these recent innovations in differentiation (Bender, 2013a).

Some of these approaches to differentiation have been discussed previously in this book, and of course many STEM teachers have already explored various approaches to differentiating the instruction. Still, some teachers, particularly in the middle and higher grades, might not have done so as yet. Therefore, this section focuses on the original approach to differentiated instruction, a variation of the traditional whole-group lesson plan. I should also note that modification of a traditional lesson plan is probably the easiest way to differentiate instruction in the upper grades, since it begins with exactly what STEM teachers are already doing—delivering a whole-group daily lesson via a well-developed, highly structured lesson plan.

Modification of a Traditional Lesson Plan

The traditional lesson plan format was briefly discussed previously in the strategy section on flipping the classroom. In that section, as in most such discussions, the traditional lesson plan includes five phases of instruction in which teachers deliver the lesson on any given day. While variations of the phases in that traditional lesson plan exist, that plan for a one-day lesson traditionally has looked something like this:

- Orientation to the topic—A three-to-five-minute orientation using an essential question, objective, or real-world example.

- Teacher-led instruction—Teacher presents additional examples and shows the content as the students' first exposure to the topic.

- Teacher-led practice—Students practice a few problems under teacher supervision.

- Independent practice—Students practice problems independently, often as homework and sometimes as small-group work.

- Check and reteach—Teacher checks student understanding on a few problems and reteaches the content as necessary.

In this lesson plan, students' attention often wanes either because the content is too difficult and they cannot keep up, or they are advanced and get bored listening to initial instructional examples that they might not need. Thus, traditional lessons typically lose students at both ends of the ability spectrum: gifted students and students with learning challenges. Still, in traditional classes, the whole class proceeds through all of these steps simultaneously, and if small-group instruction is provided, it comes following the initial instruction led by the teacher.

In order to develop a more flexible instructional option for general education classrooms, Tomlinson recommended varying the instruction through virtually every phase of this traditional lesson plan and planning instructionally varied tasks based on the learning styles and preferences of the students (Sousa & Tomlinson, 2011; Tomlinson, 2003, 1999). Tomlinson's work was quite timely, in that the instructional variation of the typical general education class has changed rather dramatically since the 1970s, when the traditional lesson plan above evolved. In particular, there are more students with special needs in general education classes than there were in the early 1970s, and this brings a variety of learning needs and learning-style preferences into focus. For that reason, differentiated instruction suggests that teachers should break classes into small groups for different work as early as the initial instructional phase of the lesson (Bender, 2013a) and not assume that the teacher must lead instruction for all students prior to differentiating the learning activities.

Thankfully, Tomlinson's work (1999, 2010) allows educators to plan lesson activities that are not based on the whole-group, one-size-fits-all lesson plan. Rather, the differentiated classroom presents a much wider array of activities targeted at individual learners in order to address the issues of more varied learning styles and learning preferences, and the wider academic diversity in today's schools.

Classroom Example: A Differentiated Math Lesson

Imagine a traditional mathematics lesson in Ms. Bower's third-grade class, a class of twenty-four students, five of whom are students with special needs. Two of those five students have learning disabilities, and the other three have ADHD with an overlay of hyperactive behavior. Further, five other students are advanced, while two of those are identified as academically gifted. In other words, this is a typical third-grade class. Ms.

Bower is teaching a math lesson concerning the aggregation of data, the creation of a tally table, and the eventual formulation of a frequency table summarizing those data. The following box shows the phases of a traditional whole-group lesson plan on the left, and a series of differentiated lesson activities on the right for the same lesson.

Traditional and Differentiated Lesson Plan Activities

Traditional Lesson	Differentiated Lesson
Orientation	
Ms. Bower introduces data aggregation.	Same activity as the traditional lesson example on students' favorite characters.
Teacher-Led Instruction	
Ms. Bower provides second example of data aggregation on the board to the entire class.	Same activity for part of the class, but a separate group, omega group, is formed and assigned an independent activity: Use masking tape and develop a grid on the floor that represents frequency table for students to stand in beside their favorite category. Meanwhile, Ms. Bower works with eighteen students in mainline group who receive increased teacher attention.
Teacher-Led Practice	
Ms. Bower gives a new data aggregation problem to the class for everyone.	Ms. Bower forms a second differentiated group of seven students for another differentiated activity, while the omega group finishes their work. Ms. Bower is then working with the mainline group of eleven students in the traditional manner, with much more individual attention.
Independent Practice and Check/Reteach Phases	
	Whole group comes back together for these activities.

Orientation to the Lesson

To begin this lesson with an attention-grabbing orientation activity, Ms. Bower might ask students to identify their favorite cartoon character from a group of five preselected characters. For example, she could project an image of each of the five characters in turn on the class SMART Board and have the students vote on their favorite. As the students vote, Ms. Bower might have one student go to the board and tally the votes beside each character. Once Ms. Bower has five pictures in one column and a tally count associated with each in the next column on the SMART Board, she has formed a tally table. She might then introduce that term to the class and say something like, "Which is the most popular character for our class? How can we summarize these data so they make sense for us?"

At that point, Ms. Bower has shown the class the advantages of aggregated data. When someone in the class mentions the idea of counting the tally marks for each character, Ms. Bower could have someone count them, and write that number in a third column beside the tally marks. She then has a frequency table on the board. She would then introduce those additional terms (tally table, frequency table) and point out to the class how much they enjoyed aggregating the data. At that point, her orientation to the class is over, and she is ready to move to the next phase of instruction.

In a traditional lesson, she would proceed to the next phase—teacher-led instruction—by saying, "Let's look at another example where we aggregate data in our class." At this point, many traditional classrooms simply lose many students' attention. While interesting orientation activities and/or first examples can, in many cases, hold students' interest for a brief time (even students with learning disabilities or attention disorders), moving into teacher-led instruction is often where they mentally leave the class. In fact, many academically challenged students are likely to lose interest in the lesson at that point. Further, some of the more advanced students may have already understood the concepts, and like their less successful classmates, they too have mentally checked out. Thus, both advanced students and students with learning problems may become less engaged with the lesson content during the whole-group lesson format.

Of course, when five students with disabilities and five advanced or gifted students cease to pay attention, Ms. Bower has effectively lost ten of her twenty-four students. In this example of a traditional lesson plan, ten students have stopped participating in the lesson, simply because Ms. Bower taught the traditional whole-group lesson plan, just as recommended in the teacher's manual!

Forming Differentiated Groups

The differentiated math lesson plan on the right side provides an alternative approach that is much more likely to keep all or most of these learners actively engaged with the lesson on aggregating data. Rather than begin the second phase of the traditional whole-group lesson, Ms. Bower could present a different lesson activity for some of the learners in the class, as she continues the traditional lesson plan phases with the other students. First, at the end of the orientation to the lesson, Ms. Bower should quickly identify several students who have probably already understood the concept, as well as others who need additional instruction. If she selects students who might work well together and have a similar learning style—perhaps learning through movement—she can form a differentiated instructional group for a different movement-based learning activity on aggregating data that is directly tied to their learning-style preference.

For example, if three gifted or advanced students and three students with learning disabilities had a learning preference for movement-based instruction, Ms. Bower could easily form a heterogeneous differentiated group for those students. She would then assign them a differentiated lesson activity to complete as she worked with others in the class. We'll call that differentiated group the omega group.

Ms. Bower might quickly check to verify that at least some students in that group have the general concept. She might ask a question like, "Do you think you could structure a tally table to collect data and then transfer those data to a frequency table just like we did on the board?" As long as some students in the omega group get the overall concept, that group should be able to work on its own in a differentiated learning activity, while Ms. Bower continues the traditional lesson format with others in the classroom. Note that while small-group instruction in traditional lessons is only used much later in the lesson plan, in a differentiated lesson plan students are doing different activities within three or four minutes of the beginning of the class, even before the teacher-led instructional phase of the lesson. Thus, fewer students get mentally lost during instruction, and fewer get bored.

Of course, the names used for differentiated groups in the class should be nonsequential and should not indicate a quantitative or qualitative judgment on the skills or the intellect of the group. However, as teachers differentiate more, the class will grow to understand that different groups are frequently formed to complete alternative learning activities, and that not all students in the class do the same activities.

In this example, Ms. Bower should have previously developed an assignment sheet for the omega group involving the structure of a frequency table. The omega group students would be instructed to move to a separate section of the room to begin their small-group work—use masking tape and develop a grid on the floor that represents the structure of another frequency table that allows groups of students to stand beside their category preferences. Thus, rather than merely copying the grid on the board, students must discuss its structure—the "tally box" column has to be much bigger, since students will stand in the boxes. As the omega group students discuss this, they are talking about how to structure a tally and a frequency table. In that way, rather than losing the attention of these six students, members of that differentiated group would be discussing and focusing on the column and row structure of a frequency table, and they will be learning content from each other.

Teachers rarely have to create these alternative differentiated activities, since most modern curricula include instructional alternatives in the teacher's manual. Ms. Bower need only preselect an appropriate activity and provide any necessary materials to the omega group.

In this example, students are assigned to review the frequency table on the SMART Board and construct a grid for a similar table on the floor using masking tape. This activity requires some floor space, an example of a frequency table (which is already on the SMART Board), and a roll of masking tape. As those students work together to create the grid, the students who do not know the concept will be learning from those who do. Students will place tape on the floor to develop an outline of a frequency table, with a five-by-three grid.

As that group of six students works on that activity, Ms. Bower will visually monitor them while leading instruction for the others in the class. Given that the teacher-directed instructional phase of the lesson typically takes twelve to fifteen minutes, the group activity for omega group should be planned with that time frame in mind. The omega group students would have to jointly plan what the frequency table must look like, using the model on the SMART Board, while planning how their grid has to differ from that example. The point is that the omega group has to figure all of this out—including the number of categories and the relative size of the boxes—while working as a group. Thus, rather than mentally withdrawing from the lesson, these students are likely to be highly engaged with the lesson content. Should this group make any errors, they are likely to be clearly visible to Ms. Bower (i.e., the grid probably needs to be fifteen feet wide!). She can then quickly coach the students to reconsider their mistake, while continuing her instruction for the other students.

The Mainline Instructional Group

In this example, Ms. Bower has provided an orientation and has already differentiated the lesson. She has formed two groups for instruction: the omega group and the mainline group. As the omega group does its work, Ms. Bower will engage in the next phase of the lesson, teacher-led initial instruction, for the mainline group. She should make certain that the activity provided for that group is at least as engaging as the work the omega group is doing.

In order to keep the focused attention of the mainline group, Ms. Bower should also consider reorienting the class. For example, if the omega group is working in the right front of the classroom, in a small-group workspace, she should have the mainline group turn their desks to face the left rear corner of the room. In that manner, Ms. Bower can accomplish two critical things:

1. She has oriented the mainline instructional group to have their backs to the omega group—and thus both groups are more likely to pay attention to their own assigned task.

2. She has placed herself in a position to lead instruction for the mainline group and still visually monitor the omega group with ease.

In this differentiated lesson, it is likely that the efficacy of Ms. Bower's instruction for the mainline group increases because she has fewer students in that group. The students working directly with Ms. Bower will receive more direct teacher attention. Also, the students in the omega group who would have probably lost attention in a traditional lesson, are much more likely to be engaged in a meaningful learning activity. This increased engagement is why differentiated instruction is effective; more students are more highly engaged with the math content.

The Beta Group

At the end of the teacher-led instructional phase, several things happen at once. First the students in the omega group might be finished with their assignment and will need another differentiated assignment. Alternatively, Ms. Bower might simply instruct them to turn their desks and rejoin the mainline group. Next, prior to beginning the teacher-led practice phase of the lesson, Ms. Bower should select another group for a second differentiated activity. We'll refer to them as the beta group. Again, Ms. Bower should take care to include both students who have grasped the content and a few who haven't. That beta group should then be given some type of assignment on data aggregation. As shown earlier, this assignment might be to test out the grid on the floor that was created by the omega group, by forming one or two new examples of a frequency table, and standing by the categories in column one.

Of course, it would also be perfectly appropriate to have the omega group work with the beta group to develop these activities for later classroom use. Or, Ms. Bower may give them a separate assignment that involves writing several data aggregation problems for subsequent classroom use. Note that when those two differentiated groups are doing separate small-group assignments, Ms. Bower will be instructing a group of only ten or twelve students in the mainline group, resulting in even more direct teacher attention for every learner.

In this classroom example, Ms. Bower is providing highly fluid differentiated instruction, targeted at individual students based on their learning styles and individual needs. In a differentiated class, small groups are frequently formed from the very beginning of the lesson, and then rejoin the mainline instruction, as appropriate. Not all groups do all the activities, but all receive small-group work tied to their learning preferences and direct teacher attention in a smaller mainline instruction group. Meanwhile, during almost all of the class, Ms. Bower will be working with smaller numbers of students and instructional efficacy is very likely to increase.

As this example indicates, rather than lecturing to the whole class, differentiated lessons offer an option to all teachers for replacing lecture with brief, intensive small-group and teacher-led instruction. In middle and high school STEM classes, which have historically been characterized by frequent lectures, differentiated instruction should be considered a more engaging instructional option.

Further, in a differentiated class, teachers should never be reluctant to form a differentiated group for brief, specific activities, or to reinclude those same students in the mainline instruction when the differentiated task is completed. This fluid, changing small-group focus with little to no whole-class lecture and different students frequently moving into different activities is the visible hallmark of a differentiated lesson.

Guidelines for Differentiated Instruction

Know your students. The concept of differentiated instruction has always focused on knowing the learning styles and abilities of each student in the class. Some students learn best through movement-based instruction; others learn visually. Some learn verbally, and some learn best in small-group discussions. Knowing the individual learning characteristics of every student, along with that student's overall achievement level, will allow teachers to form effective small groups virtually instantly, and matching the instructional activity to the individual learning characteristics is the very essence of differentiated instruction.

Take time to plan differentiated lessons. When teachers first consider differentiated lessons, they are often very concerned with the time it takes to plan multiple activities. Clearly, relying on the traditional lecture-based lesson plan is easier than planning a dynamic differentiated lesson. However, teachers must understand that the main emphasis of differentiated instruction is presentation of lesson activities that engage the learners in new and dramatic ways. At least initially, such lesson planning will take a bit more time.

In fact, good differentiated instruction takes place well before the class begins. Differentiation is based on well-planned, highly focused small-group lessons for learners with similar learning styles and needs. Teachers will need to select these activities in advance of the lesson, and prepare for them. In the example above, Ms. Bower might have continued to differentiate the lesson throughout the period by forming additional groups as necessary. However, differentiated lessons rarely involve more than three small groups in the class, because as students finish a differentiated assignment, they frequently rejoin the teacher-led instruction for a brief time.

Prepare students for differentiated group work. Many classes have historically emphasized individual, or even competitive individual, classwork, and while such activities do represent what students frequently face in the real world, they should not be the only instructional experience students have. In fact, increased small-group work improves collaboration among students, and increased collaboration tends to increase academic scores. As emphasized in the cooperative learning strategy above, teachers are well advised to increase cooperative and collaborative learning, and small-group differentiated lessons provide an excellent vehicle for doing exactly that.

In order to prepare students for these small groups, all teachers moving into more differentiation should also plan to teach small-group learning skills such as brainstorming, active listening, time-lining, and appropriate ways to offer/provide constructive criticism. These skills are critical in the modern world and directly transfer to later life experiences.

Invite students to plan and prepare differentiated activities. As shown previously, it is possible on many occasions to have one small group prepare a differentiated activity that another differentiated group might complete at a different point, either later in the lesson or the next day. As long as each of the activities focuses on the specific learning content, students can often prepare an activity for others to subsequently use.

Trust students to learn from each other. Differentiated instruction is working in classrooms around the world because students can and do learn from each other. In fact, some students may learn more effectively from each other than from a teacher. Students generally tend to pay more attention to their peers than to the teacher, and if the small groups are selected carefully by the teacher, students will learn from others in the class.

Replace lectures with differentiated lessons. Lecture is the least effective way to teach, and for that reason, many teachers have already moved to differentiated lessons rather than exclusive use of traditional whole-group lecture-based lesson plans. However, not every whole-group lesson needs to be highly differentiated. There are many whole-group activities that can and do actively engage almost all learners in STEM classes. These include gaming activities, project-based work, video/computer-based presentations, debates and role play, interactive simulations, and other whole-class activities. When a teacher is using these types of high-engagement activities, little differentiation will be necessary to keep all students focused on the learning content. To give some guidance to STEM teachers in the middle and upper grades, I suggest that teachers use high-engagement whole-group activities for one or two periods weekly and implement a highly differentiated lesson on other days.

Research on Differentiated Instruction

It may surprise many to learn that the research support base for differentiated instruction is neither particularly strong nor extensive. This lack of a strong, broad research base may stem, in part, from the assumption that differentiated instruction is a broad instructional approach rather than a specific teaching strategy. Nevertheless, teachers have responded quite strongly to the differentiated instructional concept, and many teachers report improved student satisfaction and increased academic scores resulting from increased differentiation (Bender, 2013a; King & Gurian, 2006; Lee, Wehmeyer, Sookup, & Palmer, 2010; Sousa & Tomlinson, 2011). In fact, educators generally seem to believe that differentiated instruction represents an expectation for all teachers in the future. For example, Marzano included differentiated instruction in his book on excellence in teaching (Tomlinson, 2010). Further, case study research does suggest increased academic performance when differentiated instruction is widely employed at the school level (Bender, 2013a; King & Gurian, 2006; Tomlinson, 2010; Tomlinson, Brimijoin & Narvaez, 2008).

Tomlinson, Brimijoin, and Navaez (2008), for example, described the implementation of differentiated instruction at two schools, an elementary school and a high school. These researchers documented rates of proficiency in core subjects of reading, writing, and mathematics prior to and after implementation of differentiated instruction. The faculty was provided an implementation period of one year, which included significant professional development focused on the differentiated instructional concept. Those proficiency score pre/post comparisons showed that after differentiated instruction was implemented schoolwide, students' proficiency jumped up in each subject, between 10 percent and 30 percent. That is a very significant jump in achievement scores, schoolwide!

Summary

STEM teachers who are not already providing differentiated instruction should certainly begin to do so, and many teaching strategies covered in this book can be quite compatible with differentiation. While research results are limited, this teaching strategy does represent the future of instruction simply because of the increased academic and learning-style variance in the typical classroom. At the very least, replacing most lectures with differentiated instructional assignments will increase academic engagement and performance. Further, this emphasis on differentiated instruction will provide an opportunity for both students and teachers to enjoy STEM experiences in new and novel ways.

Personally, I've become committed to this differentiated instructional strategy over the last decade, and I like to see highly fluid differentiated groups in virtually every classroom in the school. This represents a drastic improvement over the "teacher in front lecturing on science" approach to STEM, with little to no classroom activity and bored students. To prepare students for the exciting world of the future, we must all demand more of ourselves as educators. Only then can we demand more from our students in STEM classes.

STRATEGY 18

Metacognitive Strategy Instruction

Differentiated instruction results in students working often in small groups that are not directly led by the teacher. For that reason, teachers often seek a scaffolding technique to provide instructional support for students who are working relatively independently, and perhaps the most effective scaffolding approach teachers can employ involves metacognition (Bender, 2013a; Maats & O'Brien, 2015; O'Connell & Vandas, 2015). Metacognition has been receiving increased emphasis, particularly among STEM teachers, as these teachers seek ways to emphasize students' depth of understanding in STEM classes as stressed by the Common Core standards (Maats & O'Brien, 2015; O'Connell & Vandas, 2015; Rosenzweig, Krawec, & Montague, 2011). The term *metacognition* may loosely be defined as "thinking about one's thinking"; it is the inner language or self-instruction one provides to oneself while completing a complex task (Bender 2013a). Thus, metacognition represents the pinnacle of deep understanding of subject matter concepts.

> The term *metacognition* may loosely be defined as "thinking about one's thinking"; it is the inner language or self-instruction one provides to oneself while completing a complex task.

In order to emphasize the critical nature of metacognition, the National Academy of Sciences produced a white paper on learning in 2005. In that 600-page report, one concept was repeatedly emphasized as the most important aspect of learning in the hard sciences: metacognition, an in-depth thinking about the processes involved in scientific and mathematical problem solving (Maats & O'Brien, 2015). The report concluded that for STEM subjects, the critical key to all effective learning is the students' inner reflection during the learning process and that this focus on metacognition should be the basis for instruction in all of the hard sciences. Further, this comprehensive report documented the research, which over the years has shown that metacognitive instruction will increase academic success (Iseman & Naglieri, 2011; Mason & Hedin, 2011; Rosenzweig et al., 2011).

What Is Metacognition?

Metacognition has been described as an "inner language" that students use to guide their behaviors and their schoolwork, and it may include many skills. Again, different authors often list different components of metacognition, but at a minimum, the concept of metacognition includes the following:

- *Talking oneself through planning the steps necessary to complete a task*

- *Ordering those steps into the correct sequence*

- *Monitoring one's progress on those steps*

For those who may be unfamiliar with metacognition, a simple demonstration in mathematics will help. Imagine the inner language that takes place in a student's mind, while he or she completes a simple addition problem—the sequenced steps as detailed below. As this illustrates, two different "streams" of inner language are taking place, as represented by the columns below.

$$7$$

Add the digits in the ones place $7 + 4 = 11$;

$$+14$$

Write down the number 1 in the ones place, and carry the number 1 in the tens place;

Add the digits in the tens place $1 + 1 = 2$;

Write that answer down in the tens place.

Double-check the answer.

In this example, the math problem in the first column above represents the student doing the actual math, perhaps using a "counting on" procedure to add the digits in each column. In contrast, the sentences in the second column represent the inner language or metacognitive self-instructions on how to do the problem.

While the term *metacognitive instruction* is often used to represent this concept of inner language instruction, there are other terms with similar meaning, including *instructional strategies*, *learning strategies instruction*, and *cognitive strategies*. The critical element in all of these terms is that these instructional approaches involve providing a structuring mechanism focused on planning the inner language instructional support for a student to assist in completing the assigned STEM task. Metacognitive strategies help students think through their assignment, plan the sequence of steps to complete the work, and monitor how they are doing on each step.

Metacognitive Strategy Instruction

A metacognitive strategy (sometimes referred to as a learning strategy) is often presented as a mnemonic device, such as an acronym, that assists a student in understanding and completing an academic task. In many cases, this acronym specifies the series of sequenced steps to be completed when solving the problem (Bulgren et al., 2007; Lenz, 2006). In most metacognitive instruction, students are expected to memorize the strategy steps and then apply them when doing a particular type of problem. While strategies have been developed in many educational areas, a couple strategies for mathematics, from a variety of sources (Bender, 2013a; Gagnon & Maccini, 2001; Jackson, 2002), are presented in the following box.

Metacognitive Strategies in Mathematics

RIDD Strategy for Mathematical Word Problems

R   Read the problem.
I   Imagine what the problem is asking for.
D   Decide what to do.
D   Do the math.

continued →

STAR Strategy for Problem Solving

S   Search the problem carefully.
         Read the problem carefully.
         Ask, "What do I need to find?"
Write down the known facts from the problem.T
Translate the words into an equation in picture form.
         Choose a variable to solve for.
         Identify the operations necessary using cue
             words in the problem.
         If possible, use counters/manipulatives to
             represent the problem.
         Draw a picture of the equation, including known
             facts and operations.

A   Answer the problem.
         Perform the necessary operations, solving for
         unknowns.

R   Review the problem.
         Read the problem again carefully.
         Ask, "Does this answer make sense? Why?"
         Check the answer.

Steps in Metacognitive Strategy Instruction

Various proponents of metacognitive strategy instruction suggest various instructional sequences, but the steps in the box below are an abridged version of an instructional protocol developed by Don Deshler and his associates at the University of Kansas (Bulgren et al., 2007; Lenz, 2006; Schumaker & Deshler, 2003). When working with one specific strategy acronym, the teacher would have the student follow this instructional process over a period of days (Lenz, 2006; Schumaker & Deshler, 2003), while generating data on student performance.

Steps for Teaching a Metacognitive Strategy

1. **Pretest and teach the strategy:** A pretest is recommended prior to strategy instruction, and then data from that pretest should be used to help motivate the student to learn the new strategy. Students should be encouraged to "opt in" to learning the strategy, and the teacher then models the metacognitive strategy with another problem.

   The teacher should stress the conditions under which the strategy may be applied. The teacher should model the strategy using a "think-aloud" technique in which he or she talks about the steps identified in the strategy, including stressing the prompts and cues in the strategy and how they apply. Finally, students are encouraged to memorize the strategy and to identify the action to be taken in each step. This teaching process may take several class periods.

2. **Practice with controlled materials:** Deshler and his associates (Bulgren et al., 2007; Lenz, 2006; Schumaker & Deshler, 2003) stress the need to practice application of the strategy on "controlled content," by which they mean content at a slightly lower grade level. For example, if a sixth-grade student is learning a word problem metacognitive strategy, he or she should practice that strategy initially on fourth- or fifth-grade word problems in order to learn the strategy completely, prior to using the strategy on sixth-grade-level word problems. During this practice, a daily assessment is taken to measure each student's progress. This controlled practice phase may take several class periods.

continued →

3. **Assign grade-level practice:** When students demonstrate proficiency on the strategy, they should apply it on grade-level materials. This step also involves the fading out of various prompts and cues the student used in earlier steps and should continue over a period of time to ensure mastery. The charted data on student performance should be regularly reviewed with the student to point out progress over time.

4. **Stress generalization and maintenance:** As the data collection on problems using the metacognitive strategy is faded, teachers should stress that students continue to use the strategy, and find ways to generalize the strategy to similar problems. Several class periods should be used to stress generalization and maintenance.

Case Study: The STAR Metacognitive Strategy

Ms. Troop was teaching in a grade 6 mathematics class and realized that several students did not have a good grasp of how to tackle story problems. She decided to use the STAR metacognitive strategy for seven students in her class, all of whom were working at a fourth-grade level in mathematics applications. Ms. Troop understood the importance of data collection when teaching lower-achieving students, so she decided to create separate data charts for each student in that small group. For our purposes in this book, we'll discuss the performance of one student, Jamie.

To undertake the instruction, Ms. Troop planed a twenty-minute intervention for three days each week for the small group of seven target students. She created a mathematics project option for the other students to complete during that twenty minutes, which was done under the supervision of the paraprofessional, leaving Ms. Troop free to teach the metacognitive intervention to the small group. For an assessment, she created a series of story problems at fourth- and fifth-grade levels, and planned to administer five such problems for each daily assessment on intervention days.

On the first day of the intervention, she merely presented a five-problem quiz, and then discussed those results with the seven students. All of those students admitted that they needed help and agreed to apply themselves in the intervention. On the next two days of the first week, Ms. Troop taught the STAR metacognitive strategy, and no data was collected. To teach the strategy, she made a poster of the steps, similar to that presented earlier, and then used a think-aloud procedure to demonstrate how to use the strategy while doing a word problem. She also provided a worksheet with the same strategy questions, and encouraged students to write down their thoughts while they used the steps in the STAR strategy. On the Monday of week two, the students began to practice using the STAR strategy on their five word problems at grade level four while using their STAR worksheets under the supervision of Ms. Troop.

Figure 18.1 presents a data chart for Jamie, showing how many word problems (out of five) that Jamie got correct each day. These data show that Jamie took six days to practice and master the strategy (three days practicing with grade 4 word problems and three days practicing with grade 5 word problems). During that time, Ms. Troop coached him and he improved each day. Thus, after those six days of training, Jamie began to apply the STAR strategy on sixth-grade-level math problems that came straight out of his textbook! Meanwhile, Ms. Troop continued to fade her coaching and support, such that within several days, Jamie was completing word problems using the STAR strategy without any help from Ms. Troop. These data show that Jamie had learned the strategy and was continuing to use it on his math work. Therefore, after a few more days, Ms. Troop began to fade the intervention supports by having Jamie not complete the STAR reflection sheet while doing his work.

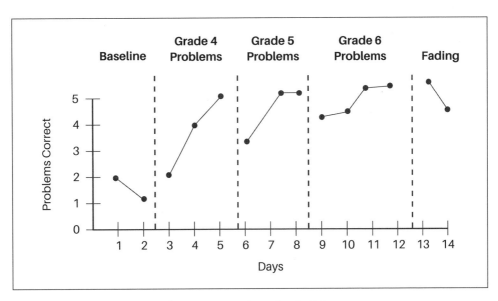

Figure 18.1: Jamie's performance using the STAR strategy.

These data show clearly that Jamie had learned a metacognitive procedure to help him solve story problems. When considering the time and effort Ms. Troop had to put in on this project, we must also consider that because of this targeted small group with seven students, each of the target students mastered a strategy that will assist them for the remainder of their mathematics careers in school and for the rest of their lives, whenever they confront a story problem. In that context, this intervention is a good use of teacher and student time!

Research on Metacognitive Instruction

As mentioned above, research on metacognitive instruction has repeatedly shown that this emphasis will increase achievement in every subject area (Bulgren, Deshler, & Lenz, 2007; Hattie, 2012; Lenz, 2006; Marzano, 2009a; Schumaker & Deshler, 2003). For example, Hattie's research (2012) identified metacognitive instruction as one of the more effective instructional strategies studied. With an effect size of .69, metacognition was number 14 on Hattie's list of most effective instructional strategies for teachers to implement. Marzano (2009a, 2007) likewise demonstrated support for several specific metacognitive strategies such as cuing, questioning, and use of advanced organizers, which together yielded an impressive 22 percent gain in academic achievement.

Research on specific metacognitive strategy acronyms has shown repeatedly that these step-by-step process acronyms will improve academic performance in virtually all subjects (Maats & O'Brien, 2015; Mason & Hedin, 2011; Rosenzweig et al., 2011). More specifically, other research has shown metacognitive instruction to be effective specifically in mathematics and science classes (Iseman & Naglieri, 2011; Mason & Hedin, 2011; Rosenzweig, Krawec, & Montague, 2011). Thus, this strategy can be implemented with confidence in virtually all STEM classes.

Summary

Metacognitive strategy instruction is certainly a tool for all STEM teachers to consider, and various science organizations have encouraged use of this strategy. While this section has focused primarily on metacognitive strategies in mathematics, many similar metacognitive strategies that emphasize reading skills can likewise be very useful in STEM classes. Strategies are available for content-area reading, writing theme papers, test-taking skills, and reading contiguous chapters in content-area texts (Author, 2005; Bulgren, Deshler, & Lenz, 2007; Iseman & Naglieri, 2011; Mason & Hedin, 2011; Rosenzweig, Krawec, & Montague, 2011; Schumaker & Deshler, 2003). As all veteran teachers realize, all of those skills are critical in many science, engineering, and technology classes. Therefore, STEM teachers should explore the many options coming from the metacognitive instructional literature. Further, given the emphasis on teaching for deeper understanding in the discussions of the Common Core curriculum, the emphasis on metacognition is only likely to increase in years to come.

STRATEGY 19

Feedback and Peer Evaluation

Feedback is essential for learning (Freemark, 2014; Goodrich, 2012; Hattie, 2012; Hicks, 2014), and in the context of STEM classes in the 21st century, feedback may be even more critical than in other classes. In the past, simple memorization was often the overall goal in education (e.g., math facts or procedural rules such as the order-of-operations guideline "Please Excuse My Dear Aunt Sally"). In those memory situations, little feedback was necessary beyond a summative assessment on student regurgitation of facts; the students either memorized the content or they didn't. In contrast, STEM classes necessitate much more feedback, since the goal of the Common Core standards in both science and mathematics is to teach content at a much deeper level. Successful students in STEM classes should be able to conceptualize the content and to evaluate each other's collaborative work in order to generate knowledge cooperatively (e.g., generation and testing of hypotheses). Students must also apply their learning across similar and different situations, and these emphases make feedback even more important.

Of course, feedback has been the focus of several strategies throughout this book, most notably the use of rubrics, Strategy 4. However, STEM teachers should use a variety of feedback options, and peer evaluation is one avenue for effective feedback. This is essential because of the collaborative nature of many modern STEM strategies, as well as the complexity of the content itself. Particularly in differentiated classes, where students are working frequently in small groups, peer evaluation will be ongoing. Further, in various strategies previously discussed (project-based learning, makerspace, wiki-based instruction, cooperative project work, and reciprocal teaching), peer evaluation is a critical component of the strategy itself (Bender, 2012). Clearly, peer evaluation should be one feedback tool in every differentiated STEM class (Bender, 2012; Crossman & Kite, 2012; Ebersviller, 2013).

Guidelines for Teaching the Peer Evaluation Process

Peer evaluation is a strategy that helps students jointly focus on producing high-quality work (Barell, 2007; Bender, 2012; Boss & Krauss, 2007; Larmer & Mergendoller, 2009, 2010), and this form of evaluation may be either informal or formal. For example, as students engage in more project-based learning teams in STEM classes, they naturally begin to offer each other informal feedback within their teams. Thus, the very nature of modern STEM instruction makes peer evaluation a critical feedback tool, and informal peer evaluation can be viewed as an extension of that naturally occurring phenomenon.

However, teachers should also prepare students for effective peer evaluation of a more formal nature, because some students have not evaluated their peers previously, and therefore, they may not have the specific skills necessary for effective peer evaluations. Thus, teachers who wish to use peer evaluation in STEM classes will need to teach these specific evaluation skills, at least initially. The following box presents several guidelines for completing peer evaluations, and STEM teachers at every grade level should feel free to adapt these as necessary. Using these guidelines students will, over time, become increasingly competent at conducting meaningful peer evaluations.

Guidelines for Effective Peer Evaluations

- Peer evaluation is intended to provide assistance for product improvement. The goal is to carefully support students and offer our best advice about how their product might be improved.

- Remember that you are critiquing the product and not the student or students who developed the product.

- Always review the entire product carefully before completing your evaluation.

- Always prepare written evaluation notes as bullet points, in order to be clear on your suggestions.

- Always seek several positive things to say and put those notes at the beginning. Those positive remarks help in getting the evaluation discussion going. You can make negative critique points later in the discussion.

- Remember to state the negative discussion points as positively as you can whenever possible. Example: "While I liked the way you did _____, I was still concerned with one aspect of that. That concern was _____."

- Be very specific in both positive and negative comments. Examples: "That was a great segment of the digital video when you discussed the point about _____ . I feel that this could have been done better if you had also presented information on _____."

- Be brief in your comments. Typically, six to ten points is more than long enough to note both the strengths and weaknesses of the product.

- Be prepared to explain any negative comments or to give examples of what you believe will improve the product.

- Before sharing those notes, review them in order to check them carefully and to remove any harsh criticisms. If you find such harsh words, reword that point carefully.

- After your comments are prepared in writing, share them with the teacher.

- At this point, share the evaluation with the student or students. This usually takes five to ten minutes, and should be done in a private conference, and the teacher may wish to observe the first several peer evaluation conferences.

- Allow students to respond to each comment you make. If they disagree, allow them to hold a different opinion.

- Do not engage in debate about the points you make. If there are serious disagreements, you should refer those to the teacher.

Peer Evaluation Formats

Perhaps the simplest format for peer evaluation involves merely an open-ended listing of comments or bullet points relative to the product under evaluation (Barell, 2007; Bender, 2012). Of course, students in some higher grade levels are probably quite capable of using the guidelines above and merely writing out six to ten brief bullet points to critique the work of their peers. However, for younger students, or for older students who are just beginning to evaluate the work of their peers, teachers may wish to provide some basic format questions or critique points to help students begin the evaluation process. The following box presents some general questions or critique points adapted from Bender's (2012) work in project-based learning. Teachers can adapt these as appropriate and provide this format for peer evaluation when students are learning the evaluation and feedback process.

Bullet Point Peer Evaluation Critique Form

- Is this product presented in a neat, organized way? Can it be improved in any way?

- Are all the necessary ideas and concepts presented? Is this product complete?

- What additional information could be included here? Are those additions critical?

- Should this information be presented in some other manner (e.g., written report? Spreadsheet? Video? Digital poster or info-graphic?)? If so, what might be more appropriate?

- Are the concepts displayed here clearly related to each other in a meaningful, understandable manner? Are those relationships clear in this product?

- Does this product reflect work that students in our class will be proud to share with the entire community?

- What is the best advice I (we) can offer for improvement of this product?

- Based on these evaluation points, what numeric grade would I assign this project, with 100 reflecting a perfect grade? Please explain/justify your answer.

Note that the final point on this form invites students to recommend a specific grade for the product under evaluation, and such an invitation to recommend a grade is a decision teachers should carefully consider. Of course, teachers may choose to invite such a grade recommendation or even make that recommendation an actual grade for the finished product. Alternatively, teachers may simply eliminate that indicator and not invite a grade recommendation at all within the peer evaluation. This choice should be based on what the teacher hopes to accomplish with the peer evaluation, as well as the maturity of the students and their fluency in peer evaluation. If the primary intent of the peer evaluation is to provide a supportive, formative evaluation, that invitation to grade the work should be left off, and for that reason, in most cases, peer evaluations do not include such an invitation. However, such an invitation can make some students take the peer evaluation more seriously, so teachers may wish to consider including this indicator on occasion.

While open-ended bullet point comments can be quite helpful as peer evaluation feedback, STEM teachers may also wish to provide some numeric scale indicators as one component of the peer evaluation process. In fact, teachers may combine a set of numeric indicators and several open questions for the peer evaluation format. The following box presents a template for peer evaluation using the Likert scale numeric scoring device. Of course, teachers should adapt this for the specific product under evaluation.

Research on Peer Evaluation and Feedback

There have been many studies over the years proving that effective feedback in general will enhance academic achievement (Freemark, 2014; Goodrich, 2012; Hattie, 2012; Hicks, 2014; Marzano, 2007, 2009a). Hattie reviewed this evidence in his meta-analysis of effective teaching strategies, and the results showed that feedback was number ten on his list of the most effective 150 instructional strategies. Research on feedback efficacy yielded an effect size of .75, suggesting it was one of the most effective instructional tools available for teachers. Marzano's meta-analytic approach coupled feedback with setting objectives and showed that the statement of specific objectives and feedback related to them was likely to increase academic achievement by 23 percent. Clearly, feedback is critical for learning and should characterize all STEM classes.

Research on the use of peer evaluation as a feedback mechanism is somewhat harder to find in the existing literature. However, Hattie's meta-analyses do show relationships that relate to this question. For example, Hattie's work indicates that peer influence yields an effect size of .53, indicating that it has a high impact on academic achievement. Of course, peer influence is not peer evaluation per se, but peer evaluation is certainly one focused way for peers to exercise influence on the learning of their classmates.

Likert Scale Numeric Peer Evaluation

This is an evaluation of the work of _____ on their product, titled _____. Please answer the questions that follow, with a 5 indicating excellent or "couldn't be done any better," and a 1 indicating "needs considerable improvement." Your teacher will discuss your evaluation with you when you finish, and points will be awarded when your assessment agrees with the teacher's assessment on the same question.

Student(s) completing this work: _____

Date: _____

Name of the assignment evaluated: _____

This person or small group:

Selected the topic components wisely

    1   2   3   4   5

Researched this topic completely

    1   2   3   4   5

Presented multiple research sources

    1   2   3   4   5

Identified and covered appropriate subtopics thoroughly

    1   2   3   4   5

Presented a reasonable summary of the information

    1   2   3   4   5

Synthesized this information well

    1   2   3   4   5

Demonstrated critical evaluation of the evidence

    1   2   3   4   5

Presented various sides of the argument or evidence

    1   2   3   4   5

Prepared work that was neat, clear, and understandable

    1   2   3   4   5

Presented the work in the most appropriate format

    1   2   3   4   5

Overall, I would evaluate this work as

    1   2   3   4   5

Signature _____

Signature _____

By signing this work, you are indicating that this is an honest, accurate evaluation. The teacher will review and discuss this evaluation with you and sign below after the meeting, prior to sharing this with your peers.

Teacher signature _____

Further, a few studies have looked directly at using peer evaluation to improve student academic performance (Crossman & Kite, 2012; Ebersviller, 2013). For example, Ebersviller (2013) studied the use of peer evaluations to improve writing among students in grade 12, and the results showed that writing improved more in the experimental group using peer evaluations. When these research results are coupled with the stated goal of the Common Core curriculum of increasing collaborative and cooperative learning experiences, it seems wise for STEM teachers to begin using peer evaluation as a routine feedback tool in their classes.

Summary

As indicated previously, feedback is essential in STEM classes, which is why several different feedback strategies have been included in this book. While teachers are quite familiar with rubrics as a feedback mechanism, they may be less familiar with using peer evaluation to provide feedback. However, the collaborative and cooperative nature of modern STEM instruction, as exemplified by a number of the instructional strategies presented herein, should motivate STEM teachers to explore peer evaluation more concretely and to teach specific peer evaluation guidelines such as those presented here. Further, over the long term, these peer evaluation techniques translate directly into the world of work in the next decades, providing yet another reason for STEM teachers to begin to implement this instructional strategy.

STRATEGY 20

Goal Setting and Self-Evaluation

As shown in the previous few strategies, the differentiated STEM class will be characterized by much more independent learning and fewer whole-class lesson activities than traditional classes, so having students set independent goals and evaluating their progress toward those goals is more important in differentiated classrooms. In fact, setting definitive goals and monitoring personal progress toward them is one hallmark of success-oriented individuals (Elias, 2013; Hattie, 2102). Therefore, it stands to reason that preparing students with these skills should be a fundamental priority in education, particularly in the sciences.

Further, the stipulation of goals and monitoring of progress toward those goals is, in many ways, a key component in the scientific process. A hypothesis, for example, might be considered a goal for a given experiment and observing outcomes dispassionately is the essence of monitoring progress in any scientific experiment. Further, it would be difficult to imagine a project-based learning project, or for that matter, an engineering project in industry, that was not based on goals stipulated in some type of timeline (Barell, 2007; Larmer et al., 2009).

Of course, educators have long realized that setting goals can help in motivating students, and research bears out the proposition that personal goal setting is an effective strategy for instruction (Elias, 2013; Freemark, 2014; Hattie, 2012; Marzano, 2009a). Thus, goal setting and self-evaluation of personal progress should be one component of instruction in virtually all STEM classes.

Over the years, many terms have been used for this basic concept of setting goals and monitoring one's progress in relation to those goals. These would include terms such as *self-monitoring*, *self-evaluation*, *self-regulation*, *progress monitoring*, and even *formative evaluation*, among others (Bender, 2013b). Marzano (2009a), for example, described this process as setting objectives and providing feedback relative to those objectives. Regardless of the terms used by various educators, however, the idea remains relatively constant. Students do better academically when specific goals are stipulated and those goals are used in tandem with a simple self-evaluation process to monitor progress regularly.

In the context of STEM instruction, I've chosen to emphasize here the self-evaluation process relative to stipulated goals, for several reasons: First, teacher and peer monitoring and feedback have been discussed in several previous strategies. Next, as noted above, constant self-reflection and self-evaluation greatly strengthens the scientific process over-all. Finally, taking data is critical in all of the sciences and should be a common characteristic of STEM classes at all grade levels.

Guidelines for Goal Setting and Self-Monitoring

There are several overriding guidelines for setting individual student goals and having students monitor them. First, setting appropriate, meaningful goals requires some instruction. Next, learning to carefully monitor and honestly chart one's own progress relative to one's goals typically requires some additional effort. Finally, teachers should ensure that the monitoring of progress against one's goals is valued and rewarded as appropriate.

Set Appropriate, Descriptive, Meaningful Goals

In many cases, young students will need some instruction in identifying and setting appropriate descriptive goals for themselves, because goal setting has not been stressed in the traditional classroom. Specifically, students should be taught that effective goals must identify specific targets for the students and should emphasize some way that the progress can be monitored. For example, "I want to improve my math skills" is not an effective goal for a fourth- or fifth-grade math student. At best, that statement is merely a statement of intention or desire, since it stipulates only a general area of study. In that example, there is little specificity on the skills within that broader area that are to be improved, and there is no suggestion on how a student might monitor progress. However, that same goal for a fifth-grade math student might be stated as follows.

> *"I will improve my performance in mathematics operations using fractions, by showing that I can add, subtract, multiply, and divide fractions with unlike denominators."*

In that statement of the goal, several specific skills are targeted, including all four mathematics operations for fractions, and those specifics help identify exactly what skills must be monitored in order to assess how well the student meets that goal.

Finally, teachers should always require students to write down their own goals in the STEM class. Goals that are written down simply become more substantive than goals that are merely discussed at the first of an instructional unit. Those hard-copy goals can then be referred to after the students have been taught the content in question.

Monitor and Chart Progress

Goal setting is virtually meaningless without reflective self-evaluation on one's performance relative to one's goals. Students must be provided with simple ways to monitor their goals, as well as time for such self-evaluation. Various charts can be used to simplify self-monitoring of students' goals. For example, an x/y-axis chart such as those presented previously in this text might provide a simple method for monitoring one's goals on a single skill. For other goals, other types of charts might be developed and utilized. Some teachers who use the goal-setting strategy choose to require that when setting a goal, students must also provide an example of the types of monitoring tools they will use to monitor their own performance on that goal. An example of this is presented in the case study below.

Help Students Value Achievement Demonstrated by Goal Setting and Self-Monitoring

Finally, teachers must help students learn to value the goal-setting and self-evaluation process. In order to encourage students to internalize this process, and make a habit of goal setting, teachers should frequently discuss students' goals with the students. The written goals should become the basis for student/teacher—or perhaps even student/student—progress evaluation conferences, in which students reflect on how well they have moved toward their goals.

Also, offering rewards for achieving goals is critical. Perhaps a pizza party for those who achieved their goals or something as simple as class recognition and a round of applause from the class can be used.

Research on Goal Setting and Progress Monitoring

Research has shown that goal setting and reflective self-monitoring will increase student achievement, and for that reason, this strategy is widely recommended in the educational literature (Elias, 2013; Freemark, 2014; Hattie, 2012; Marzano, 2009a; Moeller, Theiler, & Wu, 2012). For example, in his meta-analysis on effective instructional strategies, Hattie's research showed that goal setting was number 48 on his list of the most effective 150 educational strategies, with an effect size of .50.

Freemark (2014) studied a process he described as the "testing effect" in a recent study. The testing effect involves increased achievement associated with individuals testing themselves and assessing their own progress repetitively. Freemark (2014) documented that when students assess themselves against stated goals, achievement will increase.

As another example, Moeller, Theiler, and Wu (2012) tracked the academic impact of goal setting and self-evaluation over a five-year period at twenty-three high schools in a quasi-experimental study using 1,273 students in Spanish classes. Results indicated that setting goals and monitoring one's progress toward those goals yielded an increase in academic achievement.

Case Study: Goal Setting and Monitoring

For this case study, imagine that a sixth-grade teacher, Mrs. Hilbig, was working with a young student, DeShawn, who could not seem to master operations with fractions with unlike denominators. As this might suggest, the goal identified above would be a good goal for DeShawn to work on:

> *"I will improve my performance in mathematics operations using fractions, by showing that I can add, subtract, multiply, and divide fractions with unlike denominators."*

However, this goal is more involved than merely a "one-skill" goal, on which results can be summarized with a simple x/y-axis chart. Rather, some type of performance monitoring tool is necessary to show DeShawn's performance on each fractional operation. In essence, monitoring this goal might well require a "multiple-indicator" type of chart, where different indicators (i.e., icons) are used for each type of operation.

Mrs. Hilbig and DeShawn decided that DeShawn should work on operations with fractions three times per week (Monday, Wednesday, and Friday) for fifteen minutes each time, using an individual computer-driven program. Mrs. Hilbig set up that program to present only fraction examples that involve operations with unlike denominators and to provide DeShawn with five examples of each operation on each day. Finally, Mrs. Hilbig and DeShawn jointly decided that if DeShawn gets into trouble on any particular type of problem he should go to Khan Academy (described previously) and watch a preselected video on solving that particular type of problem. Finally, DeShawn's performance data will be printed at each sitting by DeShawn, using the computer program. DeShawn will then take the performance scores for his daily work, summarize his performance on each type of operation on his multiple-indicator chart, and present that chart to Mrs. Hilbig.

The data chart presented in Figure 20.1 shows DeShawn's performance data over a four-week period. Notice that each of the four fractional operations is summarized by a separate indicator for each day. Once DeShawn achieved a perfect score for a given operation for four straight days, that type of problem was eliminated from DeShawn's work. As these data show, DeShawn accomplished mastery in addition and subtraction relatively easily, so work on those ceased after about three weeks, whereas multiplication and division took somewhat longer. In this case, having DeShawn set a goal, and monitor his own progress toward that goal, was a highly effective instructional strategy.

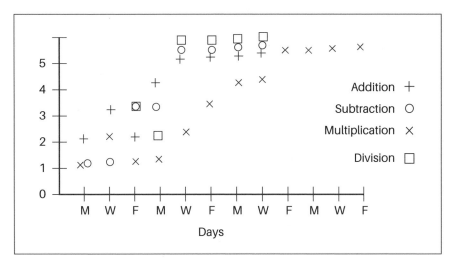

Figure 20.1: DeShawn's self-monitoring on fractional operations.

Summary

As this body of research shows, goal setting and self-evaluation is one of the most important of the effective teaching strategies for teachers to implement in STEM classes. Further, many of the proponents of goal setting and self-monitoring suggest that this is a critical skill for success in life (Bender, 2012; Elias, 2013). Like most of the effective strategies presented in this book, goal-setting and self-monitoring skills help build student clarity and prepare students for the working world. For these reasons, this is a strategy that all STEM teachers should begin to implement in all grade levels.

APPENDIX A

Meta-Analysis and Effect Size

Throughout this book, I've referred constantly to the meta-analytic work of two of the more important researchers in education, Bob Marzano and John Hattie (Hattie, 2012; Marzano, 2009a, 2007; Marzano et al., 2001). These educational leaders have used meta-analysis to summarize research on effective instructional strategies, so for a book of this nature, their research had to be quite prominent.

While many teachers are quite fluent with this research, I wanted to provide some description of this meta-analytic technique for newer teachers or for those who may not be aware of what this important research tool provides. Thus, here is a brief explanation of what a meta-analysis is, and how the effect sizes generated by that technique can be interpreted by educators in the classroom. I published one meta-analysis myself (Bender & Smith, 1990) when this research technique was still being developed, so I have some sense of the possibilities of this technique, as well as the inherent limitations and concerns.

Basically, a meta-analysis is a summarization of research data collected by many different researchers on the same question. The data is then mathematically pooled to create a large data set and to allow for certain comparisons. The original research question in all of the various studies might be something like, "How effective is reciprocal teaching compared to traditional instruction?" Because many different researchers have explored that question, there are many research studies available for a meta-analysis comparison, most of which report a mean and standard deviation for both an experimental group and a control group. Those data are necessary for the meta-analysis procedure.

Thus, using multiple studies on the same general question, the author of the meta-analysis can attack this question by combining those cumulative data and mathematically manipulating those data to draw some conclusions about the overall efficacy of reciprocal teaching. Further, the meta-analysis is a powerful technique, in that by combining data across studies, the meta-analytic research can generate extremely large experimental and comparison groups.

In a meta-analysis, the difference between groups is described as "effect size," which can best be understood as the relative effect of a specific educational intervention or strategy. This is done by a comparison of the distributions of the dependent measures between the experimental students and the control students across all of the studies.

Hattie (2012) described an effect size as a scale that allows multiple comparisons independent of the original mode of scoring in the various studies, showing the relative comparison of various independent educational interventions on achievement. He reports that for his work, he completed over 800 separate meta-analyses. Further, Hattie (2012) noted that, whereas almost all educational interventions "work" to some degree, an effect size allows the researcher to state which interventions work more effectively (Hattie, 2012; Marzano, 2007).

Effect sizes really measure how far the curve, or distribution of student scores, is moved by the specific intervention (in this case, reciprocal teaching). An effect size of .50 suggests that the distribution of scores of the students in the experimental groups was offset in a positive direction by half a standard deviation, compared to the control groups. This demonstrates that the educational intervention of reciprocal teaching is very effective, compared to the other treatments given to the control groups.

Advantages of Meta-Analyses

Most of the advantages of this technique were mentioned above. First, a combination of students across studies allows researchers to draw conclusions on the impact of a specific strategy based on very large samples of students. In that sense, meta-analyses such as those done by Hattie (2012) and Marzano and his coworkers (Marzano, 2007; Marzano et al., 2001) allow researchers to directly compare efficacy of multiple treatments including treatments that were generated from different research studies. Therefore, researchers can make definitive statements on which teaching strategies might be more effective than others.

From the perspective of teachers, it is quite refreshing to read meta-analytic research that compares educational interventions to each other, even though there may be no available research studies that directly compare the two. For example, a meta-analysis allows one to state that reciprocal teaching is more effective than whole-language instruction (Hattie, 2012). Thus, teachers seeking a new strategy should employ reciprocal teaching rather than whole-language learning.

Meta-analysis can also allow researchers to state the percentage of gain in academic achievement associated with use of a particular educational intervention (Marzano, 2009a, 2007, 2003; Marzano et al., 2001). This information, like the comparisons above, facilitates teacher decisions on what types of interventions to employ in the classroom. That is why this "percentage of achievement gain" figure has been reported for many of the educational interventions in this book.

Disadvantages of Meta-Analyses

With that noted, there are a number of assumptions that underlie any meta-analysis that are somewhat troubling. Most importantly, researchers using this technique have to determine that the differences between the various studies they include in their analysis are not substantive enough to make a meaningful difference in their overall conclusions. Here is an example.

As one might guess, there are typically many studies on the efficacy of a teaching strategy such as reciprocal teaching, particularly if the intervention strategy has been around for several decades. Further, while many different researchers have explored the question on the efficacy of reciprocal teaching, they would have explored that strategy in many different ways, so there would be many substantive differences in that research. For example, some researchers might use reciprocal teaching in an experimental design (i.e., experimental and control groups) by measuring the impact of six weeks of reciprocal teaching on students' academic achievement scores on unit tests in a seventh-grade science class. Another researcher might use reciprocal teaching in an experimental design to explore students' sense of their own learning in a fifth-grade class, as measured by student questionnaires (perhaps using a question like, How well did you learn in this reciprocal teaching lesson?). Finally, yet another researcher seeking to expand the applicability of reciprocal teaching might use it in a second-grade class lesson on the water cycle, by using reciprocal teaching only in one class period and using an end-of-class test score as the dependent variable.

In a meta-analysis, all of those studies would probably be included, even though the dependent measures (i.e., achievement scores on instructional units over time, scores on student surveys, and a one-time dependent measure score) are very different. The researcher has the responsibility in a meta-analysis to eliminate studies from the analysis that might confound the results. However, in most cases, editorial limitations (i.e., the number of pages allowed in a published research paper) prohibit the researcher from providing much detail on the decisions he or she made, and that is a second disadvantage of this technique. When reading a meta-analysis, at least in many cases, the reader is flying blind regarding the specific assumptions made by the researchers.

Use of Meta-Analyses

As noted above, there are limitations and concerns with meta-analytic research, but this powerful tool does provide much guidance to educators. For that reason, I encourage educators to read these meta-analyses by various researchers, discuss them with your peers or your professional learning network, and then reflectively implement those instructional suggestions that seem to work best in your individual situation. As always, a reflective teacher, using his or her professional colleagues as sounding boards and willing to risk trying new instructional strategies, is the most powerful source for continually improving instruction, and I have every confidence that such teachers will continue to explore new strategies such as those presented herein.

REFERENCES

Albrecht, N. J., Albrecht, P. M., & Cohen, M. (2012). Mindfully teaching in the classroom: A literature review. *Australian Journal of Teacher Education, 37*(12), 1–13.

Alstad, C. (2014, November 6). How to use cooperative learning in your classroom [Web log post]. Retrieved from http://resumes-for-teachers.com/blog/interview-questions/how-to-use-cooperative-learning-in-your-classroom/

Anderson, S. (2014, July 31). Let's build something together—maker spaces and 20% time. Retrieved from http://blog.web20classroom.org/2014/07/lets-build-something-together-maker.html

Andrade, H. G. (2000). Using rubrics to promote thinking and learning. *Education Leadership, 57*(5), 13–18.

Arreaga-Meyer, C. (1998). Increasing active student responding and improving academic performance through classwide peer tutoring. *Intervention in School and Clinic, 24*(2), 89–117.

Ash, K. (2011). Games and simulations help children access science. *Educational Week, 30*(27), 12.

Barell, J. (2007). *Problem-based learning: An inquiry approach* (2nd ed.). Thousand Oaks, CA: Corwin Press.

Bender, W. N. (2012). *Project based learning: differentiating instruction for the 21st century.* Thousand Oaks, CA: Corwin Press.

Bender, W. N. (2013a). *Differentiating math instruction: K–8* (3rd ed.). Thousand Oaks, CA: Corwin Press.

Bender, W. N. (2013b). *Differentiating instruction for students with learning disabilities* (3rd ed.). Thousand Oaks, CA: Corwin Press.

Bender, W. N. (2016). *20 disciplinary strategies for working with challenging students*. West Palm Beach, FL: Learning Sciences International.

Bender, W. N., & Crane, D. (2011). *RTI in math: Practical guidelines for elementary teachers*. Bloomington, IN: Solution Tree Press.

Bender, W. N., & Waller, L. (2011). *RTI & differentiated reading in the K–8 classroom*. Bloomington, IN: Solution Tree Press.

Bender, W. N., & Waller, L. (2013). *Cool tech tools for lower tech teachers: 20 tactics for every classroom*. Thousand Oaks, CA: Corwin Press.

Bender, W. N., & Smith, J. K. (1990). Classroom behavior of children and adolescents with learning disabilities: A meta-analysis. *Journal of Learning Disabilities, 23*, 298–305.

Benson, T., Brack, C., & Samarwickrema, G. (2012, March 21). Teaching with wikis: Improving staff development through action research. *Research in Learning Technology, 20*.

Bergmann, J., & Sams, A. (2014). *Flip your classroom: Reach every student in every class every day*. Alexandria, VA: Association for Supervision and Curriculum Development.

Berkowicz, J., & Myers, A. (2015, February 5). STEM changes the learning experience [Web log post]. Retrieved from http://blogs.edweek.org/edweek/leadership_360/2015/02/stem_changes_the_learning_experience.html

Bharti, P. (2014, May 21). How to use augmented reality in the classroom [Web log post]. Retrieved from http://edtechreview.in/trends-insights/insights/1210-how-to-use-augmented-reality-in-the-classroom

Bloom, J. S. (2015, August 25). Coding: The ultimate equalizer. [Web log post]. Retrieved from www.huffingtonpost.com/joel-s-bloom/coding-the-ultimate-equal_1_b_8032318.html?utm_hp_ref=education&ir=Education

Bold, M. (2006). Use of wikis in graduate course work. *Journal of Interactive Learning Research, 17*(1), 5–14.

Boss, S. (2011, October 6). Immersive PBL: Indiana project reaches far beyond the classroom [Web log post]. Retrieved from www.edutopia.org/blog/pbl-immersive-brings-clean-water-haiti-suzie-boss

Boss, S., & Krauss, L. (2007). *Reinventing project-based learning: Your field guide to real-world projects in the digital age*. Washington, DC: International Society for Technology in Education.

Bowman-Perrott, L. (2009). Classwide peer tutoring. *Intervention in School and Clinic, 44*, 259–267.

Breeden, J. (2015). MakerBot Replicator 3D Printer excels at enhancing classrooms [Review of MakerBot Replicator 2X Desktop 3D Printer]. Retrieved from www.edtechmagazine.com/k12/article/2015/06/review-makerbot-replicator-3d-printer-excels-small-and-durable-designs

Brown, H., & Ciuffetelli, D. C. (Eds.). (2009). *Foundational methods: Understanding teaching and learning*. Toronto: Pearson Education.

Bruns, A., & Humphreys, S. (2007, October). Building collaborative capacities in learners: The M/cyclopedia project revisited. *Proceedings of the 2007 international symposium on Wikis:* 1–10in Montreal, PQ, Canada.

Bulgren, J., Deshler, D., & Lenz, B. K. (2007). Engaging adolescents with LD in higher order thinking about history concepts using integrated content enhancement routines. *Journal of Learning Disabilities, 40*(2), 121–133.

Burnish, A., Fuchs, D., & Fuchs, L. (2005). Peer-assisted learning strategies: An evidence-based practice to promote reading achievement. *Learning Disabilities Research & Practice, 15*(2), 85–91.

Burns, M. (2014, March 24). Creating augmented reality triggers with Canva [Web log post]. Retrieved from http://classtechtips.com/2015/03/24/creating-augmented-reality-triggers-with-canva/

Caprino, K. (2014, February 12). 5 mindfulness steps that guarantee increased success and vitality. *Forbes*. Retrieved from www.forbes.com/sites/kathycaprino/2014/02/12/5-mindfulness-steps-that-guarantee-increased-success-and-vitality/

Churchill, D. (2007). Web 2.0 and possibilities for educational applications. *Educational Technology, 47*(2), 24–29.

Cook-Deegan, P. (2015, June 15). Implementing a school-wide mindfulness program [Web log post]. Retrieved from www.edutopia.org/blog/implementing-school-wide-mindfulness-program-patrick-cook-deegan?utm_content=blog&utm_campaign=implementing-school-wide-mindfulness-program&utm_source=twitter&utm_medium=socialflow&utm_term=link

Crossman, J. M., & Kite, S. L. (2012). Facilitating improved writing among students through directed peer review. *Active Learning in Higher Education, 12*(3), 219–229.

Curtis, D. (2015, June 26). Does Facebook really have a place in the classroom? *The Telegraph*. Retrieved from www.telegraph.co.uk/technology/facebook/10926105/Does-Facebook-really-have-a-place-in-the-classroom.html

Davis, L. C. (2015, August 31). When mindfulness meets the classroom. *The Atlantic*. Retrieved from www.theatlantic.com/education/archive/2015/08/mindfulness-education-schools-meditation/402469/?utm_content=buffera4dba&utm_medium=social&utm_source=twitter.com&utm_campaign=buffer

Davis, V. (2015, June 29). Year one with a 3D printer: 17 tips [Web log post]. Retrieved from www.edutopia.org/blog/year-one-with-3d-printer-vicki-davis?utm_content=blog&utm_campaign=year-one-with-3d-printer&utm_source=twitter&utm_medium=socialflow&utm_term=link

De Gree, A. (2015). Is 3D printing the next Industrial Revolution? [Web log post]. Retrieved from http://guff.com/is-3d-printing-the-next-industrial-revolution

De Pedro, X., Rieradevall, M., López, P., Sant, D., Piñol, J., Núñez, L., & Llobera, M. (2006). Writing documents collaboratively in higher education (I): Qualitative results from a 2-year project study. *Congreso Internacional de Docencia Universitaria e Innovación (International Congress of University Teaching and Innovation)*. Retrieved from http://uniwiki.ourproject.org/tiki-download_wiki_attachment.php?attId=98&page=UniwikiCongressos

Deters, F., Cuthrell, K., & Sapleton, J. (2010). Why wikis? Student perceptions of using wikis in online coursework. *Journal of Online Learning and Teaching, 6*(1).

Detroit schools choose movie maker to fuel creativity and boost test scores. (2011, August 29). *eSchool News*. Retrieved from http://eschoolnews.com/2011/08/29/detroit-schools-choose-movie-maker-to-fuel-creativity-and-boost-test-scores

Dredge, S. (2014, September 4). Coding at school: A parent's guide to England's new coding curriculum. *The Guardian*. Retrieved from www.theguardian.com/technology/2014/sep/04/coding-school-computing-children-programming

Dretzin, R. (Producer/Director). (2010, February 2). Digital nation [PBS Documentary]. *Frontline*. Retrieved from www.pbs.org/wgbh/pages/frontline/digitalnation/

Dunleavy, M., Deed, E. C., & Mitchell, R. (2009). Affordances and limitations of immersive participatory augmented reality simulations for teaching and learning. *Journal of Science Educational Technology, 18*, 7–22.

Ebersviller, J. E. (2013). *Peer evaluation as an effective tool to improve twelfth-grade students' writing*. Mankato, MN: Minnesota State University.

EdTech Team. (2015, January 15). Five new Google classroom features teachers should know about. [Web log post]. Retrieved from www.educatorstechnology.com/2015/01/five-new-google-classroom-features-for-teachers.html

Elias, M. (2013, August 16). Back to school: Goal setting with your students [Web log post]. Retrieved from www.edutopia.org/blog/back-to-school-goal-setting-students-teacher-maurice-elias

Epps, J. (2014, July 26). "Interactive Project Based Learning Using 3D" grant results. Retrieved from www.youtube.com/watch?v=bfT1AqO1qi8

Farber, M. (2015, September 8). Hands-on apps for diverse learners [Web log post]. Retrieved from www.edutopia.org/blog/hands-on-apps-diverse-learners-matthew-farber?utm_content=October15&utm_campaign=RSS&utm_source=twitter&utm_medium=socialflow%20

Fears, S., & Patsalides, L. (2012, September 11). The many benefits of teaching robotics in the classroom. *Bright Hub Education*. Retrieved from www.brighthubeducation.com/middle-school-science-lessons/17432-the-importance-of-teaching-robotics/

Ferriter, W. M., & Garry, A. (2010). *Teaching the iGeneration: 5 easy ways to introduce essential skills with web 2.0 tools*. Bloomington, IN: Solution Tree Press.

Flipped Learning Network. (2014). The four pillars of F-L-I-P. Retrieved from www.flippedlearning.org/definition

Flipped Learning Network & Sophia. (2014). Growth in flipped learning: Transitioning the focus from teachers to students for educational success. Retrieved from www.flippedlearning.org/survey

Freemark, S. (2014, October 16). Studying with quizzes helps make sure the material sticks. *MindShift*. Retrieved from http://ww2.kqed.org/mindshift/2014/10/16/studying-with-quizzes-helps-make-sure-the-material-sticks/

Frey, N., & Fisher, D. (2013). *Rigorous reading: 5 access points for comprehending complex texts*. Thousand Oaks, CA: Corwin Press.

Gagnon, J. C., & Maccini, P. (2001). Preparing students with learning disabilities in algebra. *Teaching Exceptional Children, 34*(1), 8–15.

Game based learning catching on in schools. (2012, May 8). *eSchool News*. Retrieved from www.eschoolnews.com/2012/05/08/game-based-learning-catching-on-in-schools

Gardiner, B. (2014, March 23). Adding coding to the curriculum. *New York Times*. Retrieved from www.nytimes.com/2014/03/24/world/europe/adding-coding-to-the-curriculum.html?_r=0

Georgia district implements virtual world technology. (2012, March 28). *eSchool News*. Retrieved from http://eschoolnews.com/2012/03/28/Georgia-district-implements-virtual-world-technology

Gilles, R. M., & Adrian, F. (2003). *Cooperative learning: The social and intellectual outcomes of learning in groups*. London: Farmer Press.

Ginsburg-Block, C. A., Rohrbeck, A., & Fantuzzo, J. W. (2006). A meta-analytic review of social, self-concept, and behavioral outcomes of peer-assisted learning. *Journal of Educational Psychology*, *98*, 732–749.

Goodrich, K. (2012, August 16). Dylan Wiliam & the 5 formative assessment strategies to improve student learning [Web log post]. Retrieved from www.nwea.org/blog/2012/dylan-wiliam-the-5-formative-assessment-strategies-to-improve-student-learning/#sthash.HKws6nJg.dpuf

Goodwin, B., & Hein, H. (2014, December). Research says: STEM schools produce mixed results. *Educational Leadership*, *72*(4). Retrieved from www.ascd.org/publications/educational-leadership/dec14/vol72/num04/STEM-Schools-Produce-Mixed-Results.aspx

Gorman, M. (2011, October 6). Connecting PBL and STEM: 40 free engaging resources to use in the classroom [Web log post]. Retrieved from https://21centuryedtech.wordpress.com/2011/10/06/connecting-pbl-and-stem-40-free-engaging-resources-to-use-in-the-classroom/

Green, G. (2012, January 18). My view: Flipped classrooms give every student a chance to succeed. *CNN online*. Retrieved from http://schoolsofthought.blogs.cnn.com/2012/01/18/my-view-flipped-classrooms-give-every-student-a-chance-to-succeed/

Green, G. (2014). Flipped classrooms get results at Clintondale High School [Online video]. *Techsmith*. Retrieved from www.techsmith.com/customer-stories-clintondale.html

Greenberg, M. T., & Harris, A. R. (2012). Nurturing mindfulness in children and youth: Current state of research. *Child Development Perspectives*, *6*(2), 161–166.

Greenwood, C. R., Tapia, Y., Abbott, M., & Walton, C. (2003). A building based case study of evidence-based literacy practices: Implementation, reading behavior, and growth in reading fluency; K–4. *The Journal of Special Education*, *50*, 521–535.

Grier, R., Blumenfeld, P. C., Marx, R. W., Krajcik, J. S., Fishman, B., Soloway, E., et al. (2008). Standardized test outcomes for students engaged in inquiry-based science curricula in the context of urban reform. *Journal of Research in Science Teaching*, *45*(8), 922–939.

Grisham, L. (2014, April 9). Teachers, students and social media: Where is the line? *USA Today*. Retrieved from www.usatoday.com/story/news/nation-now/2014/04/09/facebook-teachers-twitter-students-schools/7472051/

Haldane, M., & Smith, R. (2014). Using technology for active differentiation. In R. Slavin (Ed.), *Science, technology, & mathematics (STEM)*. Thousand Oaks, CA: Corwin Press.

Hamdan, N., McKnight, P., McKnight, K., & Arfstrom, K. (2013). *A review of flipped learning*. Retrieved from www.flippedlearning.org/review

Hansen, M. (2014). Characteristics of schools successful in STEM: Evidence from two states' longitudinal data. *Journal of Educational Research*, *107*(5), 374–391.

Harris, E. A. (2015, October 23). Under stress, students in New York schools find calm in meditation. *New York Times*. Retrieved from www.nytimes.com/2015/10/24/nyregion /under-stress-students-in-new-york-schools-find-calm-in-meditation.html?_r=1

Hatten, S. (2014, August 5). Engage elementary students with stop animation. Retrieved from www.iste.org/explore/articleDetail?articleid=128

Hattie, J. (2012). *Visible learning for teachers: Maximizing impact on learning.* London and New York: Routledge, Taylor, & Francis Group.

Hedeen, T. (2003). The reverse jigsaw: A process of cooperative learning and discussion. *Teaching Sociology, 31*(3), 325–332.

Hicks, J. (2015, June 18). 12 unexpected ways to use LEGO in the classroom. *Edudemic*. Retrieved from www.edudemic.com/12-ways-use-lego-classroom/?utm_source=twitterfeed &utm_medium=twitter

Hicks, T. (2014, October 14). Make it count: Providing feedback as formative assessment [Web log post]. Retrieved from www.edutopia.org/blog/providing-feedback-as-formative -assessment-troy-hicks

Holland, B. (2014). How to start using augmented reality in the classroom. Retrieved from http://edtechteacher.org/how-to-start-using-augmented-reality-in-the-classroom-from-beth -holland-on-edudemic/

Horn, M. B. (2013, summer). The transformation nature of flipped classrooms. *Education Next, 13*(3). Retrieved from http://educationnext.org/the-transformational-potential-of -flipped-classrooms/

Iseman, J. S., & Naglieri, J. A. (2011). A cognitive strategy instruction to improve math calculation for children with ADHD and LD: A randomized controlled study. *Learning Disabilities Research and Practice, 44*(2), 184–195.

International Society for Technology in Education. (2010). *How can technology influence student academic knowledge?* Retrieved from http://caret.iste.org/index.cfm?useaction =evidence&answerID-12&words-Attention

ISTE Connects. (2015, February 18). Wildly popular, then off the grid, virtual worlds are back in ed tech. Retrieved from www.iste.org/explore/articleDetail?articleid=316&category =ISTE-Connects-blog&article=wildly-popular-then-off-the-grid-virtual-worlds-are-back -in-ed-tech&utm_source=Twitter&utm_medium=Social&utm_campaign=EdTekHub

Jackson, F. (2002). Crossing content: A strategy for students with learning disabilities. *Intervention in School and Clinic, 37*(5), 279–283.

Johnson, D.W. (2009). An educational psychology success story: Social interdependence theory and cooperative learning. *Educational Researcher, 38*(5), 365–379.

Johnson, D., & Johnson, R. (1994). *Learning together and alone: Cooperative, competitive, and individualistic learning.* Needham Heights, MA: Prentice-Hall.

Jolly, A. (2014, June 17). Six characteristics of a great STEM lesson. *Education Week*. Retrieved from www.edweek.org/tm/articles/2014/06/17/ctq_jolly_stem.html

Judson, E. (2014). Effects of transferring to STEM-focused charter and magnet schools on student achievement. *Journal of Educational Research, 107*(4), 255–266.

Kagan, S. (1994). *Cooperative learning.* San Clemente, CA: Kagan.

Kamps, D. M., Greenwood, G., Arreaga-Meyer, C., Baldwin, M., Veerkamp, M. B., Utley, C., Tapia, Y., Bowman-Perrott, L., & Bannister, H. (2008). The efficacy of classwide peer tutoring in middle schools. *Education & Treatment of Children, 31*(2), 119–152.

King, K., & Gurian, M. (2006). Teaching to the minds of boys. *Educational Leadership, 64*(1), 54–61.

Klopfer, E. (2008). *Augmented learning*. Cambridge, MA: MIT Press.

Klopfer, E., & Sheldon, J. (2010). Augmenting your own reality: Student authoring of science -based augmented reality games. *New Directions for Youth Development, 128*(Winter), 85–94.

Knight, J. (2013). *High-impact instruction: A framework for great teaching*. Thousand Oaks, CA: Corwin Press.

Kuchimanchi, B. (2013, June 6). Role of animation in students' learning. *Ed Tech Review*. Retrieved from http://edtechreview.in/trends-insights/insights/367-role-of-animation-in -students-learning

Kunsch, C., Jitendra, A., & Sood, S. (2007). The effects of peer-mediated instruction in mathematics for students with learning problems: A research synthesis. *Learning Disabilities Research & Practice, 22*(1), 1–12.

Larmer, J., Ross, D., & Mergendoller, J. R. (2009). *PBL starter kit: To-the-point advice, tools, and tips for your first project in middle or high school*. San Rafael, CA: Unicorn Printing Specialists.

Larmer, J., Ross, D., & Mergendoller, J. R. (2010). 7 essentials for project-based learning. *Educational Leadership, 68*(1), 34–37.

Lederer, J. M. (2000). Reciprocal teaching of social studies in inclusive elementary classrooms. *Journal of Learning Disabilities, 33*(1), 91–106.

Lee, S., Wehmeyer, M. L., Sookup, J. H., & Palmer, S. B. (2010). Impact of curriculum modifications on access to the general educational curriculum for students with disabilities. *Exceptional Children, 76*(2), 213–233.

Lenz, B. K. (2006). Creating school-wide conditions for high quality learning strategy classroom instruction. *Intervention in School and Clinic, 41*(5), 261–266.

Lewis, A., & Thompson, A. (2010, April). Quick summarizing strategies to use in the classroom. Retrieved from www.christina.k12.de.us/LiteracyLinks/elemresources/lfs _resources/summarizing_strategies.pdf

List, J. S., & Bryant, B. (2009). Integrating interactive online content at an early college high school: An exploration of Moodle, Ning, and Twitter. *Meridian Middle School Computer Technologies Journal, 12*(1). Retrieved from https://ncsu.edu/meridian/winter2009/List /index.htm

Lund, A. (2008). Wikis: A collective approach to language production. *ReCALL, 20*(01), 1–20.

Maats, H., & O'Brien, K. (2015, April 21). Hands-off teaching cultivates metacognition [Web log post]. Retrieved from www.edutopia.org/blog/hands-off-teaching-cultivates -metacognition-hunter-maats-katie-obrien

Madge, C., Meek, J., Wellens, J., & Hooley, T. (2009). Facebook, social integration and informal learning at university: 'It is more for socialising and talking to friends about work than for actually doing work.' *Learning, Media and Technology, 34*(2), 141–155.

Mak, B., & Coniam, D. (2008). Using wikis to enhance and develop writing skills among secondary school students in Hong Kong. *System, 36*, 437–455.

Manzo, K. K. (2010, March 18). Mobile learning seen to lack rigorous research. *Education Week, 29*(26), 34–36.

Markham, T. (2011, March 7). Strategies for embedding project-based learning into STEM education [Web log post]. Retrieved from www.edutopia.org/blog/strategies-pbl-stem -thom-markham-buck-institute

Marzano, R. (2007). *The art and science of teaching: A comprehensive framework for effective instruction.* Alexandria, VA: Association for Supervision and Curriculum Development.

Marzano, R. (2009a). Marzano's nine instructional strategies for effective teaching and learning. Retrieved from www.ntuaft.com/TISE/Research-Based%20Instructional%20Strategies /marzanos%209%20strategies.pdf

Marzano, R. (2009b). Teaching with interactive whiteboards. *Educational Leadership, 87*(3), 80–82.

Marzano, R. J. (2003). *What works in schools: Translating research into action.* Alexandria, VA: Association for Supervision and Curriculum Development.

Marzano, R. J., & Haystead, M. (2009). *Final report on the evaluation on the Promethean technology.* Englewood, CO: Marzano Research Laboratory.

Marzano, R. J., Pickering, D. J., & Pollock, J. E. (2001, 2004). *Classroom instruction that works: Research-based strategies for increasing student achievement.* Alexandria, VA: Association for Supervision and Curriculum Development.

Mason, L. H., & Hedin, L. R. (2011). Reading science tests: Challenges for students with learning disabilities and considerations for teachers. *Learning Disability Research and Practice, 26*(4), 214–222.

Maton, N. (2011, November 10). Can an online game crack the code to language learning? *MindShift.* Retrieved from http://mindshift.kqed.org/2011/11/can-an-online-game-crack -the-code-to-language-learning/

Mergendoller, J. R., Maxwell, N., & Bellisimo, Y. (2007). The effectiveness of problem-based instruction: A comparative study of instructional methods and student characteristics. *Interdisciplinary Journal of Problem Based Learning, 1*(2), 49–69.

Miller, A. (2012, March 30). A new community and resources for games for learning [Web log post]. Retrieved from www.edutopia.org/blog/games-for-learning-community-resources -andrew-miller

Miner, M. (2015). Second Life lessons & classroom activities. Retrieved from www.teachhub .com/second-life-lessons-classroom-activities

Moeller, A. J., Theiler, J. M., & Wu, C. (2012). Goal setting and student achievement: A longitudinal study. *The Modern Language Journal, 96*(2), 153–159.

Moreno, R. (2009). Learning from animated classroom exemplars: the case for guiding student teachers' observations with metacognitive prompts. *Educational Research and Evaluation: An International Journal on Theory and Practice, 15*(9), 487–501.

Myers, A., & Berkowicz, J. (2015). *The STEM shift: A guide for school leaders.* Thousand Oaks, CA: Corwin Press.

Nast, P. (2015). The 10 best STEM resources: Science, technology, engineering & mathematics resources for preK–12. Retrieved from www.nea.org/tools/lessons/stem-resources.html

National Education Association. (2015). *Research spotlight on peer tutoring: NEA reviews of the research on best practices in education.* Retrieved from: http://www.nea.org/tools/35542.htm

National Research Council. (2005). *How students learn: History, mathematics, and science in the classroom.* Washington, DC: National Academies Press.

National Research Council. (2011). *Successful K–12 STEM education: Identifying effective approaches in science, technology, engineering, and mathematics.* Washington, DC: National Academies Press.

National Science Board. (2012). *Science and engineering indicators 2012.* Retrieved from www.nsf.gov/statistics/seind12/c2/c2h.htm

Nhat Hanh, T. (2010, August 23). Five steps to mindfulness. Retrieved from www.mindful.org/five-steps-to-mindfulness/

Noonoo, S. (2012, September 12). Augmented reality apps transform class time. *T.H.E. Journal.* Retrieved from https://thejournal.com/Articles/2012/09/12/Augmented-Reality-Apps-Transform-Class-Time.aspx?Page=1

Nugent, G., Barker, B. S., & Grandgenett, N. (2012). The impact of educational robotics on student STEM learning, attitudes, and workplace skills. In *Robots in K–12 education: A new technology for learning.* Retrieved from www.igi-global.com/chapter/impact-educational-robotics-student-stem/63415

Nussil, N., & Oh, K. (2014). The components of effective teacher training in the use of three-dimensional immersive virtual worlds for learning and instruction purposes: A literature review. *Journal of Information Technology for Teacher Education, 22*(2), 213–241. Retrieved from www.researchgate.net/publication/261798740_The_Components_of_Effective_Teacher_Training_in_the_Use_of_Three-Dimensional_Immersive_Virtual_Worlds_for_Learning_and_Instruction_Purposes_A_Literature_Review

Nutt, A. E. (2015, January 7). Music lessons spur emotional and behavioral growth in children, new study says. *Washington Post.* Retrieved from www.washingtonpost.com/news/speaking-of-science/wp/2015/01/07/music-lessons-spur-emotional-and-behavioral-growth-in-children-new-study-says/

Oaklander, M. (2015, February 16). Mini-meditators. *Time.*

O'Connell, M. J., & Vandas, K. (2015). *Partnering with students: Building ownership of learning.* Thousand Oaks, CA: Corwin Press.

O'Day, D. H. (2007). The value of animations in biology teaching: A study of long-term memory retention. *CBE Life Sciences Education, 6*(3), 217–223. Retrieved from www.ncbi.nlm.nih.gov/pmc/articles/PMC1964525/

Oh, K., & Nussil, N. (2014, June). Teacher training in the use of a three-dimensional immersive virtual world: Building understanding through first-hand experiences. *Journal of Teaching and Learning with Technology, 3*(1), 33–58. Retrieved from http://jotlt.indiana.edu/article/viewFile/3956/19282

Palinscar, A. S., & Brown, A. L. (1984). Reciprocal teaching of comprehension-fostering and comprehension-monitoring activities. *Cognition and Instruction, I*(2), 117–175.

Pappas, C. (2013, October 6). How to use wiki in the classroom. *TechforTeachers.* Retrieved from www.techforteachers.net/wikis-in-the-classroom.html

Parker, K. R., & Chao, J. T. (2007). Wiki as a teaching tool. *Interdisciplinary Journal of Knowledge and Learning Objects, 3*. Retrieved from www.ijklo.org/Volume3/IJKLOv3p057 -072Parker284.pdf

Pilonieta, P., & Medina, A. L. (2009). Reciprocal teaching for the primary grades: We can do it too! *The Reading Teacher, 63*(2), 120–129.

Politis, M. (2015, April 15). Augmented reality—the coolest instructional technology you haven't heard of? Retrieved from www.emergingedtech.com/2014/04/augmented-reality -emerging-education-technology/

Powell, M. (2014, October 30). Robot teachers in the classroom. Retrieved from http://iq.intel .com/robot-teachers-in-the-classroom/

Prescott, J. (2014, July 10). How professors are using Facebook to teach. *Washington Post.* Retrieved from www.washingtonpost.com/posteverything/wp/2014/07/10/how-professors -are-using-facebook-to-teach/

Pressly, A. (2014, June 14). Easy tools for using robotics in the classroom. Retrieved from www.iste.org/explore/articleDetail?articleid=93&category=ISTE-Connects-blog&article =Easy-tools-for-using-robotics-in-the-classroom

Rapp, D. (2008, August). Virtual classroom: Second Life. *Scholastic.* Retrieved from www .scholastic.com/browse/article.jsp?id=3749877

Researchers debate gaming's effects on the brain. (2012, January 11). *eSchool News.* Retrieved from www.eSchoolNews.com/2012/01/11/researchers-debate-gamings-effects-on-the-brain/

Richardson, W. (2010). *Blogs, wikis, podcasts, and other powerful tools for educators.* Thousand Oaks, CA: Corwin Press.

Robertson, W. H. (2015, January 30). The Skatepark Mathematics Extravaganza. Retrieved from http://corwin-connect.com/2015/01/skatepark-mathematics-extravaganza/

Rosenshine, B., & Meister, C. (1994). Reciprocal teaching: A review of the research. *Review of Educational Research, 64*(4), 479–530.

Rosenzweig, C., Krawec, J., & Montague, M. (2011). Metacognitive strategy use of eighth-grade students with and without learning disabilities during mathematical problem solving: A think-aloud analysis. *Journal of Learning Disabilities, 44*(6), 508–520.

Ryan, M. (2015). *16 ways to use Second Life in your classroom: Pedagogical approaches and virtual assignments.* Retrieved from http://easyamu.pbworks.com/w/file/fetch/54734557/16 _grunde_til_3-D.pdf

Schul, J. E. (2012). Revisiting an old friend: The practice and promise of cooperative learning for the twenty-first century. *The Social Studies, 102*, 88–93.

Schumaker, J. G., & Deshler, D. D. (2003). Can students with LD become competent writers? *Learning Disability Quarterly, 28*(2), 129–141.

Schwartz, K. (2015, September 28). For the hesitant teacher: Leveraging the power of Minecraft. *Mindshift.* Retrieved from http://ww2.kqed.org/mindshift/2015/09/28/for -the-hesitant-teacher-leveraging-the-power-of-minecraft/

Schwartz, K. (2013, October 14). Five research-driven education trends at work in classrooms. *Mindshift.* Retrieved from http://blogs.kqed.org/mindshift/2013/10/five-research-driven -education-trends-at-work-in-classrooms/

Sequeira, L., & Morgado, L. (2013). Virtual archaeology in Second Life and OpenSimulator. *Journal of Virtual Worlds Research, 6*(1). Retrieved from http://journals.tdl.org/jvwr/index.php/jvwr/article/view/7047/6310

Schwartz, K. (2014, May 27). Robots in the classroom: What are they good for? *Mindshift.* Retrieved from http://ww2.kqed.org/mindshift/2014/05/27/robots-in-the-classroom-what-are-they-good-for/

Shah, N. (2012). Special educators borrow from brain studies. *Education Week, 31*(17), 10.

Shapiro, J. (2014, September 5). Using games for learning: Practical steps to get started. *Mindshift.* Retrieved from http://ww2.kqed.org/mindshift/2014/09/05/using-games-for-learning-practical-steps-to-get-started/

Sharan, Y. (2010). Cooperative learning for academic and social gains: Valued pedagogy, problematic practice. *European Journal of Education, 45*(2), 300–313.

Sheely, K. (2011, November 1). High school teachers make gaming academic. *U.S. News & World Report.* Retrieved from www.usnews.com/education/high-schools/articles/2011/11/01/high-school-teachers-make-gaming-academic

Short, D. (2012). Teaching scientific concepts using a virtual world—Minecraft. *Teaching Science, 58*(3). Retrieved from www.academia.edu/1891072/Teaching_Scientific_Concepts_Using_a_Virtual_World_-_Minecraft

Singer, N. (2015, September 28). Google virtual-reality system aims to enliven education. *New York Times.* Retrieved from www.nytimes.com/2015/09/29/technology/google-virtual-reality-system-aims-to-enliven-education.html?_r=0

Slavin, R. E. (Ed.). (2014). *Science, technology, & mathematics (STEM).* Thousand Oaks, CA: Corwin Press.

Smith, D. F. (2015, September 15). Skype connects classrooms with field trips around the world. *EdTech.* Retrieved from www.edtechmagazine.com/k12/article/2015/09/skype-connects-classrooms-field-trips-around-world

Smith, R. (2015, June 15). 3D printing is about to change the world—forever. *Forbes.* Retrieved from www.forbes.com/sites/ricksmith/2015/06/15/3d-printing-is-about-to-change-the-world-forever/#4c3008a5268d

Sousa, D. A., & Tomlinson, C. A. (2011). *Differentiation and the brain: How neuroscience supports the learner-friendly classroom.* Bloomington, IN: Solution Tree Press.

Sparks, S. D. (2011). Schools "flip" for lesson model promoted by Khan Academy. *Education Today, 31*(5), 1–14.

SRI International. (2014). *Research on the use of Khan Academy in schools.* Retrieved from www.sri.com/sites/default/files/publications/2014-03-07_implementation_briefing.pdf

Stansbury, M. (2013, July 30). Does research support flipped learning? *eSchool News.* Retrieved from www.eschoolnews.com/2013;07/30/does-research-support-flipped-learning/

Subotnik, R. F., Tai, R. H., & Almarode, J. (2011, May 10–12). *Study of the impact of selective SMT high schools: Reflections on learners gifted and motivated in science and mathematics.* Paper prepared for the workshop of the Committee on Highly Successful Schools or Programs for K–12 STEM Education, National Research Council, Washington, DC.

Symonds Elementary School. (2015, October 7). Social and emotional learning: A schoolwide approach. *Edutopia*. Retrieved from www.edutopia.org/practice/social-and-emotional -learning-schoolwide-approach?utm_source=twitter&utm_medium=socialflow&utm _campaign=RSS

Teachervision. (2015). Summarizing. Retrieved from www.teachervision.com/skill-builder /reading-comprehension/48785.html?page=1&

TeachThought Staff. (2015, September 18). Education app spotlight: Contraption maker [Web log post]. Retrieved from www.teachthought.com/apps-2/app-spotlight-contraption-maker/

Thurston, A. (2014). Using cooperative learning to engage students in science. In R. E. Slavin (Ed.), *Science, technology, & mathematics (STEM)*. Thousand Oaks, CA: Corwin Press.

Tileston, D. W. (2004). *What every teacher should know about learning, memory, and the brain*. Thousand Oaks, CA: Corwin Press.

Tomaszewski, J. (2012). Fresh ideas: Using wikis in the classroom. *Education World*. Retrieved from www.educationworld.com/a_lesson/using-wikis-in-the-classroom.shtml

Tomlinson, C. A. (1999). *The differentiated classroom: Responding to the needs of all learners*. Alexandria, VA: Association for Supervision and Curriculum Development.

Tomlinson, C. A. (2010). Differentiating instruction in response to academically diverse student populations. In R. Marzano (Ed.), *On excellence in teaching*. Bloomington, IN: Solution Tree Press.

Tomlinson, C. A. (2003). *Differentiation in practice: A resource guide for differentiating curriculum, grades K–5*. Alexandria, VA: Association for Supervision and Curriculum Development.

Tomlinson, C. A., Brimijoin, K., & Narvaez, L. (2008). *The differentiated school: Making revolutionary changes in teaching and learning*. Alexandria, VA: Association for Supervision and Curriculum Development.

Topping, K. (2008). *Peer-assisted learning: A practical guide for teachers*. Newton, MA: Brookline Books.

Toppo, G. (2011, October 6). "Flipped" classrooms take advantage of technology. *USA Today*. Retrieved from www.usatoday.com/news/education/story/2011-10-06/flipped-classrooms -virtual-teaching/50681482/1

Trentin, G. (2009). Using a wiki to evaluate individual contribution to a collaborative learning project. *Journal of Computer Assisted Learning, 25*, 43–55.

Tucker, B. (2012). The flipped classroom. *Education Next, 12*(1). Retrieved from http:// educationnext.org/the-flipped-classroom/

U.S. Department of Education, Institute of Education Sciences, National Center for Education Statistics. (2011, April). Postsecondary awards in science, technology, engineering, and mathematics, by state: 2001 and 2009. (NCES Publication No. 2011226). Retrieved from http://nces.ed.gov/pubs2011/2011226.pdf

Vega, V. (2012, October 31). Research-based practices for engaging students in STEM learning. Retrieved from www.edutopia.org/stw-college-career-stem-research

Venkataraman, B., Riordan, D. G., & Olson, S. (2010, September). Prepare and inspire: K–12 education in science, technology, engineering, and math (STEM) for America's future. Washington, DC: President's Council of Advisors on Science and Technology. Retrieved from http://science.nsta.org/nstaexpress/PCASTSTEMEdExecutiveReport.pdf

Walsh, K. (2011, March 27). Facebook in the classroom. *Seriously.* Retrieved from www.emergingedtech.com/2011/03/facebook-in-the-classroom-seriously/

Watters, A. (2011). Distractions begone! Facebook as a study tool. *Mindshift.* Retrieved from http://ww2.kqed.org/mindshift/2011/09/20/distractions-set-aside-facebook-as-a-study-tool/

Walsh, K. (2012, October 10). The evolution of augmented reality applications for education and instructional use. Retrieved from www.emergingedtech.com/2012/10/the-evolution-of-augmented-reality-applications-for-education-and-instructional-use/

Welham, H. (2014, July 23). How to introduce mindfulness into your classroom: Nine handy tips. *The Guardian.* Retrieved from www.theguardian.com/teacher-network/teacher-blog/2014/jul/23/how-to-mindfulness-classroom-tips

Wiswall, M., Stiefel, L., Schwartz, A. E., & Boccardo, J. (2014, June). Does attending a STEM high school improve student performance? Evidence from New York City. *Economics of Education Review, 40,* 93–105.

Wolpert-Gawron, H. (2015, September 29). Project-based learning and gamification: Two great tastes that go great together [Web log post]. Retrieved from www.edutopia.org/blog/project-based-learning-gamification-go-great-together-heather-wolpert-gawron?utm_content=October15&utm_campaign=RSS&utm_source=twitter&utm_medium=socialflow%20

Yohana, D. (2014, August 29). 5 robots booking it to a classroom near you. Retrieved from http://mashable.com/2014/08/29/robots-schools/

Yokana, L. (2015, January 20). Creating an authentic maker education rubric [Web log post]. Retrieved from www.edutopia.org/blog/creating-authentic-maker-education-rubric-lisa-yokana

Young, V. M., House, A., Wang, H., Singleton, C., & Klopfenstein, K. (2011). *Inclusive STEM schools: Early promise in Texas and unanswered questions.* Washington, DC: National Research Council.

Zimmerman, E. (2014, March 25). 3 free ways to add animation to your classroom. *T.H.E. Journal.* Retrieved from https://thejournal.com/articles/2014/03/25/3-tools-for-animation.aspx?=FETCLN

Zubrzycki, J. (2015, October 9). New federal law means computer science is officially part of STEM [Web log post]. *Education Week.* Retrieved from http://blogs.edweek.org/edweek/curriculum/2015/10/new_law_includes_computer_scie.html?cmp=SOC-EDIT-TW

INDEX